PRAISE FOR JOAN MARIE GALAT'S

Make Your Mark, Make a Difference

"Being the change we want to see in the world isn't always easy. For parents and children alike, it can be challenging to start a conversation on how we can tackle the barriers to a better world. Joan Marie Galat's book is an excellent guide for young readers to get curious and find inspiration as our next generation of difference makers. *Make Your Mark, Make a Difference* offers a step-by-step toolkit for anyone hoping to develop the skills to create positive change within their communities! Together we truly can make a difference!"

—**Rick Hansen**, founder, Rick Hansen Foundation

"Informative, upbeat, empowering—Joan Marie Galat has created an antidote to despair in this guide to creating a kinder planet. Readers, teachers, thinkers, and community-builders will use this book as a starting point to a life of joyful action for positive change. Beautifully designed with well-researched information and terrific examples of youth activism, *Make Your Mark, Make a Difference* should be a staple in classrooms and will be a life-changing gift to kids who care. Great book!"

—**Deborah Ellis**, peace activist and author of the Breadwinner series

"Two of our world's most desperate needs right now are hope and possibility. Luckily for us, Joan Marie Galat's new book, *Make Your Mark, Make a Difference*, provides readers with both in spades! I'll surely be reading it with my own four sons, and encouraging all my students and colleagues to share this inspiring book with others!"

—**Luke Reynolds**, PhD, professor of education at Endicott College, former public middle school teacher, author, and dad

"In a world like this, with so many issues where it can often feel like you can't make a dent, we need more youth changemakers than ever. Books like this provide the necessary inspiration for youth to take that first or next step in their journey to make a difference! I can honestly say I wish I had this starting my activism when I was nine."

—**Hannah Alper**, activist, blogger, and author of *Momentus: Small Acts, Big Change*

"Encourage kids to be the change! With profiles of young people that demonstrate hope and progress on some of today's most crucial issues, *Make Your Mark, Make a Difference* is a fantastic tool for kids who want to change the world. And it's the perfect book for librarians, teachers, and parents looking to inspire them."

—**Michelle Roehm McCann**, author *Enough Is Enough* and *Reading Together*

"Joan Marie Galat's *Make Your Mark, Make a Difference* is an indispensable toolkit for young activists. It educates and inspires action, making it a critical resource for the next generation of changemakers. Including real-world initiatives like Protecting Our Students adds a layer of practicality that transforms activism from concept to achievable reality."

—**Robert Jordan**, cofounder of Protecting Our Students and the SITE|SAFETYNET℠ app

"A marvelous book that sets out to inspire and inform, *Make Your Mark, Make A Difference* should be required social studies reading. Joan Marie Galat makes notions like activism and fundamental human rights straightforward, clear, and simple, empowering young readers to envision themselves in action, and then gives them the tools they need to put that vision into action. An inspiring read for children, adolescents, parents, and educators—should be on every library shelf!"

—**Kathryn Mederos Syssoyeva**, PhD, educator and arts activist

"*Make Your Mark, Make a Difference* encourages kids to feel empowered to fight the injustices that exist in our world. It's going to take all of us working together to create the future we want to have. This book helps kids understand how they can start that change."

—**Jackson Apollo Mancini** (age eight), author of *Dr. Jon Jon Saves the Moon*

"With a wide variety of potential causes to care about, loads of stories of others who've made a difference, and plenty of good advice along the way, *Make Your Mark, Make a Difference* is a wonderful way to introduce young readers to the idea that they can be changemakers—right now."

—**Laurie Ann Thompson**, author of *Be a Changemaker* and
Emmanuel's Dream

"A thoroughly enjoyable read that is informative, insightful, and brilliant in its comprehensive review of all things that matter. This book will leave readers, young and old, feeling inspired and empowered with the knowledge that they too can make a difference!"

—**Nhung N. Tran-Davies**, author of *The Doll* and *Green Papayas* and
cofounder of Children of Vietnam Benevolent Foundation

"A comprehensive look at how kids can be confident leaders while pursuing change within a variety of important worldly issues. Joan Marie Galat provides readers with an abundance of excellent ideas for activism along with positive and thoughtful steps to achieve their goals."

—**Greg Pattridge**, PhD, teacher, writer, and creator
of the *Always in the Middle* blog

"Encouraging, supportive, and motivating, this book will inspire anyone of any age to consider how they can contribute to making the world, or just their small corner of it, a better place for all. Through real-life examples of young activists, along with a plethora of contemplative exercises that promote self-confidence, decision-making, and goal setting, the author reveals how every young person can be an advocate for positive change, on their own, in a group, or through an organization. From the abundant tips, quizzes, insights, and resources, kids will discover what is most important to them and learn how to go from feeling helpless to helpful and powerless to empowered. After reading this book, kids will come away knowing that regardless of their schedule, locale, finances, or living situation, they can make a valuable difference and have fun in the process."

—**Jo Stepaniak**, MSEd, author of *Low-FODMAP and Vegan* and
The Ultimate Uncheese Cookbook and former community and victim-
offender mediator

MAKE YOUR MARK, MAKE A DIFFERENCE

A KID'S GUIDE TO STANDING UP FOR PEOPLE, ANIMALS, AND THE PLANET

JOAN MARIE GALAT

ALADDIN
New York London Toronto Sydney New Delhi

BEYOND WORDS
Portland, Oregon

ALADDIN
An imprint of Simon & Schuster
Children's Publishing Division
1230 Avenue of the Americas
New York, NY 10020

BEYOND WORDS
1750 S.W. Skyline Blvd., Suite 20
Portland, OR 97221-2543
503-531-8700 / 503-531-8773 fax
www.beyondword.com

First Beyond Words/Aladdin edition February 2024
Text copyright © 2024 by Joan Marie Galat
Cover copyright © 2024 by Beyond Words/Simon & Schuster, LLC
Cover and interior illustrations by iStock

ALADDIN and related logo are registered trademarks of Simon & Schuster, LLC.

Beyond Words is an imprint of Simon & Schuster, LLC, and the Beyond Words logo is a registered trademark of Beyond Words Publishing, Inc.

Simon & Schuster: Celebrating 100 Years of Publishing in 2024

For information about special discounts for bulk purchases, please contact Simon & Schuster Special Sales at 1-866-506-1949 or business@simonandschuster.com.

The Simon & Schuster Speakers Bureau can bring authors to your live event. For more information or to book an event contact the Simon & Schuster Speakers Bureau at 1-866-248-3049 or visit our website at www.simonspeakers.com.

Managing Editor: Lindsay S. Easterbrooks-Brown
Copyeditor: Sarah Heilman, Emmalisa Sparrow Wood
Proofreader: Ali Shaw
Design: Sara E. Blum
Composition: William H. Brunson Typography Services

The illustrations for this book were rendered in Adobe Illustrator.
The text of this book was set in Bembo Std.

Manufactured in the United States of America 0124 MTN

10 9 8 7 6 5 4 3 2 1

Library of Congress Cataloging-in-Publication Data

Names: Galat, Joan Marie, 1963- author.
Title: Make your mark, make a difference : a kid's guide to standing up for
   people, animals, and the planet / Joan Marie Galat.
Description: Beyond Words/Aladdin edition. | Portland, Oregon : Beyond
   Words ; New York : Aladdin, 2024. | Includes bibliographical references.
   | Audience: Ages 10 and up
Identifiers: LCCN 2023033580 | ISBN 9781582708454 (hardcover) |
   ISBN 9781582708447 (paperback) | ISBN 9781665910354 (ebook)
Subjects: LCSH: Social change—Juvenile literature. | Social
   action—Juvenile literature.
Classification: LCC HM831 .G35 2024 | DDC 303.4—dc23/eng/20230804
LC record available at https://lccn.loc.gov/2023033580

For Amy, who first got me thinking about the
many ways to accomplish meaningful activism

CONTENTS

Introduction 1

PART I: EXAMINE YOUR WORLD 5

1 ○ Powerless or Powerful?: *Thinking Like an Activist* 7

2 ○ Smart Start: *Choosing Causes to Defend* 31

3 ○ Ready, Set, Action!: *Putting Your Personal Powers to Work* 59

PART II: ANIMAL AND EARTH ISSUES 87

4 ○ Justice for Animals: *Looking Out for Wildlife, Farm Animals, and Pets* 89

5 ○ We Have One Planet: *Safeguarding the Environment* 118

6 ○ Sky-High Activism: *Keeping Outer Space and Earth Safe* 142

PART III: PEOPLE ISSUES 167

7 ○ Threats and Violence: *Bringing Peace to Our World* 169

8 ○ Communities: *Ensuring Equality* 198

CONTENTS

9 ᵒ Poverty and Its Partners: *Boosting Income, Supporting Health, and Ensuring Education* 224

PART IV: CHANGE IS EVERYWHERE 253

10 ᵒ Change through the Arts: *Using Creativity to Spotlight Issues* 255

11 ᵒ Keep Going: *Accepting the Pace of Progress and Staying Positive* 284

Conclusion 315

Notes 319

Acknowledgments 341

INTRODUCTION

"You may never know what results come of your actions,
but if you do nothing, there will be no results."

Mahatma Gandhi, political activist, India

One day, my daughter came home from school talking about child soldiers—boys and girls who were forced to fight with warring groups in conflict zones. Amy had learned that armed captors in war-torn areas such as Sudan would abduct kids as young as eight and force them to fight or serve in other roles such as spies or guards. The thought of kids her age—ten years old—using rifles and killing people horrified her. She wanted to find out more about how this could happen and what she could do to help. Her research revealed that some children chose to be soldiers, believing they could protect their communities, while others were paid to fight and chose to join armed groups to help reduce their families' poverty.

Amy wanted to raise money to help child soldiers overcome the problems that forced them into lives of violence. I suggested we look for an organization already working in one of the countries where children were being *exploited*—unfairly used for another's benefit. We could research the organization's reputation, plan fundraising activities, and donate the money. Amy, however, wanted to set up her own charity and manage the project from start to finish. This approach felt complicated to me. I could imagine hosting bake sales, selling lollipops, or organizing other cash-generating activities, but I was stumped when it came to figuring out the best way to get funds to children and families in need. How could we make sure the money was actually used to help kids caught up in violence? How would we know who to trust with donated money? Another big question for me was, *How am I going to find the time to support Amy and her goal?* I didn't feel I could add this project to my other responsibilities. We talked about possible approaches, but ultimately let the hurdles stop us from pursuing a project and allowed the idea to fade.

Today, I see how these obstacles could have been overcome. Our conversations about child soldiers stayed with me and I always felt sorry that I hadn't tried harder to find a way to help Amy put her good wishes to work. In hindsight, perhaps I could have better explained the benefits of working with an established organization or steered her to get involved in helping people dealing with poverty closer to our home near Edmonton, Alberta.

Going forward, whenever I came across news stories about children and adults tackling social issues, I always read on to see how they overcame the challenges they faced, and eventually the obstructions to making a difference came to feel less imposing. In fact, it became clear—there are countless ways to be an activist, even if you do not apply that label to yourself.

I realized I had taken part in activities that fall under activism, even though I did not think of myself as an activist. There was the time I joined other families and brought my children to the school board office to march with signs in protest of the board's plan to take away the French immersion program at my daughters' school. My daughters were already taking three buses to reach their current school, and the change would have meant an even longer bus ride to a different community. I did not want them to have to change schools or endure a longer bus ride, and neither did they. It felt very unfair to all of us.

Another time, before my children were born, I had helped found and lead CURE (Community United for Responsible Environment) to start recycling and other planet-friendly activities in Lac La Biche, a small northern Alberta town where I once lived. And today, every time I promote reading at schools and libraries, I'm engaging in activism in my ongoing quest to inspire children to embrace reading and writing skills so that they can enjoy the lifelong benefits of literacy.

This journey has shown me there's an activist inside every person who has ever thought:

"That's not fair."

"We need to speak up."

"Someone needs to do something about this!"

"This doesn't seem right . . ."

I've always promoted the idea that adults who want to explore a complex topic should start with a good children's nonfiction book.

I wrote this book to help children who want to make the world a better place. I wrote this book for kids like Amy and the parents and other caregivers who want to help but need the same guidance I needed when Amy first came to me about child soldiers.

You are about to discover a great many ways to tackle injustice. The pages ahead will help you identify your own special powers and how to use them. You'll see that when you witness unfairness, you have the choice to **make your mark and make a difference**.

PART I

EXAMINE YOUR WORLD

1

POWERLESS OR POWERFUL?

THINKING LIKE AN ACTIVIST

"We're not waiting five, ten, twenty years to take the action we want to see. We're not the future of the world; we're the present, right? We're acting now. We're not waiting any longer."

Salvador Gómez-Colón, climate resilience activist, Puerto Rico

You have probably noticed that life is not fair. It can make you feel frustrated and angry—even helpless—when you come across something unjust. It might be a news story about illegal elephant hunting or families separated by war. It might be something you experience close to home, like seeing smog pollute the sky, a neighbor's dog always chained to a post, or bullying at school. Near or far, you probably wish someone would do something. You might want to help make things better but just have no idea where to start. You might even think, *What can I do? I'm just a kid.*

Let's see if you've got your facts straight.

Life is unfair.

Injustice exists in the world.

I'm just a kid.

But there is no such thing as "just a kid." Young people from around the world are tackling problems to make the world a better place. You can too! The job begins with thinking like an activist.

THINK LIKE A WHAT?

An activist is a person who fights to stop or reduce a problem. Activists also work to make life easier for those who are suffering. They understand that the way to make a difference is to take a giant difficulty and break it into smaller ones. Look at it this way—you know war is a huge issue. Can you stop countries from fighting? Probably not. Could you help people who are suffering because of war? Absolutely! You might raise money to help feed people in a refugee camp. You could collect school supplies for children in a war zone. You could encourage others to join you.

Although you might not know the best way to do these things, you can find out. Activists ask questions and play with ideas to find the best ways to help. They know problem-solving often includes these steps: practice, fail, and try again. It's annoying to fail, right? You don't hear a lot of people yelling, "Yeehaw, it didn't work!" Still, activists persist. What stops them from quitting? Knowing that what they do is important.

Right now, you are holding a tool in your hand. Use this book to discover the many steps you can take to be the kind of activist that makes the world a better place. Have you got what it takes? Find out with this Think Like an Activist quizard.

QUIZARD
THINK LIKE AN ACTIVIST

1. An activist is a person who:

   (A) signs up for acting lessons

   (B) hopes for the best

   (C) takes action to solve problems

2. An activist takes a big issue and:

   (A) makes it bigger

   (B) hides under the bed

   (C) makes it smaller

3. An activist is:

   (A) a superhero with a gold cape who always knows what to do

   (B) a wise person with wrinkles and gray hair

   (C) a person who keeps trying

What's a quizard, you ask? Is that even in the dictionary? Well, not yet, but maybe an activist could make that happen. For now, let's pretend a quizard is a teeny test that can make you a wizard of wisdom on a topic.

QUIZARD RESULTS

If you answered each question with C, congratulations! You're already thinking like an activist.

MEET A YOUNG ACTIVIST
Aakaash Anandan

Chennai is the very busy capital city of Tamil Nadu, a state in southeastern India. Cars, trucks, and buses crowd city streets. People on motorbikes and scooters, called two-wheelers, zip around other vehicles, searching for a clear path. Accidents are common, and traffic can make it hard for ambulances to reach accident victims quickly.

In 2015, five-year-old Aakaash was riding a two-wheeler with his parents. When he saw an accident occur, his mother had to explain that a young boy had hurt his head and died. She told him the child would have lived if he had been wearing a helmet.[1]

Aakaash could not forget what happened. He understood a simple decision could have saved the rider's life. Aakaash decided to take action. When people visited his home, Aakaash talked to them about why helmets are so important. He asked his friends at school to tell their parents to wear helmets too. Aakaash even began to help the Chennai traffic police. At a busy intersection called the Indira Gandhi square, Aakaash waited until drivers stopped at a long light signal. When the traffic backed up and came to a stop, he handed motorists pamphlets.

They included the message, "Uncle, please wear a helmet. It is for your safety."[2]

IT'S MY RIGHT!

Suppose you are a famous actor. (Maybe you are! Hello—can I have your autograph?) If that's not you, simply picture yourself as a star working on a big-deal project. Let's put you back in time to a film being created in 1930s California. You're getting paid for your breathtaking talent, but because you're a kid, your parents manage your money. You never even see it! When you turn eighteen—the age that makes you a legal adult—you ask for the cash. Uh-oh! Dear Ma and Pa spent every penny.

I'm not a mind-reader, but here is my best guess on what you're thinking: *They shouldn't have been able to do that! I have the right to my own money!*

You are correct. No matter how old you are, the money you earn should be saved for you. Fortunately, in 1938, actor Jackie Coogan took his mother and stepfather to court for spending his entire fortune. This led the California legislature to enact the Child Actors Bill, also known as the Coogan Law, which now ensures that child actors' rights are protected.[3] As a result, if you get a starring role in Hollywood today, your money will be safe thanks to labor laws that better protect the rights of child actors.[4]

The word *rights* refers to things you should be allowed to have, get, or do. You should *have* access to the basic things you need to survive, like clean water, nutritious food, and a safe place to live. You should be allowed to *get* an education and basic medical care and *do* and experience things like other kids, such as play, share your thoughts freely, and explore your world. You should not be treated differently because of your skin color, language, or clothes. It should not matter whether you are young or old, rich or poor, healthy or sick. Human rights are about how people treat one another. They are meant to make sure everyone has equal opportunities.

Across the globe, individuals and groups work to ensure all people can enjoy equal treatment. The United Nations (aka the UN), with 193 member countries, is the largest worldwide organization dedicated to promoting equal rights. The UN did something handy: it listed all the things people deserve to have to ensure they are treated equally. These "things" are called *fundamental human rights.*

Let's break this down:

Fundamental→ something basic and important

Human→ hopefully what you see in a mirror

Rights→ what each person deserves, in order to be treated fairly

The UN list, called the Universal Declaration of Human Rights (aka the UDHR), contains thirty articles that detail all human rights. Here's a quick look at some of them:

- All people are born free and equal.
- Everyone deserves the same human rights, no matter their race, color, sex, language, religion, or political opinion.
- No one should be placed in slavery.
- No one should be forced to marry.
- Everyone has the right to own property.
- Laws should treat all people equally.
- All children have the right to attend school.
- Anyone charged with an offense should be considered innocent until proven guilty.

○ Everyone has the right to their own opinion, called *freedom of thought*.[5]

The UN encourages all countries to use the UDHR when they create new laws, and it's been translated into more than five hundred languages!

The UN also wants to make life easier for children around the world and has made a list for kids under age eighteen called the Convention on the Rights of the Child. This document contains fifty-four articles on children's rights. Here's a quick look at some of them.

Children have the right to:

○ A name and nationality

○ Healthy food and clean water

○ A safe home

○ Protection from harm

○ Healthcare

○ Be able to play and rest

○ Go to school

○ Express opinions

○ Speak any language

○ Practice any religion[6]

Some of these rights may sound familiar, but others might surprise you. Isn't it obvious everyone should have a name and nationality? Why would anyone stop you from speaking your own language? Doesn't everyone know that the same laws should apply to everyone?

If you come from a place where laws exist to protect all citizens, these are logical questions. However, different countries and cultures around the world have their own traditions and ideas about how to live. For equality to exist, governments must support and enforce universal human rights.

GET CHATTY

Can you think of any situations that would prevent children from being able to play? Why do you think the UN included play as a children's right?

When you see a Get Chatty box, it's time to start a conversation. Your not-so-secret mission is to bring the topic points up with family or friends. You can do this at school or at the dinner table— really, anywhere you can settle in for a chat.

INJUSTICES AT HOME AND AWAY

Have you ever seen something in your school, neighborhood, or community and blurted out, "That's not okay!" Local injustices are problems that happen where you live. Suppose your school sets an unfair dress code. Imagine wanting to play on an all-boys or all-girls sports team but not being welcome because you are not the same sex. What if your local government gives builders permission to replace your favorite park with an office building? None of these things feel right.

Other difficulties exist across regions. A region could be different states or areas with less defined borders, such as "the mountains," "the south," or "the coast." A hurricane that damages homes across several states is a regional concern. Poor internet access in rural areas is another. Regional issues may even involve more than one country. You see this when Mexican citizens risk their lives to enter the United States, hoping to build a better life. Instead, they may experience homelessness, separation from family members, or unemployment once they arrive.

SPREAD THE WORD

Make a one-page brochure about an issue you care about.

Step 1—Write a paragraph that describes your concern and why it matters.

Step 2—List possible solutions. (Lists give people choices about how to help and make it more likely they'll want to get involved.)

Step 3—Talk with an adult to figure out the safest, most effective way to share your brochure.

Many concerns are global—they exist across the planet. The COVID-19 virus is a threat that has traveled around the world. Climate change—long-term changes to weather and climate patterns—impact people no matter where they live. The Black Lives Matter movement, which fights racism and violence, has spread from the United States to many other countries. Plastics, which harm wildlife, are found in every ocean. Some concerns even extend skyward, such as broken satellites that litter outer space and debates over who has the rights to mine minerals on *asteroids*—small, rocky space objects that orbit the Sun. From land to sky, you will never have to look far to find a problem that needs fixing.

COUNTRIES AND THEIR CASH

Countries are often put into categories based on their *economies*—how they make and spend money based on the goods and services they produce and sell. This is a fancy way of saying that a country's economy describes whether it is rich or poor, or somewhere in between.

A country's economy is about more than its money, though. A nation with a strong economy is better able to meet its citizens' needs for goods and services. One with a weak economy will experience greater poverty, along with other social issues. You may hear rich countries referred to as *first-world countries* and poor countries called *third-world countries*. However, new terms are now used, which better describe a country's status: *developed economies*, *economies in transition*, and *developing economies*. Not everyone agrees on the best way to classify a country. A country's wealth is not the only factor. Life expectancy, education levels, the number of people living in poverty, and other criteria may be considered. China is the largest developing economy and the world's second-largest economy, after the United States. However, other factors, such as its uneven distribution of wealth, lead to its classification as a developing economy.[7]

The world's most advanced economies belong to an informal group called the G7: Canada, France, Germany, Italy, Japan, the United Kingdom, the United States, and the European Union. The members represent democratic countries (where governments are elected by citizens) that share values. They meet annually to discuss and address matters that cross borders and affect the global economy, such as climate change, disease, peace, security, and tax evasion.

COUNTRIES AND THEIR ECONOMIES
(an abbreviated list)

DEVELOPED ECONOMIES	ECONOMIES IN TRANSITION	DEVELOPING ECONOMIES
Australia	Albania	Argentina
Canada	Armenia	Brazil
European Union	Belarus	China
France	Bosnia and Herzegovina	Cuba
Germany	Georgia	Egypt
Iceland	Montenegro	Haiti
Italy	North Macedonia	Kenya
Japan	Republic of Moldova	Pakistan
New Zealand	Russian Federation	Philippines
Norway	Serbia	Rwanda
Switzerland	Tajikistan	Syrian Arab Republic
United Kingdom	Ukraine	Türkiye
United States of America	Uzbekistan	Vietnam

Source: United Nations, 2022[8]

WHAT KINDS OF ISSUES ARE THERE ANYWAY?

A lot of different types of social concerns exist. In fact, there's a great big mess of them. One way to organize them into groups is to look at how they affect people, animals, and the planet. Some are hard to separate, though. One matter is often connected to another. It's like there is a great big string, tying bunches of them together. Take war, for example. It can make it hard to transport food to the populous or can even destroy the land and farms a country needs to produce its food supply. In this case, reducing hunger means we must also look at the subject of war.

Another drawback is that the solution to a problem can create a new problem. (You may need to read that twice!) To make this clear, think of insects crawling over a field of oats. Now picture a farmer freaking out. To protect the harvest, the farmer might use chemicals, called *pesticides*, to kill the creatures. The farmer gets a larger crop, which can help combat hunger in the world. Sounds good, right? But pesticides pollute land and water, and this harms wildlife. Pollution is not good for people either. Now the string is connecting pollution and wildlife, as well as people and hunger.

One of the reasons people face hunger is *poverty*—not having enough money to pay for the things they need to live. Poverty can make it hard to get things like clean water, housing, education, healthcare, and sanitation. Diseases thrive and spread when there's no way to get rid of sewage and trash. People living in poverty may also face another issue—*discrimination*. This is when a person is not treated well due to a personal trait, like being poor. People are discriminated against for a great many reasons. It can happen due to skin color, race, age, culture, language, and *nationality*—the country of birth or citizenship. Unfair treatment may be based on sex—being assigned female or male at birth—or *gender identity*—whether a person feels female or male or *nonbinary*, which can mean a gender outside the binary classification of female/male. The relationships people form based on their identities can also trigger discrimination.

You can see that the string-connected issues are starting to tangle.

Animals face discrimination too! People often like certain species more than others because of how they look or behave. This means popular animals, like gorillas, get more support than ugly ones, like the endangered blobfish. Of course, all creatures must be treated fairly, even if they are not everyone's idea of cute, beautiful, or wonderful.

A key problem for many wild critters is loss of *habitat*—places that contain everything an organism needs to survive. Forests, grasslands, deserts, wetlands, and other types of natural habitat ensure that a variety of plants and animals can exist. This variety, called *biodiversity*, helps ensure a balance between predators and prey. Biodiversity is an important part of a healthy habitat.

Another serious matter is the spread of *invasive species*—animals that enter a habitat where they are not usually found. Without natural predators to control their numbers, invasives bully out native organisms and make it hard for them to survive. Wildlife also faces threats from poaching. This illegal hunting, often tied to selling body parts, such as ivory or organs, can cause species to become *endangered*—at risk of dying out.

Every farm animal and pet out there deserves *humane treatment*—conditions which prevent suffering that could be avoided. All *domestic species*—those that depend on people to survive—should have the food, water, shelter, and attention they need to be comfortable and happy. Sports that involve animals, like horse racing, must ensure humane treatment. Unfortunately, not all critters get the care they need. Some domesticated species become *feral*—they escape the care of humans and go wild. Feral pigs destroy crops and pastures and can be aggressive toward people. Stray cats (and pet cats that are allowed outside) prey on wild birds and reduce their populations. In a nutshell, feral animals can take over territory, competing for food and habitat, and reducing biodiversity in the process.

The zigzagging string that connects so many issues ultimately leads to our environment. Climate change is the biggest environmental challenge facing planet Earth. We can already see how it impacts water levels through drought and flooding. Where seawater has become more acidic, we see its effects on ocean habitats. We can also see that logging and other deforestation reduces habitat and contributes to Earth's rising temperature. This increase in temperature, called *global warming*, makes the climate problem grow.

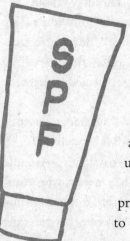

The environment is also affected by *overpopulation*—too many people living in an area. As cities sprawl outward, regions lose important farmland. More people means more pollution. This leads to a wide variety of problems, including holes in the *ozone*—a layer of Earth's atmosphere that protects us from the Sun's ultraviolet radiation.

All of these matters make the world seem pretty messy. Just remember, it is not too messy to clean up!

BE THE CHANGE

Look for everyday ways to stand up for what is right. For example, suppose you notice someone in your class is facing discrimination. One way to help is by simply demonstrating fairness. You might choose that person to be your partner for a class project, join in a game at recess, or sit with you at lunch. You don't have to make a big deal about it. Just be kind. Your effort will set an important example. It might inspire others to behave with kindness too.

WHO CARES?

Lots of people care about social issues. Around the world, kids and adults work to make a difference. Some tackle a cause on their own or with a few friends. Some get involved as a family. Others will rally a club, class, or entire school to work together. Many people volunteer or get jobs with charities or nonprofit organizations. Nonprofits operate a lot like businesses, but there is one big difference—their goal is to provide help, not make a profit.

Some activists work with *philanthropic foundations*—groups that tackle social concerns using money from donors, called *philanthropists*. Others work with *nongovernmental organizations*, called *NGOs* for short. These orgs are not part of any government.

Yes, this is a real word! An abbreviation for "organizations."

National governments, however, are often big donors to other countries facing *humanitarian issues*—situations where people are suffering. Government donations, called *foreign aid*, help reduce poverty and improve people's living conditions. Aid can also be used to teach other countries how to build their own wealth so they can meet their citizens' needs without help.

Governments give billions of dollars' worth of aid in the form of money, goods, and services. Goods, like food and emergency supplies, are common donations. Services might include training teachers or sending special soldiers, called *peacekeepers*, to provide aid during an emergency, like an earthquake or flood. Peacekeepers also help keep a region safe.

Although one country can help another and international laws do exist, no world government exists. No country or organization can enforce fundamental human rights everywhere on the planet. Instead, the United Nations helps guide relationships between countries. It also operates the United Nations Children's Fund, known by the name UNICEF. This UN agency defends children's rights in more than 190 countries and territories.

BE WISE

- Search the internet for *best charities*, *top charities*, or *reputable charities*.

- Type a charity's name into a web browser along with words such as *complaint*, *scam*, or *rating*.

- Explore websites that provide information on charities and their reputations, such as the BBB Wise Giving Alliance, Charity Watch, Charity Navigator, and the IRS Nonprofit Charities Database.

No matter where you live, you will find people and organizations working to improve our world. Seeing how others do it will help you find the best way to join in.

MORE THAN ONE WAY TO TACKLE A PROBLEM

When you see this heading, expect to be wowed by the creative ways people are working to make a difference.

BICYCLE RECYCLING PROGRAMS IN DIFFERENT PLACES

If you had to choose between walking for two hours or cycling for thirty minutes to visit a doctor, what would you pick? Bicycles make it easier for people to access opportunities like healthcare, education, and employment. Bikes cost less than cars. They don't release toxic chemicals into the air, and they boost physical fitness. Recognizing their benefits, many charities work to put bike pedals under the feet of people who need them.

KEEP BIKES ON THE ROAD
{We-Cycle-USA, Nonprofit, Arizona}

Robert Chacon began fixing bicycles and giving them to people living with disabilities. He wanted to help them become more independent. Today, We-Cycle-USA helps anyone in the area it serves who needs a bike. Sometimes they have to work for it, though. The Earn a Bike program, for ages sixteen and up, asks for eight hours of volunteering in exchange for a bike.

Robert chooses to repair bicycles, rather than buy new ones, to keep fixable bikes out of landfills. He also helps reduce waste by welcoming anyone to come in and use the fee-free shop to fix their own bikes.[9]

GET KIDS WORKING TOGETHER
{Wish for Wheels, Nonprofit, Colorado}

Wish for Wheels's mission is to bring a child's dream of a new set of wheels to life, ultimately giving brand-new helmets and bikes—always a twenty-inch Huffy—to second-grade students in low-income communities. Its founder, Brad Appel, wants kids to feel freedom and independence. Wish for Wheels's Kid2Kid program helps make that happen. It matches a second-grade class with an older class at a different school. Students meet and keep in touch as pen pals. The older students help their new friends by writing letters to businesses, asking them to donate money for bikes and help build them. Businesses, and other groups, also work directly with this nonprofit to fund, assemble, and donate bikes.[10]

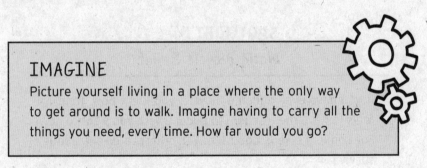

IMAGINE
Picture yourself living in a place where the only way to get around is to walk. Imagine having to carry all the things you need, every time. How far would you go?

SHIP BIKES TO REMOTE COMMUNITIES
{Polar Bike Project, Grassroots Approach, Nunavut, Canada}

The Polar Bike Project collects gently used bikes from other parts of Canada and gives them to children who live in remote arctic towns. Alison and Tim Harper founded the project after moving to the fly-in community of Kugluktuk and seeing that few families could afford bikes. Volunteers work with the Canadian Coast Guard, as well as an airline, to transport donated bicycles. They make sure the bikes are safe to ride, raise money for repairs, and donate the tools communities need to keep the bikes in good shape. After bikes are delivered, volunteers set up riding programs to encourage families to ride together and enjoy the fun of bike riding.[11]

SPOTLIGHT ON . . .
World Bicycle Relief

If you have ever ridden a bicycle, you know how great it feels to have the freedom to pedal where you want to go. For some, a bike is good fun. For others, a bike is about survival.

World Bicycle Relief (WBR) is an international non-profit organization that uses bicycles to help people escape poverty. It designed a bicycle that is so tough, riders can pedal across rough ground or bumpy roads even while carrying a heavy load. Nurses use the bikes to visit patients at their homes. Farmers use the bikes to reach customers. Children use the bikes to get to school. These rugged bikes also help keep girls and women safe. Walking can take so long that some don't get home until after sunset. With bikes, girls and women can travel during daylight hours instead of walking in the dark, through dangerous out-of-the-way areas. WBR has provided bikes in developing countries including Colombia, Malawi, and Zimbabwe. Using these bicycles also allows more time for education as well as more choices when it comes to earning money and getting healthcare. In Zambia, WBR hires people in the communities it serves to assemble, repair, and distribute the bikes. By creating jobs and hiring locals, WBR also helps reduce poverty.[12]

GET CHATTY

What's good about donating new bikes? Can you also think of reasons for giving used bikes? Aside from getting a bike, how might volunteering in exchange for a free bike help someone?

ONE THING YOU CAN DO NOW
Design a poster that promotes cycling safety or a bike-recycling program. Post it on community bulletin boards or ask an adult to share it on social media.

SKILLS YOU MIGHT HAVE AND SKILLS TO BUILD

Even if you want to help, you might wonder if you have any skills to offer. It is useful to remember that everyone, including you, is good at something. You might be an ace at dreaming up ideas. You might have a talent for keeping track of details. You might excel at signing up volunteers.

If you are interested in activism, you are probably enthusiastic. You care about your world and want to make it better. You might also be *self-motivated*. That means no one has to talk you into fighting for the issues you care about. You are ready and willing to get started. Figuring out what to do will take some *critical thinking skills*, which means considering a matter from every angle instead of diving in with your first idea. When it comes to dreaming up plenty of ideas, it helps to have creative skills. The idea of "being creative" might make you think about arts and crafts, building models, or other pastimes. However, there are many ways to be creative, and each one is important because creativity helps with problem-solving.

If you would like to be more creative, try doing something in a different way than you usually would. For example, you might eat cereal out of a mug instead of a bowl, using a fork instead of a spoon. By escaping a routine, you remind yourself that there is more than one way to do things. And, when the milk runs through your fork and down your chin, you will be able to practice other skills—patience, along with acceptance when things don't quite go as planned. You've heard about not crying over spilled milk, right?

Do you think you could talk other people into trying this creative experiment? If you do, you will be practicing public speaking skills and leadership. If your family does not want to take part in this cereal investigation, you might have to work on problem-solving. How can you get them to see this as a useful exercise? Can you use your communication skills to negotiate and find a way to make everyone happy about doing the activity? Perhaps you could get them to agree to use a mug if they do not have to use a fork.

It will be easier to find a solution that makes everyone satisfied if you have *empathy*—the ability to understand other people's feelings. Perhaps your parents do not want to drip milk onto their work clothes. Using empathy can help you solve the worry. Why not suggest playing the creativity game on a weekend? You will have to be organized to make this happen. Think of the best way to remember the change of plans. Should you write it on a calendar? Put a sticky note on the fridge? Make a note in your journal? As an activist, you will want to find ways to keep track of your plans. You will also want to have fun. You are more likely to finish what you start when you're having a good time. One of the fun  things about activism is that you get the chance to try new things and practice new skills. It is also fun to be creative and see your efforts lead to results. So, have fun!

SATISFY YOUR CURIOSITY

Craving more details? Sit down with an adult and satisfy your curiosity by digging deeper into researching the following topics on the internet. Find child-friendly websites more easily by adding "kids" to your search terms.

- Child Actor's Bill USA
- UNICEF
- World Bicycle Relief
- Wish for Wheels
- We-Cycle-USA
- The Polar Bike Project

2

SMART START
CHOOSING CAUSES TO DEFEND

"Every action, no matter how small, is like drips on a rock—
over time, they can carve a canyon through even the thickest,
most immovable layer of rock."

Shannon Watts, founder of Moms Demand Action, United States

It's exciting to share space with the many activists trying to make our world better. Whether you are pumped about a cause or unsure where to throw your energy—brace yourself! Your curiosity is going to get a workout as you encounter the laundry basket of issues in the pages ahead. Be warned! This can create a conundrum. Your heart might want to fix everything, and all that emotion can trigger brain freeze. How do you choose a matter to focus on? Must you pick only one? Luckily, Part 1: Examine Your World provides the answers. The tips you find within these chapters will help you narrow down your options and choose an approach. That frozen part of you is sure to thaw as you discover how to get started, research your concern, and tell fact from fiction. It will be a mind-blowing experience, and we are about to have some fun!

"Wait a minute," you might say. "Mind-blowing? Is this fiction you speak of?"

It does seem like an exaggerated claim, doesn't it? You could even say it's *unsubstantiated*—a statement not supported by evidence. Every activist must be able to tell the difference between facts and *misinformation*—false or misleading information that is often shared with the deliberate intention to misinform or deceive.

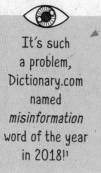

It's such a problem, Dictionary.com named *misinformation* word of the year in 2018![1]

Lucky for you, you'll be a pro at identifying reliable sources of information by the end of part 1. You'll also be ready to head into parts 2 and 3, where you'll be introduced to a number of issues around the planet. Some you'll already know about, while others might make you think, *I didn't know that was even a thing!*

And maybe there will be a little voice in your head whispering, *This is all so sad. I don't know if I want to keep reading.* That thought is EXACTLY why you should persist. Your *utterly* valid reaction makes you the perfect person to stand up and help.

Why you should not put this book down. Ever!

If you stop reading, you'll miss discovering the amazing ways people—with concerns like yours—work to improve lives and our planet. In this book, you'll see how actions add up and create change, and you'll learn that your contributions can be a catalyst too. If you ever feel this is going to be too hard, remember one thing: **If you make a difference in even one life, you've made a contribution that matters.**

It is now my pleasure to introduce part 4. (If only books could have drumrolls! This section truly deserves some fanfare.) The final section of this book showcases unique and creative ways people are making change. We're talking artsy activism. Think poetry, dance, photography, and theater. You might find yourself reaching for a pen, camera, or costume in support of your favorite cause too! You'll also find tips to help you set goals, stay motivated, and work with other volunteers. Part 4 might even help you answer the big question: What are you going to be when you grow up? And that is not an unsubstantiated claim. Drumroll, please!

GOING FROM HELPLESS TO HELPFUL

The first time an environmental issue bothered me, I was in fourth grade. My science assignment was to write a report on land pollution, and the horrifying facts I uncovered made me more observant. I began noticing trash on the ground, and I started speaking out if anyone with me littered. One rainy afternoon, as we walked home, a friend dropped her gum on the ground. I tried to explain why littering was bad, but her glazed eyes made it clear my speech wasn't working. Determined to change her mind, I refused to walk another step unless she picked it up. Perhaps the downpour was more convincing than my words, but she did retrieve the gum. I made a difference in my own small way.

As you look for causes to defend, start with matters that have touched your own life. Next, think about problems that affect the area where you live and the people you care about. Organize your thoughts by listing your concerns under these three headings:

Home

School

Community

A list might look like this:

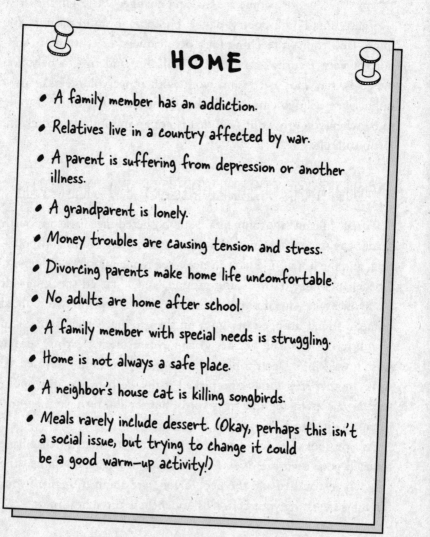

HOME

- A family member has an addiction.
- Relatives live in a country affected by war.
- A parent is suffering from depression or another illness.
- A grandparent is lonely.
- Money troubles are causing tension and stress.
- Divorcing parents make home life uncomfortable.
- No adults are home after school.
- A family member with special needs is struggling.
- Home is not always a safe place.
- A neighbor's house cat is killing songbirds.
- Meals rarely include dessert. (Okay, perhaps this isn't a social issue, but trying to change it could be a good warm-up activity!)

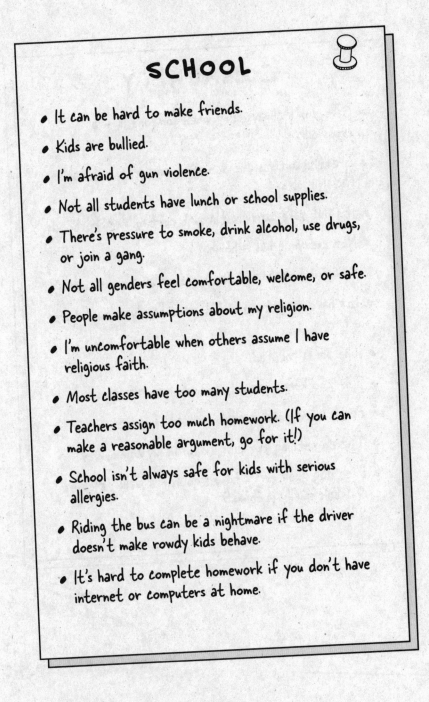

SCHOOL

- It can be hard to make friends.

- Kids are bullied.

- I'm afraid of gun violence.

- Not all students have lunch or school supplies.

- There's pressure to smoke, drink alcohol, use drugs, or join a gang.

- Not all genders feel comfortable, welcome, or safe.

- People make assumptions about my religion.

- I'm uncomfortable when others assume I have religious faith.

- Most classes have too many students.

- Teachers assign too much homework. (If you can make a reasonable argument, go for it!)

- School isn't always safe for kids with serious allergies.

- Riding the bus can be a nightmare if the driver doesn't make rowdy kids behave.

- It's hard to complete homework if you don't have internet or computers at home.

COMMUNITY

- Cars don't always stop when someone is in a crosswalk.

- Graffiti artists are damaging property and making racial insults.

- It's not safe to walk through certain neighborhoods.

- Not everyone has a home.

- People in wheelchairs can't get up and down curbs.

- It's hard to get around if your family doesn't have a car.

- The air is polluted.

- The zoo keeps marine mammals in small aquariums.

- People feed pond ducks unsuitable foods.

- There's nothing for kids to do in my community.

- I see dog poop every time I go for a walk. (Please end this smelly problem!)

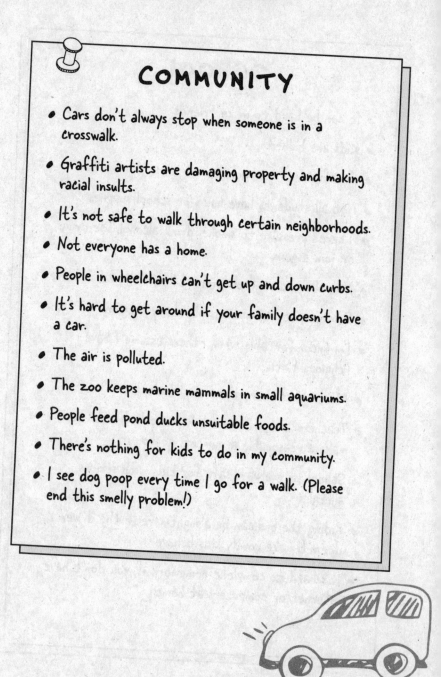

As you can see, many possibilities exist. Whenever something bugs you, consider it an *aha!* moment. Revisit your list now and then and add new observations. Imagine spending your time on different issues and how leading change would make you feel. Narrow down your choices even more with this handy quizard.

QUIZARD
WHAT DO YOU CARE ABOUT?

1. If I were going to give my last $20 to a good cause, I would pick one that helps:

   (A) Save endangered wildlife

   (B) Make healthcare affordable

   (C) Locate missing children

   (D) Promote renewable energy

2. If I were choosing a summer camp with a social justice theme, I would pick one that focuses on ways to:

   (A) Prevent animal cruelty

   (B) Support LGBTQ youths

   (C) Make sure all children can go to school

   (D) Stop people from cutting down forests

3. If I were going to give a speech to my class, I would prefer to talk about:

   (A) How pesticides impact birds

   (B) Ways to make life easier for immigrants

(C) The dangers of drug use

(D) How to stop plastics from reaching bodies of water

4. If I were going to watch a show or movie that demonstrates how one person can make a difference, I would pick:

(A) *The Supervet* (how a vet uses technology to save animals)[2]

(B) *The Boy Who Harnessed the Wind* (a thirteen-year-old boy protects his family and village from famine)[3]

(C) *Wadjda* (a ten-year-old Saudi girl stands up against traditional gender roles)[4]

(D) *I Am Greta* (the girl who became a global activist for climate change)[5]

5. If I were going to take part in a protest, my sign would say:

(A) Be a Friend to Elephants—Skip the Circus

(B) Black Lives Matter

(C) Protect Kids, Not Guns

(D) The Climate Is Changing, Why Aren't We?

QUIZARD RESULTS

If you answered mostly:

A, your interests lean toward animal matters.

B, your interests lean toward concerns that affect communities.

C, your interests lean toward problems that affect children.

D, your interests lean toward planet-wide environmental issues.

If your answers jumped around a bit, don't worry. A five-question quizard is not enough to fully analyze your mind. (Be suspicious of quizzes that try to tell you otherwise!) The exercise is still useful, though. It helps steer your thinking toward your interests and takes you to the next step—posing questions of your own. Asking questions helps you understand situations better and narrow down the many choices. To begin, put on your reporter glasses and prepare to do some digging. Asking reporter-style questions is the fastest way to find out what you need to know. It works like this: start with a blank page, pick your peeve, and interview yourself.

BE A REPORTER

1. WHAT is the problem?
2. WHO is affected?
3. WHERE is this happening?
4. WHEN does it happen?
5. WHY do I care?
6. HOW have people tried to solve this?
7. HOW are current solutions working?
8. WHAT else can be done?
9. WHAT can I do?
10. WHO else can help?
11. WHO is responsible for making change?
12. HOW can I take one part of this issue and make it better?
13. WHEN can I get started?

You'll immediately know the answers to some questions. Others will call for research. Digging up facts is an important skill. The more you do it, the better equipped you will be to take on the world. Research can stop you from making mistakes and wasting time. If money is involved in accomplishing your goal, research can help you spend more wisely. Knowing all the facts will help you strengthen your ideas. You'll see what others are doing and get ideas on what you might do too. The more you know about your cause, the easier it will be to make the greatest difference. Plan to do some deep digging to get a well-rounded perspective on your problem!

I recently explored a situation that bothers me—frogs getting run over by vehicles. In case you haven't heard, some frog species migrate between the habitat where they feed and the wetlands where they breed. This is risky business. At a single road crossing, thousands of frogs may die. If you want to help protect the little hoppers, you can organize a team of friends to carry them across the road. Volunteers at hundreds of sites throughout Maine do this on the rainy nights when the frogs migrate, and it can make a big difference.[6] It can also harm frogs if people don't first research how to best help. Frog helpers need to know that amphibians are delicate creatures. They must be handled with care. Amphibian skin is permeable—it has pores that allow liquids to pass through it. Frog helpers with lotions, soap, insect repellant, perfume, hand sanitizer, and other chemicals on their hands can harm their amphibian friends. Informed frog handlers know they must start with clean hands, and then moisten them in a puddle of rainwater or on wet ground foliage, keep their hands wet, and be extremely gentle.

Gathering frogs without first gathering information can be dangerous in other ways too. You might drop a frog if it does something unexpected. That's why it's helpful to know that startled frogs may pee on you when you pick them up. This clever defense mechanism

EXPLORE MORE

If you find useful information on the internet, you might wonder whether you should bother to look further. After all, the web is a handy tool that allows you to access information and research from around the world. Still, you might miss important information if it's all you rely upon. Make sure you get the big picture by visiting a library or bookstore's non-fiction shelves. Seek out books and newspaper and magazine articles on the matters you want to explore. Most of these published materials go through an editing process. In addition, they may be *fact-checked*—reviewed to ensure that the information presented is accurate. It's easy to find the date of publication too. Ask librarians and bookstore staff to steer you toward current and reliable sources of information. They might show you hard copies of newspapers, magazines, journals, or other *periodicals*—written works published at regular intervals. They might also refer you right back to the internet, as many periodicals are published online. If you do get the chance, though, flip through a paper copy. Browsing this way can sometimes lead to the discovery of valuable new facts.

is meant to make you drop the frog so it can escape. Knowing this peeing trick in advance can spare a handler from falling for it.

You might want to express your love for frogs with a big slobbery kiss. Research will tell you this is not a good idea either. Frogs secrete toxins that can make you ill. They can also have bacteria or parasites. Frogs are creatures you definitely do not want on your lips.

As you research, you'll discover other ways to help too. Instead of handling frogs, you might choose to encourage governments to install culverts that allow frogs to cross beneath roads. You might suggest they put up warning signs for drivers or invest in barriers that direct frogs toward under-the-road passages. Your efforts could save hundreds of thousands of amphibians at a single location.

Begin by gathering information. Check out books as well as reliable online resources. You know typing questions into a browser will lead to all kinds of answers. However, not all answers may be as helpful as you hope. Anyone can post information online, and not all of it is trustworthy. Before accepting written words as fact, look deeper into who wrote the information. Ask these two questions: Am I reading facts supported with evidence, or an opinion? If it's an opinion, does the writer have the education or experience to make sure these statements are accurate?

Let's give this a try with investigating frog migration:

1. Who is the writer of the information? If it's written by well-known journalists, scientists, or scholars, or comes from a website sponsored by an organization that is known to be reputable (such as state and federal organizations; national museums; and journals, magazines, and television channels that are known to rigorously fact-check), you can accept the information as fact. If you are unable to verify if the writer or website has appropriate credentials or if the writer lists an association that appears to have a bias, you'll need to cross-check your facts with additional resources before coming to a

conclusion. A bias is a personal (and sometimes unreasonable) judgment or opinion. For example, if a blog promotes using culverts to save frogs, but the blog writer owns a business selling culverts, you can tell the writer has something to gain (money) by convincing people that culverts save frogs. Although the writer may present factual information, it may be slanted to serve the writer's personal interests. Therefore, you cannot rely solely on this particular source.

2. Look for the date the content was written. It's important to always seek the most current data. Look also at the quality of the website. Is it easy to navigate, modern-looking, and up-to-date? Or is it clunky to use and full of outdated information? Poorly designed websites aren't always a sign of unreliable information, but they should nudge you to take a closer look.

BE THE CHANGE

Activism can be loud, but it can also be quiet. You can help frogs by providing shelter, water, and *native plants*—species naturally found in your area. All you need to get started is a quiet patch in your backyard or on your school grounds. Choose a damp, shady spot, such as near a gutter, in a place where pesticides are not used. Fill a terra-cotta plant saucer with water, set it in your habitat, and plan to change the water daily. Next, pile sticks to create additional shelter. You could even make a frog abode.

For the froggy house, dig a shallow hole, set a clay pot on its side in the depression, and add dry leaves. Show the habitat to visitors and guests, and tell them why it is important. Quiet examples can have a powerful impact!

Now let's hop away from the frogs and get back to those reporter-style questions. Having investigated frog migration, you should find it much easier to fill in any blanks in the who-what-where-when-why-how list. Thanks to your research, your answers might look like this:

1. **WHAT is the problem?** Frogs trying to cross roads on wet, rainy nights are getting struck, injured, and killed by vehicles, pedestrians, and cyclists.

2. **WHO is affected?** Species include the spring peeper, wood frog, Columbia spotted frog, California red-legged frog, and others, as well as toads, spotted and mole salamanders, and other migrating amphibians.

3. **WHERE is this happening?** Problems occur on roads that separate wetlands and forested foraging areas. Frogs may only need to hop a few hundred feet. In other places, they migrate more than a quarter mile.

> Could you hop
> that far?

4. **WHEN does it happen?** Frogs migrate on warm and rainy spring nights after the ground thaws and temperatures stay above 40 degrees Fahrenheit (5 degrees Celsius). A heavy evening rain sparks the migration. In some places, it's called the *Big Night*.

5. **WHY do I care?** I can't stand it when animals suffer. It's not fair that frogs die because human-made roads separate their habitats. It doesn't have to be this way.

6. **HOW have people tried to solve this?** People have tried carrying frogs to safety, erecting frog-crossing signs, lowering speed limits, using fences that steer frogs toward under-the-road crossings, and installing culverts.

7. HOW are current solutions working? In some places, hundreds to thousands of frogs are saved.[7]

8. WHAT else can be done? More frog crossings need to be identified. People need to know about this problem.

9. WHAT can I do?

- Find out what species live nearest to me.
- Look for roads near wetlands where amphibians cross, and register sites with an organization that runs a safe-crossing program.
- Ask transportation departments to make roads more frog friendly.
- Join or start a volunteer group.
- Raise awareness about the problem.
- Participate in a program that helps carry frogs across roads.
- Get involved in *citizen science*—projects that involve collecting information and sharing it with scientists.

10. WHO else can help? I can ask friends, classmates, family, scouts, guides, Junior Forest Wardens, and other nature-related groups.

11. WHO is responsible for making change? Government departments involved in managing transportation, fish and wildlife, conservation, and natural resources can tackle this problem.

12. HOW can I take one part of this issue and make it better? I can improve awareness by starting a school club and urging members to share frog safety information with their families and friends. We can put up posters in the hallways and ask parents and teachers to use their social media to spread the word. The club can write letters to people in government and ask for change. Volunteers can contact local newspapers, radio stations, and other media to ask them to cover the upcoming migration. Every spring, we can encourage people to detour around roads that frogs cross.

13. WHEN can I get started? The best time to begin is now!

IMAGINE

Picture life without frogs. Need a little help? Frogs eat pests such as mosquitoes, helping to spare you from the bites and diseases these stingers spread. By studying frogs and their unique characteristics, including the ability to regrow limbs, scientists gather important information about ways to treat cancer,[8] depression, high blood pressure, heart disease, Alzheimer's disease, AIDS, pain, and other problems.[9]

SHRINK THOSE PROBLEMS!

Number twelve on the previous list is a key question that can help you take a giant issue and make it smaller. Sometimes you may want to help out with the immediate difficulty. In this case, that's helping frogs cross roads. Other times, you might want to tackle the root of the matter—the fact that roads interrupt habitats. Both ways of helping are important. If you decide ahead of time what success looks like, it will be easier to achieve your goals. Remember, it's easier to shrink a problem to something you can tackle than it is to completely eliminate the problem. It would be wonderful to save every frog, but instead, you can do your best to save as many as possible.

One way to narrow down your goals is to take general ideas and make them more precise.

INSTEAD OF ...	TRY BEING SPECIFIC ...
I will save *all* the frogs!	I'll help spring peepers within 25 miles of my home.
I'm going to put frog crossing signs at every pond.	I'm going to raise enough money to erect signs at one new location each spring.
I'm going to tell the world how roads are making migrations deadly to amphibians.	I'm going to make sure every newspaper and radio/TV station within 40 miles of my neighborhood knows about this matter.

Now outline the steps you'll need to take to achieve your goal. Your list might look like this:

1. Find out which species of frogs live and migrate closest to where I live.

2. Research whether an organization is already working on the situation in my area. Ask how I can get involved.

3. If no local organizations are assisting, look for sites where frogs are at risk.

4. Research how to best handle frogs when helping them across roads.

5. Plan a frog-helping event:

- Choose a road that amphibians need help to cross.

- Figure out how to make sure volunteers stay safe when saving frogs on dark, wet roads in rainy weather. I might ask the local transportation department to temporarily close the road. If the road must stay open, ask police to help direct traffic.

- Put out the word and invite people to volunteer.

- Provide participants with clear instructions on how to help and stay safe.

6. Find out whether I need permission to erect signs.

7. Raise funds to pay for frog-crossing road signs by buying and reselling frog-shaped gummy candies.

Do this step before raising any money.

8. Ask local newspapers, radio, and television stations to report on my topic.

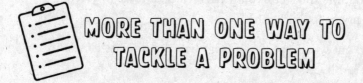

MORE THAN ONE WAY TO TACKLE A PROBLEM

You've probably noticed that the word *research* keeps popping up. Examining an issue from every angle is incredibly useful. It can help you get where you want to go faster and with fewer upsets. Despite these benefits, you may start to feel that this book is mighty bossy. *Find out this! Find out that! Look stuff up. Ask questions!* To counter that feeling, replace *mighty bossy* with *a fine example of leadership.*

SPREAD THE WORD!

How many people do you know? It probably feels like too many to count. Friends, family, and other people you interact with form your personal network.

Invite your connections to help spread news about your cause and activities. They're like free megaphones! If you're working with a group, grow your network even more by asking each person to tell three others. Guide them to include a specific request to help out. If you're aiding frogs, for example, volunteers might ask: Can you make a frog habitat in your yard? Will you please support us with a donation? Are you able to help carry frogs across roads?

HELPING AMPHIBIANS IN DIFFERENT PLACES

Around the world, people are using their imaginations to help frogs and other amphibians. Check out the following enterprises and see if you too might find ways to improve habitat, breed frogs to boost populations, or add to scientific knowledge by sharing your observations in nature. If you read or hear about a frog-friendly initiative, explore how you might make it work in your area.

GIVE AWAY MONEY
{SAVE THE FROGS!, Charity, California}

Around the world, amphibian populations are in trouble due to habitat destruction, pollution, and disease. Climate change, which alters water levels and temperatures, is a problem too. Dr. Kerry Kriger is a biologist who set out to help by founding SAVE THE FROGS! This charity helps protect amphibians and inspires people to care about frogs and nature. Based in California, SAVE THE FROGS! hosts events around the world and works to create, restore, and protect habitat.

In 2009, Dr. Kriger founded Save the Frogs Day, an international day of amphibian education and action aimed at inspiring more people to become involved. The charity assists groups across the globe that organize events on the last Saturday of April. Funds have been used to remove non-native weeds from frog habitat, take people on educational frog walks, and hold rallies calling for a ban on the use of atrazine, an herbicide that is harmful to frogs. Since 2009, SAVE THE FROGS! has provided more than $100,000 of funding to forty-seven amphibian conservationists in sixteen countries.[10]

RAISE FROGS TO FIGHT EXTINCTION
{Frogs & Friends, NGO, Germany}

More than three thousand frog species are viewed as threatened.[11] Frogs & Friends is a nongovernmental organization working to prevent frog extinction through its Citizen Conservation program. Based in Germany, Frogs & Friends wants to establish a scientific frog-breeding program using zoos and private animal breeders to raise frogs in captivity. Experienced breeders would raise species most at risk while beginners would be invited to raise easier, less threatened varieties. As well as ensuring that populations are not wiped out, the program would educate and inspire others about the importance of amphibians.

ONE THING YOU CAN DO NOW

Protect water. When you use less of it, treatment plants do not need to draw as much from the environment, thus leaving more water in natural areas. Another way to help is to dispose of medicines at hospitals, pharmacies, and police departments that collect unwanted or expired drugs. If that's not an option, ask an adult to help you find out what local and regional disposal guidelines are for your area rather than making them disappear down a toilet or drain. This approach prevents medicines from entering wastewater treatment plants, which can't always remove the chemicals that drugs contain before the treated water is returned back to the environment. Your actions can help protect frogs, fish, and other wildlife that could be harmed by chemicals found in treated water.

REPORT DISEASE

{Partners in Amphibian and Reptile Conservation, a Partnership of Organizations, United States}

Habitat destruction is a serious threat to amphibians and reptiles—called herpetofauna. Around the globe, diseases are also causing populations to decline.[12] The US-based organization Partners in Amphibian and Reptile Conservation (PARC) works to conserve herpetofauna and their habitats. It collects information on diseases and asks people in the United States and Canada to share their observations when they see species impacted by disease. If you find dead amphibians or reptiles, or live ones that seem sick, you can report them using the Herpetofaunal Disease Alert System (HDAS). The information is used to understand the spread of diseases or *pathogens*—microorganisms that cause disease. It is also used to analyze the severity of emerging diseases. As well as monitoring and controlling the spread of diseases, PARC may also take actions to protect habitat and reduce the spread of harmful bacteria, viruses, and other pathogens.

DECISION DILEMMA

As you get *active* in activism, you'll have some decisions to make. One of your choices is whether to tackle a cause on your own or to involve others. Pros and cons exist for both options.

If you decide to manage your own project, a pro is that you'll get to do it your way. A con is that you'll be responsible for all the work! But, even if you want to run the show, remember you can still ask others for advice or assistance. If you get stuck, talk things over with a pal or family member.

If you join a group or invite other people to be part of your activities, you might find it's possible to get more done. (Thus, the phrase *Many hands make light work*.) For some people, teamwork is energizing. It can lead to fresh ideas and new ways of dealing with glitches. Team efforts can also bring challenges. Starting your own group means you'll have to figure out who should do what. Volunteers might not complete tasks the way you like or always finish what they start. Although this can be frustrating, finding ways to manage these problems will give you important skills that will help your activism. Whether you work on your own or with others, you can be effective. Choose what works best with your personality and don't forget—you can always change your mind!

FIND YOUR CAUSE

Do amphibian woes make you feel like you've got a frog in your throat? If they do, you may have found the perfect situation to tackle. If they don't, that's okay. You can direct your energy in another important direction. When you decide to commit your courage to a cause, you'll be more likely to succeed if you truly care about the problem. That sounds easy, but you may feel pressures—real or imagined—to choose or avoid an issue for other reasons. For example, many people are willing to support charities that help children, cancer patients, or animals. It can be harder to find volunteers to help those addicted to drugs or living in prison. If you pick a cause you feel you *should* pick—maybe because it's in the news a lot or your friends and family care about it—you'll probably lose interest. Instead, go for the project you can't stop thinking about. Your research will help you narrow down the choices. In fact, sometimes it will clearly make you think, *Nope, this is not for me.* Other times you'll simply know, *This is where I belong.*

BE WISE

If activism pursuits lead you to collect or spend money, you'll need a quick and easy way to track it. Find an empty notebook and get into the habit of recording every dollar and coin that comes in and goes out. Start by marking four columns with these headings:

Date

Activity/Event

Purpose

Amount

As you tally donations and expenses, add notes about your activities and events. This will achieve two things. One, you'll see if you're spending enough time on your most important activities. Two, when reporters or donors want to know what you've been up to, you'll have all the dates and details in one place.

YOU'RE IN BUSINESS!

Running a charity is a lot like operating a business. You'll need to make short- and long-term plans, organize volunteers, and deal with donations and expenses. You might find yourself forced to spend time on tasks not directly in line with the ways you want to help. One way to bypass chores relating to *administration*—the management of an organization or business—is to volunteer with an existing group. An internet search will show you many choices, but be sure to research your options. You want to make sure you donate energy, time, or money only to groups with good reputations. Sadly, some people try to take advantage of others' generosity. After a natural disaster, for example, phony charities appear. They ask for donations to support those in need but do not deliver the money where promised. With a little effort, however, you can tell if a charity is legit or more likely the efforts of someone running a *scam*—an attempt to collect donations by deceiving people.

Look for warning signs. Phony charities often:

- Try to rush you into donating
- Request that money be paid in forms that are hard to trace: gift cards, cash, or *wire transfers*—money transferred electronically
- Do not have a website or online presence, or only have a poorly designed website without names, phone numbers, email addresses, or a contact page
- Claim that 100 percent of funds go to the cause (Although this can be true, it does cost money to run an organization. Use the Be Wise tips on page 22 to research whether the charity is legit.)

SPOTLIGHT ON . . .
Amphibian Migrations and Road Crossings Project

When you're as small as a frog, traveling a quarter of a mile from your forest habitat to your breeding habitat is a big deal. Every spring, volunteers in New York's Hudson Valley prepare to help these little fellas out. Knowing amphibians need wet conditions for their migration, frog-friendly folks watch the weather and wait for word that the *Big Night* migration has begun. Those willing to volunteer in the dark and rain find there are many ways to assist. They track weather, monitor traffic conditions, and note locations where frogs cross roads. Clad in rain gear and safety vests, helpers identify and count the species they encounter before gently carrying amphibians to safety. Since 2009, Hudson Valley volunteers have recorded 21,000 live amphibians, as well as 9,500 killed by vehicles. They have found twenty different species and aided more than 17,000 animals in reaching safety on the other side of the road. As well as saving amphibian lives, the project brings attention to the need to protect small wetlands and connecting forests as habitat for both plants and animals.[13]

MEET A YOUNG ACTIVIST
Leo Berry

Marshes, swamps, bogs, and fens provide key habitat to thousands of plant and animal species, including migrating birds. Since the 1970s, however, a chief cause of extinction has been the loss of wetland habitat. Swampy areas are important for other reasons too. They filter sediments, nutrients, and pollutants from water as it flows to lakes, rivers, and other water bodies. They also help slow floodwater.[14]

In Indiana, fifth-grade student Leo Berry was eleven years old when he discovered that a government *bill* had been introduced that would take away state protections for more than seven hundred thousand acres of wetlands.[15] He organized a *petition*—a written request that calls for change, which interested people can sign. After enough signatures are collected, petitions are delivered to those with the authority to make the change.

This is a draft of a law that will be presented to government.

Leo's petition, posted on Change.org, called for Indiana's governor to cancel the anti-wetlands bill. His efforts helped raise awareness about how the law would impact wetlands. After collecting more than thirty-one thousand signatures, Leo took the petition to the governor's office. Despite his efforts, the bill passed in April 2021. It was, however, later amended to restore some wetland protections. Leo continues his activism efforts through a nonprofit he had previously founded with his mom called Helping Ninjas. It works to inspire youths to be active citizens that portray kindness, while supporting the environment and other global issues.[16]

SATISFY YOUR CURIOSITY

Do you want to gather more *un-frog-ettable* facts? Hop
over to a computer and search these terms:

- Amphibian migration
- Frogs and biodiversity
- Frogwatch USA
- Volunteer with frogs
- Frog crossing sign images
- Protecting wetlands
- Misinformation
- Charity scams
- Steps to setting up a charity
- Creating a petition and Helping Ninjas

3

READY, SET, ACTION!

PUTTING YOUR PERSONAL POWERS TO WORK

"Do better. Your words and actions have weight, and they can inspire change when used correctly. Recognize the power you have to move the needle on issues that matter."

X González, survivor of the Marjory Stoneman Douglas High School mass shooting and cofounder of March for Our Lives, United States

Suppose the fountain of amphibian facts has you thinking about water in a big way. You might *leapfrog* to the thought that water impacts people too. Even though it covers about 71 percent of Earth's surface, not everyone has enough clean water to drink or use. In fact, one in three people around the world can't access safe drinking water when they need it.[1] This is called *water scarcity*—the lack of clean and safe water in a given area.

Ready, set, action! Let's find a way to reduce this problem.

Suppose you've already done your research and turned the thought *Nobody should go thirsty* into the focused plan *I want to help a rural community in Kenya access safe water.* Next, how will you help? If you're like most kids, you can't simply fly to another part of the world and start digging wells. Even if you had handfuls of cash and a plane ticket, how would that work? You would need experts to tell you how and where to build the well. You might have to arrange permits or rent special machines to dig through soil and rock. If you don't speak the local languages, you'll need to hire translators too!

Despite these obstacles, solutions exist. The most direct route is to aid people already working in Kenya. Let's suppose you've done research and discovered a group called Charity: Water. You found out it manages water access projects in Kenya and invites kids to raise money by running campaigns. You see that the process to run a campaign is four simple steps: register with the charity, set a fundraising goal, invite others to help, and start earning money for the cause. When the goal is reached, Charity: Water will send you a report about the people and community who benefited. You feel this approach could be a good fit for you. To be sure working with this organization is a safe choice, though, you check its status on the Charity Watch website and see it is described as "top rated." In other words, you can feel good that any cash you collect will go where it's supposed to go. Now you need to raise the money! How exactly is that going to work?

GET SOME ATTENTION!

Before you start trying to rake in the dough, think of questions you'll probably be asked along the way and prepare your answers.

You'll need to decide the best way to describe your project when you seek volunteers, ask for donations, or plan fundraising events. Plan to create a message that gets people's attention, and remember, it can't just touch their hearts—it needs to touch the hands that will reach for piggy banks and purses and wallets. It's got to prod the part of the brain that tells the mouth to shout yes when you ask for help.

Inspiring others to care about your cause is an important part of being an effective activist. People will be more likely to volunteer with you or donate money if they understand three things:

○ Why the issue is important

○ Why it matters to you

○ How their contribution will help

That may sound like a lot to communicate, but you've got talents that will help you do it.

USE YOUR VOICE

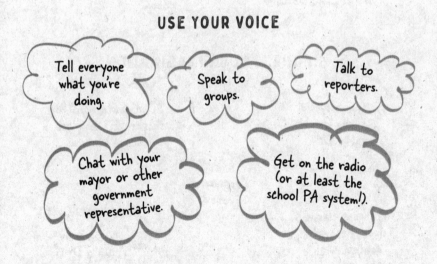

Tell everyone what you're doing.

Speak to groups.

Talk to reporters.

Chat with your mayor or other government representative.

Get on the radio (or at least the school PA system!).

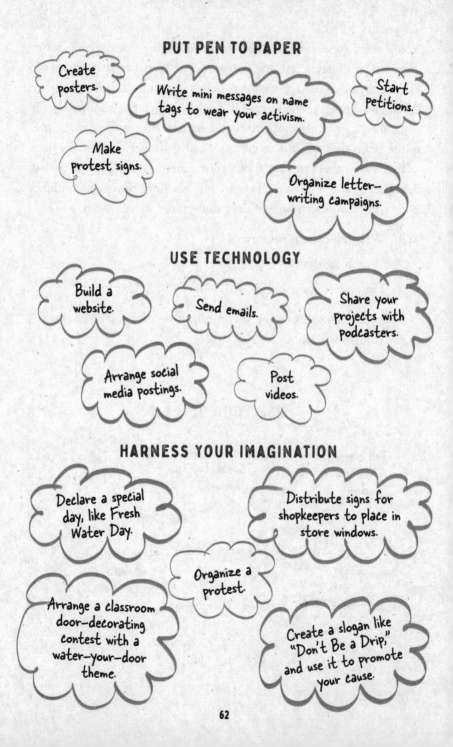

PUT PEN TO PAPER

Create posters.

Write mini messages on name tags to wear your activism.

Start petitions.

Make protest signs.

Organize letter-writing campaigns.

USE TECHNOLOGY

Build a website.

Send emails.

Share your projects with podcasters.

Arrange social media postings.

Post videos.

HARNESS YOUR IMAGINATION

Declare a special day, like Fresh Water Day.

Distribute signs for shopkeepers to place in store windows.

Organize a protest.

Arrange a classroom door-decorating contest with a water-your-door theme.

Create a slogan like "Don't Be a Drip," and use it to promote your cause.

As well as your personal genius, you've got four key tools you can use to broadcast your message—facts, questions, stories, and pictures.

SPREAD THE WORD!

Create a banner and hang it in a place where your target audience will see it. You could use water-proof markers to write your message on a vinyl tarp, or glue colorful felt letters on burlap and stitch the material around a dowel to make a hanger. If you have access to a computer with a large-paper printer, try using a banner *template*—a file that helps you follow a pattern to create a design. Before diving in, become an art investigator. Examine signs to see how others use color and images to attract attention. Notice the size of lettering and make sure your own sign will be readable from a distance. Now get creative!

LET'S START WITH THE *FACTS*

Facts, they're an ideal way to make a good first impression. When you share information, you show you understand the issue. This makes you appear reliable! If you want people to care about your topic, be straightforward and dial down excess emotion, which can make you appear less convincing. Writing "OMG People are DYING of Thirst" will not be as effective as "Every year, hurricanes and floods leave families without safe drinking water." Sometimes, though, you just need to get your ideas out of your head and onto paper before you forget them. If you find yourself writing "Dirty, poopy water is making people puke," consider that a necessary rough draft. It's rare for someone's first effort to be a keeper, and in fact, it's a useful start. You've narrowed down what you want to say and gotten words onto paper. Don't stop. Add some details as you revise, and you might come up with a message that packs serious punch, perhaps something like "About two million people around the world get water from a source contaminated with feces, according to the World Health Organization (WHO)."[2] Appealing to logic and reason will prove most effective, and sharing your source will demonstrate that you're *credible*—someone people can believe and trust.

LIKE THIS, SEE?

- Safe drinking water is not always available at schools and healthcare facilities in developing countries. (WHO)[3]

- Unsafe drinking water, along with poor hygiene and sanitation, causes diarrhea—a condition that kills 700 children under five years old every day. (UNICEF)[4]

- Living without a reliable source of safe water can affect children's physical development and contribute to stunted growth. (UNICEF)[5]

- Only 25 percent of people in Kenya are able to wash their hands with soap and water at home. (UNICEF)[6]

- Adding water and sanitation facilities in a home reduces the need for and cost of healthcare. (WHO)[7]

QUESTION, QUESTION, *QUESTION*

Now you have facts that pack a powerful punch, but be sure to work questions into your chitchat too. Questions are a bit like invitations that welcome people to get involved. The right phrase can

IMAGINE

Imagine living 83 miles north of the Arctic Circle during a water shortage. One winter, residents in the small Alaskan community of Kivalina were forced to melt snow and ice every time they needed water to wash or cook. Normally, they pump water from the Wulik River into two large storage tanks. They have to be filled before freezing temperatures make the water slushy and hard to pump. In 2012, however, repair work combined with storms that muddied the river delayed the community's ability to store clean water. Everyone watched as temperatures continued to drop. Unable to completely fill the tanks, residents were forced to ration their water use for six months.[8]

inspire others to talk about your topic. Conversation boosts interest in your subject and can make it feel more personal. After you ask questions, remember to listen to the answers! That may seem obvious, but it's easy to get focused on what you want to say next and forget to pay attention.

When the time feels right, steer the conversation toward ways people can get involved in your campaign. The easiest way to harness help is to be direct about what you want. People are more likely to say yes and follow through when you make your "ask" specific. Simply asking "Can you help?" leaves possible participants wondering what they're signing up to do. They may decide it's easier to say no than to squirm out of a commitment that is bigger than they expected. Instead of letting people wonder how they can chip in, tell them exactly what you need.

LIKE THIS, SEE?

YOU: If you had to spend three hours a day fetching clean water, what activities would you have to give up?

SOCCER SAM: Three hours! I'd have to quit the team and say good-bye to hanging out with friends. I probably wouldn't finish all my homework.

YOU: It sounds like you wouldn't have much fun, plus you'd get behind in school. You can see that the need for water would really interrupt your day. Would you consider donating five or ten dollars to my campaign?

YOU: If your family had to spend fifty dollars a month for clean water, what would you have to give up so that you could pay for the water?

POPCORN PARKER: Fifty dollars! I guess we'd have to stop going to the movies and ordering sodas and snacks. Or we could skip haircuts or mobile phone data plans or stopping for ice cream.

YOU: Imagine if it wasn't only luxuries you had to give up, but things like clothes or shoes or food. Would you be willing to spend two hours a week to help with my plan to build a well in a Kenyan village?

YOU: How do you think your health would be affected if you could only wash in dirty water or only drink unpurified water?

CLEAN JEAN: I guess that would make me sick. Maybe I'd end up in the hospital.

YOU: You're right. Bacteria in the water can cause infections, diarrhea, and other serious problems. Can you help us prevent illness by coming to our fundraising party and bringing two or three friends?

I'VE GOT A STORY FOR YOU

Suppose the facts you share and the questions you raise don't convince your audience. All is not lost. You still have your secret weapon—*stories*! If you've watched a news clip on television or read a news article, you've probably seen this technique in action. The reporter spotlights someone affected by the matter being discussed. During a drought, for example, a reporter might interview a farmer about how the lack of water is affecting livestock. The human connection creates interest and suspense. You can't help but wonder how the farmer will deal with this circumstance. What will happen if the animals don't get enough water? How will the story end?

Whether you're talking one-on-one or speaking to a group, you can use stories to help listeners understand your issue and remember why it's important. If you have personal experience with water shortages, you could describe how you came to be in that situation. You could include how it affected your daily life and made you feel.

Even if you've never faced a serious water shortage, you may still have a story to share. To discover it, start a list about water-related experiences you've had. Have you ever been thirsty but unable to get a drink? Have you ever had to go without water when you wanted it, even for a short time? Did you forget to bring a water bottle on a field trip or to a sports team practice? Have you been in a situation where there were no water fountains or toilets? Close your eyes. Go back to that place in your head and think about how it affected your day. Use your experience to bring feeling to your story.

LIKE THIS, SEE?

Even though I've always lived in places where water is as close as the nearest tap, I remember once wanting more than we had. It happened on a wilderness camping trip. My parents brought all the water they expected us to need. The blue plastic jugs reached up to my waist, and it was hard to just tip out a glassful. I was trying to pour myself a drink when I dumped ten gallons of water. It fell like a waterfall. As cold as a glacier, the water soaked my clothes and splashed dirt up my legs.

Now we only had twenty gallons for three people for three days. It was the kind of weather where your clothes stick to your skin and your mouth feels full of cotton. Mom set aside enough water so we'd each have a gallon a day to drink. That added up to nine gallons, leaving only eleven for cooking, washing dishes, and keeping our-

Bring feeling to your story.

selves clean. Every time someone went for a drink, I looked away. I knew better than to complain out loud, but the water was warm and tasted like plastic. It was impossible to wash properly, and I always felt grubby. It wasn't much fun, but at least it was only three days. Soon I'd be home and have all the water I wanted.

But that's not the case for everyone. In parts of Kenya, kids and their families live without enough water every single day. My life was never at risk, but some kids in other countries get sick because they don't have water that is safe to drink or to use for washing.

Share a fact.

Can you think of a time when you had to go without water?

Use a question.

If you don't have a personal experience to share, you can solve the problem the same way reporters do—by presenting other people's experiences. Find stories by reading news articles and visiting the websites of charities that focus on your issue. Enter search terms like "stories about [your topic]," then choose one that shows how the matter impacts an individual, family, or community. If you're preparing a speech, plan to tell the story in your own words. If you want to use the exact story found in a brochure or other written materials, you must write to the content owner and request permission. It's vital to respect *copyright*—the legal right to reproduce or publish a literary or artistic work. If given permission, you may be asked to list the organization as your source.

Whether you're sharing *facts*, asking *questions*, or telling *stories*, you are sure to find that words are mighty. Still, there's one more trick you'll want to take advantage of—the power of *pictures*.

BRAIN NUGGET

The United Nations defines the human right to water as having the ability to access a safe source within one thousand meters of home. It should not take longer than thirty minutes to collect water, and thirteen to twenty-six gallons (fifty to one hundred liters) should be available to each person every day. To be affordable, water should not cost more than 3 percent of the household income.[9]

GET THE PICTURE!

Human beings can't help but feel drawn to images. Pictures hold our attention and help us understand information. From photos and illustrations to charts and diagrams, think about how you might use images to make posters, a website, or social media posts more interesting. You can take photos, draw illustrations, make your own charts, or find content online. Search your topic along with the phrase "images in the public domain." (See the Be Wise on p. 72 to learn more about "public domain" law.) This will allow you to find pictures you can legally use without the need to pay royalties or copyright licensing fees. You can also search "images with a creative commons license" to find content that is free to use if you follow certain rules such as crediting the creator. Sites like Pexels, Pixabay, and Unsplash offer plenty of choices without requiring users to sign in.

LIKE THIS, SEE?

Suppose you want to create a poster to draw attention to the lack of safe water in certain North American communities, after discovering it is a too-common problem in Native American households in the United States and First Nations reserves in Canada. Follow these steps to make your message pop.

1. Set an objective. What do you want your poster to accomplish? Are you inviting people to an event, or asking them to vote on an issue, donate, or participate in some other way?

2. Consider your target audience. What kind of images and wording will attract their attention? You might choose something bold and rousing for children and teens, but use more formal elements for a poster aimed at professionals.

3. Create a rough copy of your message, including a call to action where you state exactly what you want readers to do. Now rewrite it! Play with the words. Make a list of possible headlines and simple key messages, and then pick your best ones.

4. Create or gather one or two supporting images. If you are planning to print black-and-white copies on a computer or with a photocopier, test whether the images will appear clearly.

5. Choose a color scheme that works well with your image. Lay out your rough copy, aiming to keep the poster uncluttered and easy to read. Use large lettering to grab attention and a smaller font for details such as the date, time, and location of an event.

40 PERCENT
of people do not have access to **CLEAN WATER**

6. Once you're happy with all the elements, decide how many posters you need to print, and then get out there and put them up! Remember to check with businesses, your school office, and private property owners before you start taping.

BE WISE

Around age twelve, I began to work on a secret plan to run my own nature center. I wanted to teach people how to conserve wildlife habitat, prevent pollution, and care for the environment. As well as collecting feathers, minerals, and mushrooms for my displays, I began recording television shows about nature. I pictured a small theater where visitors could watch videos and be transformed into *conservationists*—people who work to protect animals, plants, and the environment from being damaged by human activity. At the time, I didn't know it would be illegal to charge people admission to watch my recorded TV shows. I didn't know I would need to get permission from the copyright owners.

If you find the perfect video or picture or story to help your cause, check to see who owns the content. It may be in the *public domain*—unprotected by copyright and available for anyone to use. If it's not, you can explore using it under the fair use doctrine. In certain conditions, fair use allows small excerpts of works to be shared for nonprofit education that is *noncommercial*—not meant to earn money for profit. As an activist, you fight for what is right, and people look to your example. Set a good one by never breaking laws in the quest to make a difference.[10]

MAKE CONNECTIONS

You've got plenty of tools to help you with your to-do list. Now you need volunteers. How are you going to convince people to give you their valuable time? Try telling possible helpers about the benefits of getting involved with you. You might promote advantages like:

- We're a friendly bunch.
- Lots of volunteers become buddies.
- You can learn new things like how to build a website or be an *emcee*—the person who acts as the host of an event, introducing public speakers.
- We always have fun when we work as a group.
- It feels satisfying when everyone is focused on the same goal.
- You can help us make a real difference.
- Volunteering can make you feel happy. It can give you the chance to spend time around people with the same interests, provide a place to practice your social skills, and boost self-confidence.
- Working for free can make it easier to get paid jobs when you're older. Volunteering gives you work experience that you can include when preparing future *résumés*—documents job seekers create that list education, work experience, and other qualifications.
- Contributing your efforts to a cause can aid you in getting accepted into a college or university. It could even help you win a *scholarship*—funds given to students to help pay for post-secondary education.

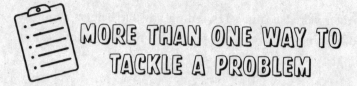

MORE THAN ONE WAY TO TACKLE A PROBLEM

When you shake a can of soda and pull the tab, you know what to expect: the liquid will explode in a fountain of fizz. The results of your efforts will be immediate. When you raise your voice in protest, you want to see quick results too (although less sticky ones). Unfortunately, activism doesn't work like a pop can. It rarely occurs with clear start and end dates or focuses on an issue that can be solved in weeks. Instead of letting drawn-out processes frustrate you, look at how the organizations and activists in the pages ahead helped others by staying involved.

ENSURE ACCESS TO CLEAN WATER

Can you feel liquid sloshing inside of you? It might not be obvious, but up to 60 percent of your body is made up of water. It serves a bunch of purposes, from protecting your brain to building your cells. You need sweat to control your temperature and saliva to digest your food.[11] Water is vital, but not everyone can get it with the turn of a tap. Around the world, activists are finding ways to help ensure that more people can access clean water.

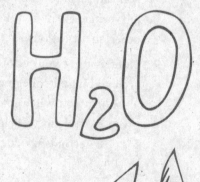

INVENT A GADGET

{Hippo Roller, Business and Social Enterprise, South Africa}

The chore of fetching water often falls to children and women. The Hippo Roller is a low-tech invention that allows users to push a steel handle to roll a sturdy, barrel-shaped container of water along the ground. The ninety-liter (twenty-four-gallon) drum makes it possible to carry more water in a single trip—enough for a family of five for one day. Water can be moved longer distances and over rough ground more easily. Households that own a Hippo Roller may also find opportunities to earn an income by delivering water to others for a small fee, thus allowing more people to benefit from a single unit. So far, more than sixty thousand Hippo Rollers are being used in fifty-one countries, where they aid millions of people. The company helps run campaigns for communities who ask for fundraising help, and partners with NGOs, sponsors, and others interested in assisting. Community leaders usually aim to ensure that households with the greatest need—the elderly, homes headed by children, and those living farthest from water—are the first to get their own Hippo Roller.[12]

SET UP MICRO LOAN PROGRAMS
{Water.org, Global Nonprofit, Missouri}

What do you do if you don't have enough money to pay for clean water and sanitation? One solution is to borrow the funds you need. Unfortunately, that's not so easy. Traditional banks do not usually lend money to people living in poverty. The nonprofit Water.org came up with a solution called WaterCredit. It helps people in areas where it is common to live on less than $6 a day. Water.org sets up partnerships with local financial institutions and teaches them how to set up micro financing programs for water and sanitation. These programs are designed to lend small amounts of money to pay for plumbing. The small loans enable participants to afford the cost of installing a tap or toilet in their homes. When they pay back the loan, the money becomes available for another family to borrow.[13]

PUT SCIENCE AND TECHNOLOGY TO WORK
{Water Is Life, Nonprofit, Hawaii}

Use science. Imagine a book that cleans water! That's exactly what chemist Dr. Theresa Dankovich did when she devised a type of paper that can stop deadly water-borne diseases including typhoid, cholera, and E. coli. The book's pages, printed with food-grade ink, contain water safety tips in English and Swahili. Each page can be removed, inserted into the book's  packaging to create a filtering device, and used to make water safe to drink. One page provides thirty days of clean water. One book equals four years of water that is safe to drink! Developing the Drinkable Book served as a foundation for a new product called the Nano Bucket, which uses a built-in filter to trap harmful bacteria and other microorganisms. The Nano Bucket can provide a family with an unlimited supply of safe water for several years.[14]

GET CHATTY
Imagine you're the leader of a small village when the community well dries to a trickle. You must decide how to handle the crisis. Will you choose to control how much each family takes or find a way to supply more water? How will your village pay for your solution?

FUNDRAISING

Projects to distribute Hippo Rollers, set up loan programs, and develop water-filtering tools have one thing in common: they all require money. You might need cash to get your project rolling too. That's why I'm hoping the word *fun* in *fundraising* is popping out at you. It's a perfectly placed reminder—you can have a good time making money for your cause. (If you also notice *raisin* and *sing* in *fundraising*, draw your own conclusions.) One way to bankroll your projects is to dream up money-making activities that offer a good time. Aside from their entertainment value, fun activities offer an important benefit. They help erase any awkwardness you might feel about asking people to donate money. Instead of making a direct call for cash, you're giving something in return—a fun time or a service people want.

Suppose you're ready to start raising funds for water in Kenya. Pull out your waterproof pen and make a list of possibilities. It might look like this:

- Ask a hairy-faced teacher if you can sell raffle tickets allowing the winner to shave the teacher's moustache or beard.

- Host a talent contest. It could be Saturday night with family and friends or a school-wide event. Charge an entry fee to attend, or collect donations.

- Plan a fundraiser called It's-Not-Halloween! Ask permission to dress your principal, coach, or librarian in a costume or old wedding dress. (Also ask if it's okay before raiding anyone's closet!) Use the school PA system to announce what's happening, and tell students you'll be visiting each classroom to collect donations before allowing your victim to change back into regular clothes. (Before the event, remind students and staff to bring money on event day.)

- Plan a face-painting event. You might paint your teachers' faces in weird ways and collect donations from staff and students before allowing them to clean the paint off. Or raffle the opportunity to paint the face of an adult who works at your school.

- Issue a challenge to school sports teams in your region, and see who can raise the most money for your cause.

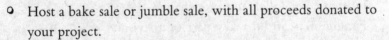

- Plan a game night with everyone chipping in $5 to play.

- Host a bake sale or jumble sale, with all proceeds donated to your project.

- Organize a water-themed contest. Advertise a $2 entry fee, and promise 25 percent of the proceeds to the winner. All you need is a water supply, bucket, length of rope, marker, posterboard, and two trees. Each contestant must fill the pail, run three laps around the first tree, and stop at the rope line to toss the water on the second tree. (This approach will prevent players from running on slippery ground.) Time your contestants, mark the results on a posterboard, and see who is the fastest.

- Raise funds through a Dog, Dishes, and Dirt Wash. Ask friends, classmates, or even every student in your school to offer to do dirty jobs in their own homes in return for donations. Keep adults in the house happy by telling participants that the chores they offer to complete can't be ones they're already expected to do. Post a chart recording how many dogs, dishes, and other dirty areas get cleaned. Make it fun by encouraging classes to compete for the Best Dirt Busters Award. (Make an ugly but fun trophy by upcycling used cleaning supplies—like an old mop with homemade googly eyes glued on.)

- Ask a local grocery store to donate eggs for a special contest. For a small fee, sell participants an egg. Instruct them to name their new friend and spell the name out on the shell with a marker. Contestants must keep their eggs from breaking for one full school day and promise to clean up if there's a crash. When the time's up, anyone with an unbroken egg gets their name in a drawing for a chance to win 25 percent of the proceeds.

It often takes dollars to make change.

Fundraising can be a key part of activism, but you should always consider whether your project really does call for cash. If your activities include attending protests, letter-writing campaigns, or volunteering your labor, you probably won't need to collect moola to accomplish your goals. Materials like envelopes and stamps might be found around the house, and you may be able to arrange for many services, like photocopying, to be donated. Take a thoughtful approach to raising money, and know what you will use it for before asking people to cough up dough. Only spend your money after careful consideration. That way you won't need to raise as much!

Is there an award for great puns?

BE THE CHANGE

What if you want to donate to a cause but don't have any money to chip in? You could solve the problem the next time you have a birthday or celebrate a holiday where gift-giving is typical. Let the gift-givers in your life (parents, siblings, grandparents, and so on) know that if they were planning on giving you something, you would appreciate a monetary donation to your favorite charity instead. Make sure you express your wish with *tact*—in a manner that avoids offense. You don't want to appear as though you expect a present or are demanding one. If the gift-givers in your life agree to the idea, be sure to send thank-you notes that include information about how the donations were used to help. This approach to raising funds offers the added bonus of making your chosen issue more visible to others. Your special-occasion activism might even get more people personally involved in your charity.

SPOTLIGHT ON . . .
Thirst Project

Nobody should have to drink out of a swamp or mud puddle. When Seth Maxwell and seven college friends learned about the water problems many face, they decided to pool their money and find a way to help. With only $70, the nineteen-year-olds talked a grocery store manager into selling them $1,000 worth of bottled water. They took the water bottles to Hollywood Boulevard in Los Angeles and began to give them away, hoping people would stop and talk with them. It worked! They asked those they met whether they knew about the water crisis—how millions around the world are unable to access safe drinking water. Though the students only set out to raise awareness, some passersby began to offer donations for the water. The students raised $1,700 after chatting with more than one thousand people, and donated the cash to a nonprofit organization building freshwater wells in Uganda.

Some of the young people the students met that day asked if the college students would come to their respective schools to talk about water scarcity and speak on how their schools could help. The friends realized that while many charities tackle water issues, no one was focusing on getting young people involved. In 2008, they set up the Thirst Project and challenged students across the United States to get involved. This worked too! In the project's first ten years, students helped raise more than $10 million. Funds, raised by school groups and individual students, have been used to help more than five hundred thousand people in thirteen countries access clean water.[15]

ONE THING YOU CAN DO NOW

Gather up a gaggle of friends and two empty ice-cream pails per person. Fill the buckets with water and take a thirty- to forty-five-minute walk. How many times did you stop to rest? If that were all the water you had for the day, what would you use it for?

MEET A YOUNG ACTIVIST
Mari Copeny

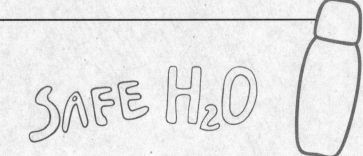

In 2016, people living in Flint, Michigan, were told their water was no longer safe to drink. It contained dangerous levels of lead and other contaminants, putting the health of tens of thousands of residents at risk. A disease outbreak led to the deaths of at least twelve people. At age eight, Mari Copeny wanted to fight for safe water. She wrote a letter to President Barack Obama, letting him know that she was one of the people affected. In his reply, the president told Mari that he would visit Flint and that she was the first to know! He examined the crisis firsthand and later approved $100 million in relief funding. Mari, also known as Little Miss Flint, continues her activism. She set up *crowdfunding*—a web page that enables people to donate to her cause—using the GoFundMe platform. Mari set a goal to raise $500,000 for water filters to help anyone in the United States who needs to filter toxins from their water. After meeting her target on Earth Day in 2021, Little Miss Flint reset her goal to $1 million. As of September 2023, she had raised $750,352.[16]

MEET A YOUNG ACTIVIST
Ryan Hreljac

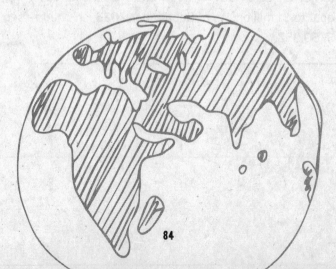

Ryan Hreljac was in first grade in 1998 when his teacher explained the problems people in some parts of Africa face in obtaining safe drinking water. Hoping to earn enough to drill a well, he asked for extra chores around the house. Ryan raised $70 but soon learned that would not be enough. He began speaking to school groups, service clubs, and anyone else who would listen about his goal. In less than a year, he collected enough donations for a well to be built at Angolo Primary School in Uganda.

An organization called Canadian Physicians for Aid and Relief (CPAR) partnered with Ryan to build the well. Afterward, Ryan's second-grade teacher arranged for her students to become pen pals with students attending Angolo Primary School. Ryan asked his pen pal—Jimmy Akana—about his water situation. He learned that before the well was built, Jimmy often woke at midnight to fetch water for his aunt and her children. Carrying a small pail, he sometimes made the five-kilometer trip three times before going to school! In 2000, Ryan traveled to Agweo, a village in Uganda, to see the well his funds built and personally meet his pen pal. Ryan's family later adopted Jimmy, who moved to Canada to live with his new family. From that point on, the boys grew up together. Ryan's family helped Jimmy claim refugee status, and in 2006 he became a Canadian citizen. He still does some volunteering with Ryan's Well from Alberta, Canada, where he works in the trades of welding and pipefitting and lives with his wife and children.

Today, Ryan's Well Foundation continues to build wells. It raises funds and works with nongovernmental and community-based nonprofits in the areas it focuses on to provide water, hand-washing stations, and latrines in countries where they are most needed. The foundation has built more than 1,724 water projects and 1,321 latrines and helped more than 1.4 million people. It also educates the public on water safety, such as the importance of using clean water containers and keeping domestic animals out of water sources. It even offers training on how to maintain and repair wells, allowing communities to manage their own water after a project is completed. Ryan's Well Foundation invites kids to take part in the annual School Challenge to raise money for specific projects.[17]

SATISFY YOUR CURIOSITY

Next time you find yourself at a computer with internet access, explore water issues and solutions by tapping out these keywords:

- Water scarcity
- Charity: Water
- Safe water for Indigenous communities
- UNICEF
- World Health Organization
- Hippo Roller
- Water.org
- Water Is Life
- Mari Copeny
- Ryan's Well Foundation
- Charity Watch

PART II

ANIMAL AND EARTH ISSUES

4

JUSTICE FOR ANIMALS

LOOKING OUT FOR WILDLIFE, FARM ANIMALS, AND PETS

"The basis of all animal rights should be the Golden Rule: we should treat them as we would wish them to treat us, were any other species in our dominant position."

Christine Stevens, founder of the
Animal Welfare Institute, United States

You've heard it! Humans are superior to every other animal. We're at the top of the food chain and proud of it. No other species can speak words, learn multiple languages, or write text. Sure, elephants, chimpanzees, and dolphins are super intelligent, but you won't see *them* reading a book. They won't build fires, invent smartphones, or wear clothes either. Our brains, so capable of complex thinking, also give us the unique ability to brag about being this fabulous. As a bonus, we're flexible enough to reach around and pat our own backs after a job well done.

Here's one remarkable feat you may not have thought too much about: *Homo sapiens* are the only life-form to *domesticate* other species—bring them from a wild state to one under human control to meet our needs. You don't have to look very far to see how important domesticated animals are to humans. When it comes to feeding a population, it's easier to raise livestock and poultry than hunt wild creatures. Farmers and ranchers keep animals to obtain some of the materials we use, like sheep, llamas, and alpacas for fiber; ducks and geese for feathers; and domestic foxes and mink for fur. Animals are also reared to guard property, transport loads, and carry us around. Dogs aid police, rescue workers, and people living with disabilities. Critters are trained to perform in shows, pose with people for photos, and fight—all for human entertainment. Think of rodeo sports, bull fighting, and greyhound racing. Even homing pigeons were put to work during World Wars I and II, delivering important messages in canisters tied to their legs.[1]

Domestic members of the animal kingdom make our lives easier and more interesting. Unfortunately, humans don't always return the favor. In addition to food, water, and shelter, domestic animals have important needs that are not always met. This includes room to exercise, social time with members of their own species, and other types of physical and intellectual stimulation.

GET CHATTY

Whenever you see captive creatures, ask yourself, what are this species's overall needs? Are they being met here?

Wild critters, on the other hand, know how to care for themselves. The act of survival keeps their bodies and minds active. Some wild animals, however, are forced to endure lives in captivity—in cages, pens, or other fenced areas that prevent free movement. They may be on farms, like deer raised for their antlers, meat, or even urine.

Yes, people buy urine. Deer pee is sold to hunters who use it to lure bucks during hunting season. It's collected in pens with grated floors.

Other captive wild animals live in zoos, aquariums, and theme parks. Some travel with circuses. Businesses catering to tourists offer exotic encounters such as the opportunity to ride elephants, feed giraffes, hold koalas, pose with alligators, or swim with dolphins. These activities sound fun for people, but are they truly good for the animals? It is important to consider how human interactions impact animal well-being.

In some countries, especially Japan, cafés exist that offer customers the chance to feed, pet, and photograph captive creatures like owls, hedgehogs, rabbits, snakes, cats, and dogs. Some businesses limit the number of visitors at one time or make other efforts to reduce animal stress, but coffee shops are unnatural settings for these animals. Solitary, nocturnal species like owls and hedgehogs are forced to live among other animals and under artificial lighting. Hedgehogs, which run, climb, and swim in the wild, are unlikely to get enough exercise. Owls, which may be tethered, cannot fly or hunt. Captive fauna cannot follow their natural instincts.

Animals captured in the wild are often sold in other countries as exotic pets. Local laws may allow residents to keep certain species, but *legal* does not always mean *ethical*—the best moral choice. Even when prohibited, people often keep exotic creatures without facing penalties. If you live in Texas, you may own tigers, even though they are endangered. The *Austin American Statesman* reports that after the country of India, the state of Texas is home to the largest population of pet tigers, many living right in suburban backyards.[2] In natural conditions, tigers roam large ranges, and apart from mothers raising young, tigers are solitary.

BRAIN NUGGET

Perhaps you have a dog or cat in your home, or guinea pigs, canaries, or fancy rats to keep you company. Species that are domesticated have been selectively bred to ensure that certain traits exist. The bichon frise, for example, is a dog breed reared to be friendly. Its people-loving personality appears in every generation. A single wild animal that becomes tame is different. Although it loses its fear of humans, it does not pass this adaptation to offspring.

ARE YOUR ACTIVISM STRIPES STARTING TO RIPPLE?

As you discover the issues animals face, you may realize you've witnessed mistreatment that you did not identify at the time. Suppose you visit a city where horse-drawn carriages share roads with cars and trucks. It's so nice to watch these glorious beasts with their rippling manes and prancing hooves. But wait a minute—how many hours do these horses work each day? And those clip-clops are rather loud. How do hard pavement, pollution, and the effort of pulling heavy loads hour after hour impact working horses? Do they ever get to graze in open pastures?

You might ask similar questions at events where animals serve as entertainment. Perhaps you've seen horses in parades walking with an exaggerated gait. These equines, known as Tennessee walking horses, step differently because they've been subjected to soring—the deliberate infliction of pain to force an artificial gait. It can be accomplished by applying a harsh chemical to a horse's legs or *pressure shoeing*, which involves injuring the hoof. Racehorses are subjected to injuries too. They might occur from the use of whips, spurs, or *tongue ties*—devices that tie the tongue to the horse's lower jaw to keep it in place.[3] Zebras, camels, ostriches, frogs, falcons, pigs, and dogs including greyhounds, huskies, and other breeds are also raced.

BE WISE

People sometimes take activism to levels considered radical by using extreme measures to try to achieve change. Rather than advocate in ways that are peaceful and lawful, extremists choose direct actions. They might do things like release lab animals, throw paintballs at people wearing fur coats, or vandalize property. Those who engage in radical activities may find supporters backing away from their cause. They may also face harsh penalties. Be careful to avoid taking actions that could be viewed as radical.

Another troubling activity is the inhumane practice of putting animals together to fight. Dogs, hogs, canaries, crickets, and bettas are some of the species that have been forced to brawl. Onlookers often take part in illegal gambling, placing bets on their favorites. In cockfighting, roosters typically fight to the death. This brutal "sport" is a crime in every US state, yet underground fights still occur.

It's troubling to discover the many ways cruelty and neglect occur. With 8.7 million species on our planet to consider, you might wonder where to start.[4] As you find your way, draw on the animal in you. Bring the strength of elephants and the persistence of mosquitoes. Stay as determined as a salmon swimming against the current. Inch around obstacles like earthworms, work like beavers, and solve problems like pigs (they're very smart!). Stay tuned. The quizard ahead will help guide you.

ANIMAL RIGHTS

Not everyone agrees on what rights animals deserve or what laws should be in place to protect them. Many feel it's all right to use critters for food and clothes, but that treatment must be *humane*— delivered with compassion and sympathy. Others would like to see animals protected from all human *exploitation*—deeds or acts that take unfair advantage. The physical and mental states of animals, which arise from their living conditions, are collectively called *animal welfare*. Those who keep creatures, both domestic and wild, have a responsibility to ensure that the animals live without preventable pain and distress.

As you zero in on animal activism, consider the things that motivate people to treat critters the way they do. For example, scientists experimenting on mice may focus on important positives—ways to increase knowledge, advance science, and improve lives. They may truthfully argue that experiments are the most effective way to develop medicines and valuable health treatments for people, as well as other animal species. It is also a fact, however, that animals are exploited to test products that are not vital to our survival, such as cosmetics.

Biology teachers focus on goals too, like ensuring students learn *anatomy*—the parts of living things. Every year, a great number of animals are killed and preserved so that students can perform *dissections*—the act of cutting dead animals open to explore how their bodies work.[5] Some argue that models of frogs made from synthetic materials and online dissection programs could be used to replace killed specimens. Others say in-person experiences are key to learning and building scientific interest.

MONEY, TRADITION, AND HABIT

Animal welfare is often impacted by the need and desire to make money. Farmers, for example, may choose to house more livestock closely together to increase profits. Long-held customs can also impact how species are treated. At rodeos, competitors demonstrate traditional ranching skills. One event—calf roping—involves participants on horseback chasing calves to lasso them, toss them to the ground, and tie three legs. On ranches, roping is used for branding, tagging, and providing medical treatments. At rodeos, roping is a sport that stresses animals for human entertainment.

Another tradition, often passed down through families, is trapping. People may inherit family *traplines*—routes where generations

EXPLORE MORE

My research found estimates suggesting that twelve to twenty million animals are sacrificed for dissection annually in the United States,[6] but I have been unable to verify these numbers with unbiased sources. As an author doing my homework, I cannot present these numbers as factual. When you read statistics, pay close attention to wording such as "estimates" as well as to the bias of those making claims. As an activist, you must do your own thinking and sometimes your own math. Suppose you want to know how many dissections take place in your school district. You could count high schools, track down how many biology classes are offered each year, and find out the average class size. You could even look up science curriculum guidelines. Still, it would be difficult to confirm how many actual dissections take place. Local teachers might provide useful insights, but in the end, you would need to make an educated guess to work out a total. Although it can be difficult to narrow dissections down into statistics, estimates do provide rough guidelines on the scope of the problem. Just be sure to remember—in all your activism research—numbers are not always free from imperfection.

of owners have permission to set traps. In certain regions around the world, including Alaska, northern Canada, and *First Nations* (peoples Indigenous to the North American continent) communities, trapping may be a traditional way of providing food and fur, as well as an income. Supporters argue trapping can be achieved humanely, while opponents view the practice as cruel.

Sometimes, suffering that occurs is the result of simple human laziness or indifference. Think of dogs whose owners don't provide opportunities for exercise or parrots that are housed in small cages. People are not always aware of how their actions impact animals' well-being.

FACTORY FARMING

If you've ever enjoyed a country drive, you've probably spotted farm animals grazing in fields and pastures. Farmers and ranchers are tasked with meeting our demand for affordable food, and some keep farms where critters enjoy room to roam. Much of the food on store shelves, however, comes from animals raised indoors at large-scale commercial operations. The goal at these industrial facilities, commonly called *factory farms* or *feedlots*, is to produce the most meat at a minimal cost. To achieve this, animals are packed into small spaces only slightly larger than their bodies. Pregnant pigs are kept in housing too tight for them to turn around. Calves in veal crates may be chained at the neck and unable to lie down. Chickens are unable to alter the direction they face, spread their wings, or follow their natural desires to roost off the ground, lay eggs in nests, and bathe in dust. Living without sunshine, fresh air, or freedom, creatures on large commercial farms are typically denied the opportunity to roam, socialize, and behave in ways natural to their species.[7]

You can help by learning about domestic-animal welfare and educating others. One way is to let shoppers know that labeling can contain phrases that sound good but actually mislead the consumer. Terms like *free range*, *cage free*, and *pasture raised* suggest good living conditions. These descriptions, however, are not a guarantee that humane care was provided. That's because anyone can use these words. Instead, look for products that have been *certified*—guaranteed to meet a set of criteria, by organizations that promote animal welfare standards. In the United States, you can look for labels like *Certified Humane,* which require farmers to meet standards and submit to inspections.[8]

Many people live their activism by choosing to eliminate animal-based foods from their diets. They may become *vegetarians*—people who do not eat meat—or *vegans*—people who do not eat any food that comes from animals, including eggs and dairy products. Those following a vegan lifestyle might also avoid leather, wool, feathers, or other animal products. Asking people to turn their backs on all animal products may be less effective than starting with a smaller step—encouraging the use of fewer animal products. You could promote Meatless Monday or the idea of being a *flexitarian*—someone whose diet is usually meatless but sometimes includes fish or meat.

BE THE CHANGE
The Meatless Monday movement encourages people to eat less meat for both personal and planet health. Choosing plant-based foods over meat, even once a week, can help reduce the number of animals raised on factory farms. It also cuts down on the amount of greenhouse gases that arise from livestock production.

FRIEND OR FOOD?

Have you ever wondered why it's considered okay to eat some animals but not others? Species that serve as companions in some cultures are readily eaten elsewhere. Dogs and cats are considered fair game throughout much of Asia, and some of those eaten are stolen pets, crammed into small cages for transport to traders or restaurant owners. Humane Society International reports that every year thirty million dogs and ten million cats are killed for food, with ten million dogs[9] and four million cats[10] slaughtered annually just in China.

You might not think of horses as food either, but they are shipped as live exports from the United States to other countries where they are killed in slaughterhouses. *Kill buyers* purchase unwanted horses through private sales and auctions. They buy retired racehorses as well as young and healthy animals. Travel to distant slaughterhouses involves cramming horses into trucks, or onto boats or airplanes, without enough room to move. They travel without food, water, or protection from aggressive stallions. Many become injured during transport. Upon reaching their destinations, stressed horses endure cruel killing methods rather than euthanasia.

Horses are generally not raised for food. Their meat can contain medicines that aren't safe for human consumption. Buyers do not know the history of the animals they purchase, making horse meat a risky choice for consumers.

If you would like to help end the practice of eating companion animals for food, look for national and international organizations that aim to stop these practices. For example, in 2017, Taiwan banned killing, selling, and eating cats and dogs. See what other examples you might follow. Join forces with groups that provide rescue services for horses, as well as burros, which are also sold to kill buyers. Seek charities for wild horses and burros, and support horses by learning about the Safeguard American Food Exports (SAFE) Act, which aims to prohibit the sale or transport of horses for human consumption.[11]

SPREAD THE WORD!

The word *blog* may sound like a fish-ball being coughed up by a dolphin, but it's a great tool to reach internet users. Short for *weblog*, a blog is a website or section of one where people share personal thoughts, opinions, and information. It may include pictures or videos, links to other pages, and the option for visitors to add comments. You can start your own, or you can take a shortcut to reach readers more quickly. Look for blogs that already exist on your topic, and offer to write guest posts about your cause or activities. The site owner will get free content, and you'll get to spread your message to a ready group of readers who are already interested in your topic.

MORE THAN ONE WAY TO TACKLE A PROBLEM

So many animals need helping hands. You might start by encouraging others to rescue individual creatures. Or you might dive into activism that helps entire flocks, schools, and herds. You might get your hands dirty at a rescue facility or keep them clean by tackling issues from a computer. One way is not better or more important than another. For some, there are benefits to activism from a distance. If the species you love make you sneeze, wheeze, itch, or erupt with hives, you can still befriend and assist the furred, beaked, and finned creatures of the world.

MAKE ANIMALS' LIVES BETTER

From the dogs and cats in your own neighborhood to wild species in crisis, there are so many causes in need of aid and so many ways to make change. Check out how these creative kids and organizations got started.

TEACH OTHERS HOW TO HELP
{Lobby for Animals, Nonprofit, Florida}

For Thomas Ponce, one of the best feelings is knowing he's doing everything he can to help animals and the environment. One of his first efforts was in kindergarten—a poster about tiger poaching. His project won first place at his school and went on to be judged at the county level.

It was exciting for Thomas to know his message was reaching more people. He was inspired to learn all he could about ways to improve the treatment of animals and the environment. He took online classes from the Humane Society of the United States and attended conferences on animal rights and environmental issues. Thomas reached the conclusion that effective *legislation*—the process of establishing laws—would be the best way to make a difference.

In 2012, at the age of twelve, he founded Lobby for Animals, a nonprofit that teaches people how to *lobby*—the process of influencing governments, especially lawmakers, to create laws that support a cause. Thomas uses his website to share information about his concerns and offer training on how to effectively approach government officials on matters you feel passionate about.[12]

RESCUE FARM ANIMALS

{Farm Sanctuary, Nonprofit, California and New York}

Farm Sanctuary is a nonprofit focused on stopping farm animal abuse. It operates two sanctuaries: a 275-acre farm in New York that is home to more than eight hundred farm animals and a twenty-six-acre sanctuary in Southern California, with about one hundred animals. As well as rescuing cows, goats, lambs, ducks, chickens, and other species, this nonprofit educates people about responsible animal welfare. It offers sanctuary tours and work group parties that allow participants to spend time with critters while learning about ways to reduce their abuse. Farm Sanctuary also advocates for change, including better animal product labeling, legislation to prevent inhumane confinement, and banning the sale of eggs from hens kept in cages. It invites people to sponsor a sanctuary animal and arranges adoptions with people who can provide safe spaces.[13]

BE THE CHANGE

Volunteer at an animal shelter. Rescued critters find themselves in unfamiliar environments with strange smells and noisy neighbors. You can make their stays more pleasant by volunteering to walk dogs, fill water bowls, scrub floors, and clean cages. Some people even foster pets—keep them temporarily at their home—until permanent homes are found. You may need to use your sweet-talker skills to get the adults in your home to agree to this idea!

INSPIRE OTHERS

{Kids Against Animal Cruelty, Nonprofit, United States}

In 2010, fourteen-year-old actor Lou Wegner visited an animal shelter for the first time. He was shocked to discover how many critters were euthanized at crowded shelters every year. Determined to help, Lou founded Kids Against Animal Cruelty. He wanted to inspire other young people to get involved. Thanks to Lou's efforts, kids, teens, and young adults in sixteen states and four other countries run KAAC chapters. Members work to ban puppy mills and educate others about responsible pet care, including the importance of spaying and neutering. They use social media to find homes for animals in need of both foster and permanent homes.[14]

IN THE DOGHOUSE

One of the most popular companion animals is one of the first species ever domesticated. Dogs have been around since about 13,000 BCE. It's exciting to get a new puppy, but sometimes things do not go as expected. The pup may be too barky, active, or expensive to keep. Unwanted dogs often end up at shelters where they contribute to canine *overpopulation*—the issue of too many dogs in an area. Every year, about 3.3 million dogs go to shelters in the United States. About 670,000 are euthanized due to overcrowding, aggression, or lack of adopters.[15]

Another tail-between-the-legs problem is that many canines originate from *puppy mills*. Dogs at these facilities are bred in crowded, inhumane conditions. Operators run mills in ways that allow them to save money and make greater profits. Females live their lives in unsanitary, cramped cages, with no regard for their health. Breeding dogs get little or no personal attention and are often killed or abandoned when they become too old or ill to produce puppies. The Humane Society of the United States estimates the United States is home to at least ten thousand puppy mills. Dogs raised this way are often sold through websites that present owners as small, family breeders. Puppy mill dogs are also sold at pet stores and through newspaper and magazine ads.[16]

You can help curtail puppy mills. Encourage people to give homes to *rescue dogs*—those found in shelters—and only support responsible breeders. Research ways to locate trustworthy businesses and share what you learn. (Hint: start with the puppy-friendly pet stores listed on Humane Society websites.) You can try to influence local pet stores too. Ask them to provide evidence to patrons that shows they only purchase from responsible breeders.

If you encourage people to learn about the needs and characteristics of different dog breeds before choosing a pet, you can also help reduce overpopulation. Promote the benefits of *spaying* and *neutering*—surgeries that prevent animals from reproducing. Ask people to vote for political candidates who are active in tackling animal issues. You might even organize a bark-in-the-park event to raise funds for the people and organizations working to help your tail-wagging friends.

BRAIN NUGGET

Parrots, including parakeets, are undomesticated species that may be raised in bleak conditions at bird mills. Birds need space for flight and more stimulation than allowed by the small cages they are often kept in. While regulations in the United States were amended in 2023, bird breeding remains a largely unregulated industry with limited protections under the federal Animal Welfare Act. Birds make up the largest population of captive wild animals.[17]

IN THE WILDERNESS

Wild creatures know how to care for themselves, but our activities often interfere with their ability to function naturally. Animals are called *endangered* if they are at risk of becoming extinct. Species that might become endangered in the foreseeable future are classified as *threatened*.

In some habitats, a direct and deadly threat is *poaching*—the illegal killing or trafficking of game or fish. Millions of animals representing thousands of species are taken from their natural habitats. Elephants, rhinoceroses, and monkeys are just a few that are commonly harvested. Poached animals may be killed for ivory, antlers, tusks, hides, meat, bones, or organs. Their parts may be used for questionable medicinal purposes or to make jewelry, figurines, or other decor. Some, including parrots and other birds, are sold as exotic pets. Buyers purchase live animals and their parts through *black market transactions*—the buying and selling of illegal goods.

Poaching is big business. Around the world, animal products are sold for great sums of money. As well as having an enormous impact on species' survival and their ecosystems, poaching is an economic problem comparable to selling drugs and weapons. It sometimes even plays a role in violent armed conflicts. Militant groups kill animals to provide food for soldiers and use poaching profits to pay soldiers and purchase weapons.[18]

When it comes to trafficking wildlife, the WorldAtlas lists these countries as the worst:

1. Kenya

2. Tanzania

3. Uganda

4. South Africa

5. China

6. Thailand

7. Vietnam

8. India

9. Malaysia

10. The Philippines[19]

As you seek creatures to champion, research species that interest you and issues that attract your attention. Begin with ethical fishing, trapping, and hunting. Also look up unethical *trophy hunting*, where the largest animals are sought, and *captive hunting*, where patrons pay for the right to shoot animals in enclosures. A new concern is *internet hunting,* where game species may be lured with food to a spot near a mechanized tripod with a live camera. The "hunter" clicks a mouse to trigger a computer-enabled rifle. Another unsporting practice called *bear hounding* involves using hounds equipped with radio collars to help hunters locate and pursue bears.

As you research, don't forget about all the life-forms that make water their home. You might explore whale and shark hunting, as well as *shark finning.* This involves cutting a fin from a shark, often while it's still alive, for use in shark fin soup, a dish served throughout China, Taiwan, and Southeast Asia.

ONE THING YOU CAN DO NOW

Certain types of tuna fishing equipment can also trap and kill dolphins, seabirds, sea turtles, sharks, and other marine species. To avoid supporting fishing that harms other animals, only purchase tuna that is pole- or troll-caught or captured by pole-and-line. How can you tell when you're holding a can of tuna? Look for dolphin-safe labels that certify compliance with tuna fishing laws and regulations.[20]

If you find that examining how humans treat animals is a lot to take in, remember this: the best way to respond is to take action. Begin with this quizard, which is designed to help you explore where your interests lie.

QUIZARD
WHAT IF?

1. If I could pick a class field trip, we would go to:

(A) an insect sanctuary

(B) an elephant refuge

(C) a marine mammal rescue center

(D) a dog shelter

2. If I was going to spend a month helping one species, I would pick:

(A) honeybees

(B) chimpanzees

(C) leatherback turtles

(D) chickens

3. If a millionaire offered to donate $1,000 to my favorite animal charity, I would give it to:

(A) the insect sanctuary at Te Manahuna Aoraki, New Zealand

(B) the Wild Camel Protection Foundation

(C) Sea Life Trust

(D) American Society for the Prevention of Cruelty of Animals (ASPCA)

4. If I was going to design a T-shirt, it would say:

(A) I BEE-lieve in planting flowers

(B) Go wild for wildlife

(C) Whale, now what?

(D) For Pet's Sake

No matter what T-shirt you'd like to wear, reach your arm around and give yourself a pat on your back. There are no wrong answers when it comes to figuring out the best way to direct your activism. You get points for trying!

QUIZARD RESULTS

If your most frequent answer was:

A, you'll be a good friend to the insect world.
B, the large mammals of the world welcome you to their team.
C, expect to get wet. You're headed for the sea.
D, domestic animals are your jam.

If your answers jumped around, you either have many interests or need to explore further. After all, the quizard made no mention of birds, fish, amphibians, reptiles, small mammals, or other critters. (I wanted to write a quizard including all 8.6 million known species, but my editors had other ideas.)

As you dive into problem-solving, encourage others to follow your example. Be prepared to sometimes play teacher. (You might prefer to call yourself an expert, guru, or whiz kid.) No matter what title you choose, take pride in leading others to make change. Be sure to arm yourself, and your team, with the best weapon—information that is *evidence based*—facts supported by proof, such as scientific studies that show something is true.

Facts are a powerful way to sway people who are new to an issue. Changing the beliefs and behaviors of people with long-held opinions is harder and not always possible. As an activist, you can expect to find yourself responding to different viewpoints or arguments. That doesn't mean getting in people's faces and insisting you're right. Instead, aim to win others over by focusing on solutions. Be calm. Be charming! But also, be exactly what you are—a *vertebrate*—an animal with a backbone.

If your best efforts still lead to roadblocks, don't give up. Simply take a different approach. Devise a plan to meet your goal. This is called strategy! For example, if you feel adults are not taking you seriously, bring your message to people your own age. Ask them to share your message with the grown-ups in their lives. Though it can be a challenge to dream up the right strategy, it is also part of the thrill of activism.

IMAGINE

Imagine going a full day without eating or using any animal products. As well as skipping foods from ice cream to screaming-hot chicken wings, you'll go without products that contain animal-based ingredients or use them for processing. This includes some perfumes, plastic bags, sugars, nail polishes, crayons, red candies, cake mixes, and bagels.[21]

SPOTLIGHT ON . . .
Performing Animal Welfare Society

Pat Derby was a Hollywood actress, dancer, and singer who became a film and television animal trainer. After witnessing animal neglect and abuse on set, Pat developed her own training methods based on trust instead of fear. She tried to make life easier for the creatures in her care, but it wasn't always easy. She wrote the 1976 book *The Lady and Her Tiger*, which exposed how the industry treated performing animals and shared her story from trainer to rescuer. Determined to save captive wildlife too, Pat and her partner, Ed Stewart, cofounded the Performing Animal Welfare Society (PAWS).

Founded in 1984, this nonprofit operates three sanctuaries for captive wildlife in Northern California, including the first elephant sanctuary in the United States (established in 1986). The bears, elephants, big cats, and other species that live out their lives on PAWS properties include victims of the exotic pet trade and mistreated or abandoned animals from circuses, zoos, traveling shows, captive breeding, and the film and television industry. PAWS works to educate the public about captive wildlife issues and the importance of protecting natural habitat. It is an international leader in animal welfare, and the elephant handling techniques Pat and Ed developed became a model for other elephant handlers.[22]

BRAIN NUGGET

Sometimes, a mental condition leads people to mistreat critters. One such condition is *animal hoarding*—an obsessive need to collect animals, which results in their neglect or abuse.

MEET A YOUNG ACTIVIST
Duncan Jurman

Around the world, insect populations are declining. Florida high school student Duncan Jurman is aiding his favorite species—butterflies—one plant at a time. One of the ways he helps is by handing out flower seed packs to neighbors, classmates, and other students and reminding them that butterflies are important pollinators.

Duncan's fascination began around age five, when he became intrigued by the way caterpillars manage to stay hidden by blending into their environments and how they transform into butterflies. A young researcher, he began to collect facts about his favorite insect family and share what he learned with others. In fourth grade, Duncan started delivering butterfly education sessions at schools to encourage audiences to set up butterfly gardens on school grounds. Then at the age of sixteen, he set up a twenty-eight-species butterfly garden at his own high school, complete with a sustainable irrigation system.

Duncan created a website to provide information on how to identify species and ensure butterflies have the food and habitat they need. He shares which flower species help the most and asks people to stop using pesticides and herbicides. Duncan's campaign, Bring Butterflies Back, encourages people to plant flowers, take part in community gardening, and transform Florida's Broward County from weedy suburbs to a butterfly sanctuary. In 2020, Duncan was recognized with a Young Eco-Hero award for his important environmental activism.[23]

MORE THAN ONE WAY TO TACKLE A PROBLEM

The more you learn about an animal species, the more likely you are to take an interest in its survival. From tentacled creatures that live in shells to seabirds with blue feet, it's easy to grow fascinated with the organisms that share our planet.

Species preservation often means working to save animals that you never get to see outside of maybe a zoo or live webcam. Don't let that stop you, though. If you want to throw your energy into helping endangered animals but are not sure how to join the cause, look at how others use education and fundraising to make an impact.

EFFORTS TO STOP EXTINCTION

Many activists put effort into educating others about the risks creatures face. They know that curiosity leads to knowledge and awareness leads to action. From urging governments to make change to selling merchandise with a message, kids are finding ways to raise funds and put the money into good hands, just like the young activists highlighted in this chapter.

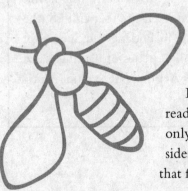

When you visit an organization's website, you learn what it says about itself. When you read news articles, you learn what others say about the organization. Be sure to explore both, and when reading news, remember, reporting is only fair if it is *nonbiased*—tells both sides of a story. Choose news sources that follow this basic standard.

SUPPORT RESEARCH
{Save the Nautilus, Nonprofit, Montana}

Josiah Utsch was seven when he became interested in the nautilus, a marine mollusk with a spiral shell, up to ninety tentacles, and the ability to move by expelling water. The nautilus, which has survived in Earth's oceans for 500 million years, is often called a living fossil because of its shape, which is similar to its fossilized ancestors.

At the age of eleven, Josiah read a *New York Times* article that said the chambered nautilus could face extinction. He was determined to take action. With help from his friend Ridgely Kelly, Josiah created a nonprofit called Save the Nautilus. Its goal is to support research and raise awareness about nautiluses' chief threat—being killed for their tiger-striped orange-red shells, which are used to make jewelry and decor.

Since 2011, the charity has raised more than $24,000 by collecting donations and selling notecards, shirts, bumper stickers, and other merchandise. Thanks to the efforts of Josiah, Save the Nautilus, and scientists' conservation efforts, scientists were able to do something particularly important. They gathered the evidence needed to ensure that CITES (the Convention on International Trade in Endangered Species of Wild Fauna and Flora) regulates all varieties of nautilus. As a result, the US Endangered Species Act lists one type of nautilus as threatened.

SUPPORT RESEARCH (CONTINUED)

Save the Nautilus also works with partners who help promote the cause. One partner— professional entertainer Nymphia the Nautilus Mermaid—based one of her costumes on this animal and has donated a portion of mermaid show proceeds to saving nautiluses. Josiah and Ridgley have raised awareness in the United States, Canada, Spain, Australia, and the Netherlands. They ask others to join them by sending letters to governments to help spread awareness.[24]

SELL A UNIQUE PRODUCT

{The Blue Feet Foundation, Charitable Foundation, Massachusetts}

Will Gladstone was in fifth grade when his science teacher, Mr. Banister, told his class about the shrinking blue-footed booby population on the Galapagos Islands. About the size of a large seagull, blue-footed boobies waggle their blue feet at each other during courtship displays. The shade of a male's feet is important to the female.

It occurred to Will that selling socks the same color as the birds' feet would be a way to raise funds to help the species. Will and his ten-year-old brother, Matty, established the Blue Feet Foundation. They held a contest for a unique sock design based on the blue-footed booby, picked a winner, and, with help from their parents, found a supplier and set up an online store. The first sale took nearly three months, but business picked up as people discovered what the boys were doing.

Since 2016, the Blue Feet Foundation has sold more than twenty thousand pairs of socks and raised more than $150,000. It has sold socks in all fifty US states and fifty-four countries. Funds are donated to the Galapagos Conservancy and the Charles Darwin Foundation to help support scientific research on the blue-footed booby.[25]

SATISFY YOUR CURIOSITY

Search these topics for an internet safari of issues:

- International Marine Mammal Project
- Owl cafés
- Exotic pets
- Tennessee walking horses
- Racehorse welfare
- Understanding Animal Research
- Factory farming
- Puppy mills
- Certified Humane
- Performing Animal Welfare Society (PAWS)
- Save the Nautilus
- The Blue Feet Foundation
- Poaching
- Animal rights

5

WE HAVE ONE PLANET

SAFEGUARDING THE ENVIRONMENT

"When viewed in total, Earth is a spaceship just like Apollo.
We are all the crew of spaceship Earth and, just like Apollo, the crew
must learn to live and work together. We must learn to manage the
resources of this world with new imagination."

James Lovell, NASA astronaut, United States

S tep outside and find a place where you can stand in nature.
Lose your shoes and curl your toes into the ground. The soil
and minerals beneath your feet are part of the environment. Tip
your face upward. Is it warm, cool, or breezy? The air you feel is
part of the environment too. Scan the sky for clouds. The water
droplets they hold, along with all the water on Earth, are also your
environment. These nonliving parts of our planet are vital. They
allow the living parts—plants, animals, and people—to survive.

We use *natural resources*—things found naturally on Earth—to meet our needs. Two major types, plants and animals, provide all our food. We use resources like oil, coal, natural gas, sunlight, and wind to create heat, light, and power. The basic materials in every human-made object come from natural resources. Think of tree fibers made into toilet paper, minerals used to build computers, and plastics rendered from oil.

Since our lives depend on natural resources, it seems obvious to say we must take care of our environment. Yet around the globe, human activities threaten what we need to live. Side effects from our use of natural resources include climate change, pollution, and waste creation, as well as habitat loss, extinction, and other challenges. Protecting the environment must involve better resource management. We need to care for soil and minerals, water and air, plants and animals, and every other aspect of nature. The best approaches are *sustainable*—they do not damage resources or let them run out.

Think of sustainability this way: Two families with peach trees decide to bake pies. Taking an ax, family one chops down their tree. They gather enough fruit for two pies, and then burn the wood. Family two picks enough peaches for two pies. They try to avoid harming the tree in any way. In fact, throughout the year, they care for the tree. They water it, pull pesky weeds, and prune branches, helping it to produce more fruit. The family even saves peach pits and plants an orchard. Repeating this cycle makes the peach crop sustainable. Family two's children and grandchildren will be able to pick peaches far into the future. Family one, however, will never enjoy peaches from their tree again.

This sad tale might make you wonder—couldn't they see they were only hurting themselves?

In places untouched by humans, plants and animals maintain stable populations. The natural environment is good at caring for itself. But 7.8 billion people live on Earth. We take up a lot of room! Environmental problems are often tied to our need for food, water, fuel, and shelter. Local and national economies may depend on jobs related to harvesting or processing natural resources. It is not real-istic to leave all of nature alone. Instead, we must manage Earth's resources in ways that protect the environment. As an activist, your challenge is to explore ways to meet today's needs without ignoring the needs of future generations.

IMAGINE

Picture your life without anything made from trees. These plant giants give us wood, paper prod-ucts, and food, but that's not all. Without trees, you'd have to kiss good-bye chocolate, maple syrup, cork, latex gloves, and even some life jackets and hair dye. If we don't protect and manage the trees, how will we survive?

GLOBAL WARMING AND CLIMATE CHANGE

Have you ever heard anyone decades older than you insist, "It was a lot colder when I was a kid!" You might have wondered if that could be true. Doesn't the same weather more or less repeat year after year? Are these cold-weather storytellers just trying to sound Arctic-tough? Maybe not.

Keep in mind that climate and weather are two different things. *Weather* refers to daily conditions. *Climate* describes the average weather over a period of thirty or more years. It's natural for Earth's climate to experience gradual changes over time. The past one hundred years, however, have seen temperatures warm more quickly than ever before, meaning your storyteller was right! Science shows that Earth's average surface temperature is creeping higher. Since the late nineteenth century, it has increased about 2.12 degrees Fahrenheit (1.18 degrees Celsius).[1]

All regions on Earth, from low-lying coasts to the highest mountains, are experiencing climate change. Some places are becoming warmer and drier. Others are getting more rain. This rapid change is occurring because of human activities, which include burning fossil fuels and clearing land for agriculture. These practices release carbon dioxide, methane, water vapor, ozone, and other gases, called *greenhouse gases*, into the atmosphere. Just as the clear walls of a greenhouse trap heat to keep plants warm, the gases trap the Sun's heat around Earth. It's like an invisible blanket surrounds the planet, making everything warmer. In the last 150 years, human activities created almost all the greenhouse gases warming our planet.[2]

If you live in a place with cold winters, you might like the idea of warmer temperatures. Unfortunately, when an entire planet heats up, serious problems occur. Climate change is a matter that needs immediate action.

CAN YOU ADAPT?

If you wonder why a few degrees are such a big deal, try this experiment. Ask an adult in your home if you can lower the temperature a couple of degrees. You may need to adjust a thermostat or turn off fans. (Notice how this experiment could saves fossil fuels?) Now take the test a step further. Ask to drop your hot water tank's temperature. See how long it takes before the change makes you uncomfortable. (If your family isn't thrilled about this activity, practice your persuasion skills! If they still won't cooperate, sleep with extra blankets, and monitor how the temperature change makes you feel.)

QUIZARD
WHAT ARE YOU TALKING ABOUT?

1. You want to know if it's a good day to hang out at the beach.
   You're talking about (A) weather or (B) climate.

2. You wonder about the annual level of snowfall in Fairbanks, Alaska.
   You're talking about (A) weather or (B) climate.

3. You notice that spring occurs earlier each year.
   You're talking about (A) weather or (B) climate.

4. You text about how one minute it's sunny, but the next it's raining.
   You're talking about (A) weather or (B) climate.

QUIZARD RESULTS

If you answered A, B, B, A, you know what you're talking about! You deserve an imaginary gold crown. (A real one would use too many natural resources.)

GET CHATTY!

Some of us wear shorts when it's snowing. Other people are always bundling up. Identify your personal comfort zone, and then start a conversation on human reactions to temperature changes. How do you feel when you're outside your zone? Is it harder to concentrate on the things you need to do? How might changing temperatures impact plants or wildlife?

CLIMATE CHANGE IMPACTS PEOPLE AND ANIMALS

We can observe the effects of climate change. Animals are moving into new habitats. Plant-growing ranges are shifting. Winter ice on rivers and lakes is melting earlier in the spring. Summer heat waves are stronger. Sea ice is melting, making sea levels rise. Superstorm events are more windy, wet, destructive, and costly. Hurricanes that come ashore are causing more intense rain and increased flooding.

Climate change can impact our food supply and where we can live. When it causes severe weather, human health and safety are threatened. Picture powerful hurricanes with more rain and higher wind speeds than ever before. The planet is seeing more droughts, which lead to freshwater shortages and wildfires. UNICEF reports that hurricanes, cyclones, and other powerful storms, along with rising sea levels, are putting around 500 million children at risk.[3]

Sea levels rise when global warming melts too much ice. As well as sea ice, Earth is home to thick masses of ice on land, called *glaciers*, and *ice sheets*—ice that covers millions of square miles. Melting sea ice exposes darker surfaces, and these surfaces absorb and release heat, warming the oceans. Warm water takes up more space than cold water, and the expanding water means sea levels are rising even more. Normally, bright ice reflects sunlight back into space, and this helps keep Earth's overall climate mild, but when Earth's ice masses shrink and disappear, temperatures rise.

By the end of the century, sea levels are expected to rise at least one foot (0.3 meters) higher than levels in the year 2000.[4] This is enough to cause problems for the billions of people living and working along coastlines. As well as forcing people to move, rising seawater can seep into freshwater, making it undrinkable. Salty seawater can contaminate *groundwater* (the water below Earth's surface), which is needed to irrigate and grow crops. It can also change the chemistry of soil, causing plant species to disappear. Shorebirds, sea turtles, and other life-forms will also lose important habitat when beaches flood.

As oceans warm, marine creatures adapted to cooler temperatures become stressed. Life is harder for animals that don't feel well. They may face health and reproduction issues. When warm water stresses coral, it expels the algae it needs to survive and turns white. This process, called bleaching, can be deadly not only to coral but also to many ocean species that call the coral reefs home. Climate change could kill all of Earth's coral reefs. A threat to coral reefs is a threat to humans. More than 500 million people depend on reefs.[5] They provide habitat for a quarter of all saltwater fish species, many of which are used as human food. Coral reefs also protect shorelines from storms.[6]

On land, climate change is affecting crop yields. Farmers in some regions are facing drought in the growing season and too much rain when they need to harvest. Heat waves are killing poultry, cattle, and other livestock. Warmer temperatures are allowing insects to spread farther and faster. They are entering areas where they have no natural predators, making it easier for them to damage crops and infect forests.

Plants are impacted by climate change too. Some may produce seeds or berries earlier than normal. When migrating birds appear at their usual time, the food they need may no longer be available. Animals may become extinct if they cannot adapt to changing climate conditions.

Some species of animals will face unique issues, such as problems with *parasites*—organisms that live in or on another living thing. Parasites, which are usually harmful, get food or shelter from their hosts. Moose will suffer from ticks more because mild winters make it easier for the ticks to attack. Salmon on North America's Pacific coast are experiencing a lethal parasite—*Ceratonova shasta*—known to thrive in warmer water.

When seasonal conditions occur at the wrong time, species that depend on camouflage to keep them hidden are in trouble. Snowshoe hares, for example, have fur that changes from brown in the summer to white in the winter. This makes it easier for them to avoid predators. When snow melts earlier than it should, the ground is brown, but hares are still white. Hungry predators spot this prey more easily, and hare populations can drop. The result is an unbalanced *ecosystem*—the community of species that live in an environment.

These are just a few examples of how climate change impacts our world. If you want to help reduce global warming, explore and promote ways to reduce heat-trapping gases, and use fewer fossil fuels and electricity. To get started, adopt new daily habits. Turn the power off when you're not using lights, televisions, computers, video games, and other electric equipment. Reduce vehicle emissions by choosing to walk, bike, use public transit, or carpool instead of riding in cars. Campaign for governments to use fewer fossil fuels, reduce deforestation, and limit the amount of pollution that industries can emit.

GET CHATTY!

Help your pals understand climate change with some T-shirt talk. When you are in the sun, white T-shirts reflect light, making you feel cooler. Black T-shirts absorb heat, making you feel warmer. In the same way, Earth's ice masses help cool the global temperature by reflecting light away from Earth. That's why they are so important.
Tell everyone!

MORE THAN ONE WAY TO TACKLE A PROBLEM

When you join the fight against climate change, you unite with a cause that will affect every living thing on the planet—from monarch butterflies to the great southern right whales, and even your neighbors across the street. The climate impacts all of us, and no matter where you live, you play a role in what the future will hold for generations to come. Will you be part of the solution?

CLIMATE CHANGE CHANGERS

The next three activists share a noble characteristic: dedication. If I were going to throw words around—after all, that's what authors do—I might whip out my thesaurus to see what other vocabulary might fit. My favorites, *effort*, *focus*, and *persistence*, fully describe what a weight lifter, hermit, and former US vice president have in common when it comes to finding ways to combat climate change.

BUST A MOVE
{Individual, Grassroots Approach, Kiribati}

Kiribati is a nation of small tropical islands between Hawaii and Australia. Severe weather, changing rain patterns, and other climate effects are affecting crops, fishing, and fresh-water supplies. The rising sea level could make the country disappear as early as 2050.[7]

David Katoatau, an Olympic weight lifter from Kiribati, has used dance to bring attention to climate change. After competing at weight lifting events, David would immediately leap right into a dance routine, but not to celebrate a win. Instead, he used his dancing to get people's attention and the media talking about the rising sea levels that are affecting Kiribati. David also wrote a letter to world governments, asking them to help stop his country from disappearing beneath the sea.[8]

PAY ATTENTION AND RECORD OBSERVATIONS
{Individual, Grassroots Approach, Colorado}

Some people call the hermit in Colorado's Rocky Mountains the Snow Guardian. His real name is billy barr (shown here the way he writes his name—in lowercase letters). At age twenty-one, billy became the sole resident of the mountain ghost town of Gothic, Colorado. He decided to measure snow levels and other weather conditions to pass the time. Twice a day, for more than forty years, billy tracked the weather. He kept detailed notes on animals and their behaviors too. Near the end of the 1990s, a scientist learned of billy's records. He realized they showed important climate change trends, so billy shared his notes, helping scientists who need historic data to understand our changing planet.[9]

SET UP AN ACTIVISM SCHOOL
{The Climate Reality Project, Nonprofit, Washington, DC}

The Climate Reality Project teaches anyone—including children in middle school—how to be a climate change activist. Former US vice president Al Gore founded the project to get the world talking about climate change. It seems to be working! The three-day program has trained more than thirty-one thousand people[10] in 154 countries[11] to be climate advocate leaders. Trainees find out how global warming is affecting people around the world. They learn how to share the science and solutions to reduce greenhouse gas emissions and shift to clean energy, as well as how to talk to reporters and encourage communities to act.

EXPLORE MORE

If you are feeling eco-anxiety, you aren't alone. Climate change is a worry, but experts around the world are tackling the situation. Remember, the first step to activism is understanding the issue. Exploring the impacts of climate change in your region will help you find the best way to personally chip in. Facts give you power!

MEET A YOUNG ACTIVIST
Desmond (Dessi) Sieburth

Did you know that a building project could change a life? Building a bird feeder at the age of eight led Desmond (Dessi) Sieburth to grow interested in birds.

By age ten, Dessi was working to raise awareness of how climate change, lead poisoning, and litter affect birds. He also raised money to support research and conservation by hosting a Big Photo Day. Dessi asked sponsors to make donations based on how many different bird species he could photograph within Los Angeles County in one day. He took pictures of eighty-four species and raised $727.

Over time, Dessi noticed bird populations growing smaller and realized western bluebirds were a species he could help. Western bluebirds need dead trees with old woodpecker holes or other cavities to raise their young. This habitat, however, is hard to find. People often clear dead, standing trees. Dessi began to build bluebird nesting boxes. He set them up at three different locations in the Los Angeles area and checked them weekly during the nesting season. In six years, from 2014 to 2019, Dessi saw 579 young birds, called *fledglings*, leaving the nest.

Dessi also works to protect wild birds and their habitat by taking part in research, leading bird walks, and writing articles on birds, their habitat, and conservation. He organizes an annual fundraiser to raise money to protect and create bird habitat. Dessi also runs a website called Protecting Our Birds. In 2019, the John Muir Association named Dessi the Youth Conservationist of the Year. (Pretty cool for this sixteen-year-old!)[12]

A WORD FOR *HOME*

In chapter 1, we learned that a habitat is a place that contains everything an organism needs to survive. Your home is a huge part of your habitat. You eat, sleep, and do much of your daily living in this place. Imagine what would happen if your home was demolished and you had no place to go. This is what creatures face when their habitat is destroyed.

Organisms live in specific habitats because they have *adaptations*—special behaviors or physical characteristics that help them survive. Take the snowshoe hare's changing fur color based on the season—that is an adaptation. Animal species cannot just move to a different type of habitat. Their adaptations, which protect them from predators and help them find food, match their natural surroundings. That's why mountain dwellers need high elevations, marine life needs seawater, and rainforest critters need wet, tropical woodlands.

Sometimes a habitat becomes *fragmented*—separated by barriers. Imagine you live on the third floor of an apartment building. Unfortunately, aliens came along, cut the apartment in half, and built a new road right through the middle. Your refrigerator is now on one side of the block, and your bed is across the street. Every night, you must take three flights of stairs down, cross a busy street, and climb more stairs to go get a glass of milk. Traveling between the different parts of your habitat puts you in danger and wastes energy. Animals trying to use split habitats waste energy too. It becomes hard to find food, reproduce, and raise young. Unfortunately, on Earth, humans are the aliens destroying animal habitat. This destruction is the leading cause of species extinction.

Humankind's quests for natural resources cause much of this loss. When people drill mines, clear forests, and fill in wetlands, they destroy habitat. Roads, dams, walls, fences, and railway tracks fragment places where critters need to live. Wildfires, rising sea levels, flooding, drought, and other climate change also damage habitats.

But you can tackle habitat loss! Raise awareness about the importance of biodiversity, or work with groups that preserve or rebuild habitats. Encourage actions that reduce habitat loss—use recycled paper, reduce water use, and choose rainforest-friendly products.

SPREAD THE WORD

Choose a place in your community that matters to you, like your school, public library, swimming pool, or hockey rink.

Step 1: List ways your chosen facility could reduce its impact on the environment.

Step 2: Respectfully share your ideas in a letter, signed by you and others who care.

Step 3: Send your letter to those with the authority to make change. It might be a principal, school board, or manager. Share it with local media too!

WHERE DO YOU GET YOUR ENERGY?

Natural resources fall into two groups: *renewable* and *nonrenewable*. Coal, oil, and gas, for example, are nonrenewable. They take thousands to millions of years to form, and we'll run out if we use these stores too fast.

Renewable resources are more plentiful. We have flowing water to make hydroelectric power, and heat found deep inside the Earth to generate geothermal energy. Sunlight, air, plants, and animals are renewable too. We will always have these resources. It sounds great! Unfortunately, human activities may create issues even when resources are plentiful. Pollution can block sunlight, making it harder to generate solar energy. Too much logging can cause forests to disappear. Overhunting can lead to animal extinctions.

One solution is to get more creative about our resource use. Consider these renewable energy resources: human waste and animal manure. It might make you shudder, but these stinky sources could save trees. Why? Because more than two billion people depend on wood for cooking and heating. Like wood, human waste and animal manure are biomass fuels. Using these alternate biomass fuels could reduce human reliance on wood.

Energy that doesn't pollute is often called *clean* or *green energy*. Renewable energies are usually better for the environment, but pros and cons always exist. While biomass fuels are plentiful, it is costly to build and run the needed facilities to create a product that is safe and easy for people to use. Wind energy is clean but creates noise pollution. Wind farms also can destroy habitat and kill birds and bats that fly into blades. Nuclear energy, created by splitting atoms, is cheap to produce and does not emit greenhouse gases, but building nuclear plants is often too costly for poorer nations. Plus, nuclear energy creates radioactive waste, which can cause cancer and other diseases if not properly contained.

Despite these renewable options, nonrenewable fossil fuels like coal, petroleum, and natural gas are still the world's main sources of energy. Our use of fossil fuels, from heating buildings to driving cars, produces carbon dioxide and other greenhouse gases. Methods used to collect these fuels result in pollution, habitat loss, and other problems. There are reasons why fossil fuels are so popular, though. They are plentiful, easy to store, and efficient, and it only takes a little bit to produce a lot of energy. Located in almost every country, fossil fuels are easy to find and can be transported by truck, train, or pipeline. They can be moved to processing facilities, unlike cleaner energies like wind, sun, and hydroelectricity, which are most easily turned into usable energy in the regions where they are harnessed. This is often far from the urban centers in need of power. Cleaner energies can only be moved through power lines. In the United States, the existing transmission line infrastructure is not enough to enable clean energy on a large-scale basis. Another problem for clean energy advocates is that other people sometimes engage in activism to stop power line expansion. They may be concerned about habitat loss, unsightly infrastructure, ecosystem health, or other issues.[13]

Technologies and infrastructure, such as refineries and pipelines, already exist for using fossil fuel energy. This typically makes them cheaper to use. However, clean energy advocates reported that things changed in 2021 for *G20 countries*—a group of nineteen countries and the European Union representing the world's major economies. The price of fossil fuels rose, and two-thirds of newly installed renewable power became cheaper than the least expensive coal-fired power.[14] The price of oil is also constantly changing, and activists must pay attention to ensure that any financial claims are up to date.

No matter what price oil is trading at, a fight for clean energy is a fight to combat climate change. If energy is a matter you would like to tackle, find out all you can about possible solutions. Take part in activism that encourages people to use less energy, choose clean energy, and reduce pollution. Ask governments and industries to lower dependence on fossil fuels and put the environment first.

ONE THING YOU CAN DO NOW

Can you think of a creative way to collect neighborhood garbage without using plastic bags? How much litter can you gather in an hour? Repeat the following week and compare.

WASTE IN OUR WORLD

Have you ever been asked to take the garbage out? Was it heavy? Think on this...in 2018, the US Environmental Protection Agency (EPA) estimated that each person in the United States generated 4.9 pounds of garbage a day.[15] All that garbage adds up, and managing it is a challenge! Some countries don't have garbage collection services. Others have old or ineffective systems. Poor practices can contaminate drinking water, spread disease, pollute air, and create greenhouse gases.

Many communities deal with trash by building *landfills*—places where waste is placed between layers of soil. A liner separates waste from the surrounding environment. This is different from a dump, where trash is only piled. Both, however, create *leachate*—a solution that results when liquid percolates through matter. In this case, the leachate is a toxic liquid that forms when rain or melted snow passes through waste. Imagine water seeping through dirty diapers, plastics, and rotting food. Leachate that escapes dumps and landfills can pollute soil, groundwater, and waterways. Piles of garbage also release what you might call nose pollution—gases including hydrogen sulfide (smells like rotten eggs) and ammonia (smells like cat urine). Odorless methane escapes too. This flammable gas can leak into buildings and become explosive. According to the UN, about 5 percent of greenhouse gases comes from decaying solid waste, which includes all the objects we throw out daily in our trash bins.[16]

Some waste is hazardous before it even reaches a landfill. It may be flammable, poisonous, *corrosive* (able to dissolve things), or *reactive* (able to cause a chemical reaction). Bleach, batteries, motor oil, prescription drugs, and other common products must be disposed of safely. The waste from electronics is a growing challenge around the world.

BE THE CHANGE

Did you know your actions leave a *carbon footprint*? This is the amount of greenhouse gases, like carbon dioxide, you create. You can shrink your footprint with everyday choices. Choose products with less packaging. Donate reusable items. Recycle what can't be reused. Choose a refillable water bottle over single use plastics, or even better, use a glass. Instead of asking for a ride, walk or hop on a bike. Plant flowers, trees, or an entire garden.

Water is also an ingredient in waste. Think of sewage! If you live where water is as close as the nearest tap, you have probably wasted water. This is an environmental concern because it takes natural resources to make water safe to drink and use and even reclean it. Many industries use vast amounts of water to cool equipment or create products. It takes water to produce food, to refine gas and oil, to make paper, to process wood into lumber, and to produce metal items. It takes so much water to produce nuclear energy, plants are usually built near lakes and rivers. Water treatment plants clean dirty water and return it to the natural world. Unfortunately, there aren't enough of them. The UN has found that about 80 percent of the wastewater returned to ecosystems has not been treated.[17]

If you decide to be a champion for waste management, promote the responsible use of water. Encourage practices that create less waste. Support programs that reuse and recycle products. Ask governments to ensure these are safe waste management facilities and to upgrade landfill sites.

PUTRID POLLUTION

You have probably stepped over it or smelled it in the air. Pollution exists when harmful materials, called *pollutants*, contaminate the environment. It is found everywhere—even in remote Antarctic ice. Pollution threatens all forms of life.

On land, trash is part of the crisis. Mountains of it can be deadly. In 2000, a giant pile of garbage collapsed at the Payatas dump site in the Philippines. The trash buried and killed 232 people and left 655 families homeless.[18] Trash is a threat to wildlife, pets, and farm animals too. They may die if they eat litter or get their heads stuck in containers, and even one small cigarette could cause a wildfire.

Liquid wastes add to the problem. Soapy water dripping from a washed car on a driveway allows detergents to enter storm drains that lead to waterways. Sewage, gasoline, pesticides, and fertilizers affect soil habitat when they enter the environment. Land pollution becomes water pollution if it seeps into groundwater and enters *surface water*— the water bodies we see. Garbage often ends up in surface water too, endangering creatures and humans alike. Many industries return heated water to the environment, which can stress or kill plants, fish, and other aquatic life by raising surface water temperatures.

Oceans face additional challenges like oil spills and *acidification*— when seawater becomes more acidic. Carbon dioxide in the air naturally dissolves in the ocean. Unfortunately, there's too much carbon dioxide. Oceans have become 30 percent more acidic in the past two hundred years.[19] Acidification weakens coral reefs and the shells of oysters and other shellfish. It upsets food chains and ecosystems, reduces biodiversity, and threatens *food security*—the ability of people to access food. Lakes and reservoirs are becoming more acidic too.

BRAIN NUGGET

All liquids, except pure water, are either *acidic* or basic (also called *alkaline*). Sour-tasting liquids like lemon juice are acidic. Soap and ocean water are basic. A liquid's acidity or alkalinity is measured on a scale of 0 to 14, called its *pH* number. Liquids with pH numbers below seven are acids, while pure water is neutral, at seven. Alkaline liquids have pH numbers eight and up.

The carbon dioxide causing ocean acidification is invisible. (Other contaminants, like smog, are visible.) As well as causing health issues, air pollution can react with chemicals in the atmosphere. It may form acid rain, which is harmful to creatures, habitat, crops, and human-made structures.

Noise and artificial light also pollute the environment. They can interfere with animals' abilities to meet their needs. (Read more about light pollution in chapter 6.) Noise and artificial light make it harder for species to seek prey and avoid predators as well as to communicate with each other. Both noise and light can also create habitat loss by impacting pollination, seed disbursement, and other activities that keep ecosystems healthy.

Our planet needs your pollution solutions! Look for ways to prevent problems as well as ways to clean up the mess. You might encourage people to take simple steps around the home, you might join others who battle for a cleaner world, or you might lead a protest for change.

SPOTLIGHT ON . . .
Plant-for-the-Planet

Felix Finkbeiner was nine years old in 2007 when he started the Plant-for-the-Planet Foundation with his friends. Today this organization in Germany leads a movement to plant a trillion trees around the world. The organization's reforestation efforts also help it tackle its other chief concerns—biodiversity loss and the climate crisis.

One of Plant-for-the-Planet's activities involves training children and older youths to be Climate Justice Ambassadors. Kids learn how to plant trees and how to keep them alive. They find out that species must be matched to the right habitats and that preserving existing forests is as important as planting new saplings. Ambassadors also gain important activist skills, including how to motivate others to get involved. They learn how to deliver speeches, reach out to politicians, and lead effective protests. With *dendrophiles* around the world, the foundation also makes sure ambassadors have the chance to learn from one another. It organizes online video get-togethers and hosts speakers who can mentor kids.

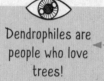

Dendrophiles are people who love trees!

Another Plant-for-the-Planet activity is a campaign called *Stop Talking. Start Planting.* Ambassadors invite the public to get involved by taking a photo of themselves holding a leaf to their mouth and sharing the image on social media. They're asked to include a message on how tree planting buys time for humankind to reduce the emissions that cause global warming and to use Plant-for-the-Planet hashtags.

As well as empowering young people, Plant-for-the-Planet conducts research on restoring forests. It shares data and software tools with organizations around the world. The foundation has national organizations in Brazil, the Czech Republic, Ghana, Italy, Mexico, Spain, Switzerland, the United Kingdom, and the United States, and it works with young leaders around the world who are dedicated to planting trees. It has trained more than ninety-five thousand children ages nine to fourteen at over 1,700 academies in seventy-five countries.[20]

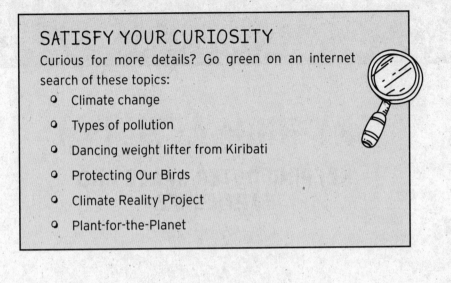

SATISFY YOUR CURIOSITY

Curious for more details? Go green on an internet search of these topics:

- ○ Climate change
- ○ Types of pollution
- ○ Dancing weight lifter from Kiribati
- ○ Protecting Our Birds
- ○ Climate Reality Project
- ○ Plant-for-the-Planet

6

SKY-HIGH ACTIVISM

KEEPING OUTER SPACE AND EARTH SAFE

"But you also must remember that science and technology are changing our world dramatically, so it's important to ensure that these changes are heading in the right directions. In a democratic society, this means that everyone needs to have a basic understanding of science, to make informed decisions about the future."

Stephen Hawking, physicist, United Kingdom

What's the first thing you do when you visit a new place? Do you duck your head down and stare at the floor? Hide in a box? Hopefully not!

Humans are driven to explore. We need to know what is going on! And we don't just itch to find what's over the next hill. We want to know what's above the treetops and beyond the clouds, all the way to the farthest reaches of outer space.

Inspired by the urge to discover, exploring the cosmos delivers a rocket full of benefits. Scientific knowledge is a big benefit. Engineers and scientists continually develop new technologies to enable people to live and work in space. Thanks to their efforts, we have satellite communication, more accurate weather forecasting, and global positioning systems (GPS). You've experienced space technology if you've ever had your picture taken with a cell phone camera, worn invisible braces on your teeth, or jumped up and down in sneakers containing memory foam.

Super! So, where does the activism come in when it comes to space? Well, for starters, some people question why governments spend money on exploring beyond our planet when we have serious problems—such as war, starvation, homelessness, and climate change—to solve here on our home planet. Defenders point out that space exploration helps us tackle earthly issues. They show how its research has saved lives, pointing to examples that range from cancer therapies and implantable heart monitors to ventilators designed specifically to aid COVID-19 patients. Space tech has led to the development of robotics that are used during brain surgeries, along with solar panels, water purification systems, and cordless tools. It improves human safety through satellite data that is used to predict severe weather, aid emergency responses, measure pollution, and gather climate change information. Some space-based experiments can even quickly generate data that would take years to collect on Earth.[1]

SPACE, THE FINAL FRONTIER OF WORLD-CHANGING TECH

In the United States, NASA—or the National Aeronautics and Space Administration—is the part of the government responsible for science and tech related to space and airplanes. Its work has led to more than two thousand space industry *spin-offs*—products, technologies, and processes that arise from exploring beyond our atmosphere.[2]

In addition to direct spin-offs that benefit our lives, space advocates might bring up how space exploration has helped with *national security*—the protection and defense of a country. Satellites collect data that is used to monitor air space and support military operations. Governments recognize that mastery from sky-high places will allow them to gain advantages in wars and smaller conflicts. Some nations are developing space systems to command military forces worldwide and monitor and target the forces of other countries.[3]

If non-peaceful countries gain too much power in the cosmos, what might happen? And how can you help?

Begin by exploring the opinions of *futurists*—people who study current trends and predict what might happen. Futurists and the UN Committee on the Peaceful Uses of Outer Space (COPUOS) have a lot to say on how space could be used for warfare. Check out the 1967 Outer Space Treaty, a milestone document which declares:

○ Space shall only be used for peaceful purposes.

○ No country may place nuclear weapons on the Moon or other bodies in space.

○ All countries have the right to use and explore space.

- No country may claim the right to own or govern space.

- Countries exploring space are *liable*—responsible—for any damage that results from objects they have launched into space.[4]

More than one hundred countries have signed the Outer Space Treaty, but a great many others are uncommitted. To expand and reinforce its ideals, the United Nations General Assembly (UNGA) adopted four additional outer space treaties:

1. The 1968 Rescue Agreement sets standards for the return of objects launched into space and for aiding astronauts in emergency situations. (It may seem surprising that guidelines are needed to state obvious things—like astronauts in dangerous situations must be rescued. However, setting policies before disaster strikes makes it easier and faster for nations to know how to respond when unexpected situations occur.)

2. The 1972 Liability Convention describes legal responsibilities. It looks at who should pay for damages (called liability) if launched space objects cause injury, loss of life, or harm to property.

3. The 1976 Registration Convention outlines the requirement to register all objects launched into outer space with the United Nations. We need to know what's out there!

4. The 1984 Moon Agreement reinforces ideals in the Outer Space Treaty to better ensure that the Moon and other celestial bodies are only used for peaceful purposes. From 1963 to 1996, the UNGA also developed five declarations and legal principles on space-related activities. These include

Yes, television can be an outer space issue.

addressing the use of space for international direct television broadcasting, *remote sensing* of Earth (using satellites to collect data on our planet's physical characteristics), nuclear power sources in outer space, and the use of space in ways that benefit all states, particularly developing nations.[5] COPUOS adopted guidelines on reducing the hazard of space debris (2007)[6] and ensuring that space activities are conducted in ways that strengthen long-term sustainability (2019). It recognizes that future generations must also be able to enjoy peaceful access to outer space.[7]

The work of COPUOS and its more than one hundred member nations is ongoing.[8] If you'd like to get involved in out-of-this-world

BE THE CHANGE

Do you remember the story of Chicken Little? She went around shouting that the sky was falling, but it turned out the poor bird was only hit by a falling acorn. Chicken Little could have investigated what truly happened, but instead she spread misinformation. She even set out to tell the king! If you come across organizations making suspicious claims, examine whether their messages are *objective*—expressing facts rather than opinions. Consider whether the writer or speaker is trying to convince you to believe something without presenting opposing sides of the story. Ask whether claims can be proven. When promoting your cause, be sure to let people know how careful you are when it comes to research. It's better than being a chicken little!

activism, one way to get started is by lobbying governments to make safety beyond Earth a priority.

Another way to help is to join activists promoting *space-based solar power*. This is clean, sustainable energy that would be harvested beyond the planet and relayed to Earth. While ground-based solar panels provide some of the energy we use, obstacles exist. They cannot generate energy at night, on cloudy days, or in regions without enough sunny weather. Space-based solar projects would not face these limitations. However, new technologies are needed to make this solution a reality.

LIFE IN SPACE

Activists also work on planning and promoting *space settlements*— places where people, including entire families, could permanently live on the Moon, Mars, or habitats in orbit around Earth. These habitats, sometimes called space colonies, orbital colonies, or space cities, do not yet exist. Fears about climate change, the COVID-19 pandemic, and other crises are inspiring people to explore how living off our planet can be achieved on a greater scale. Many believe advances in rocket science and other technologies will make this possible.

Can you imagine a nation beyond Earth? Asgardia—also known as the Space Nation—is an international community of people devoted to establishing a peaceful country in space. The Space Nation aims to be a single society without states, countries, or religions. It wants to avoid bringing Earth's existing problems into its realm and to protect our planet from the militarization of space. Asgardians already have a currency, called the *solar*, and a *constitution*—a document that outlines the laws and principles used to govern. People who accept the constitution and meet other criteria can pay an annual resident fee to obtain the right to vote and hold office. So far, 1,087,276 people from 203 countries are part of Asgardia. Founded by Azerbaijani-born Russian scientist Dr. Igor Ashurbeyli in 2016, Asgardia collects funds to research ways to create artificial gravity and protect future residents from space radiation.[9]

Another option for space activists is supporting the search for alien life. Why advocate to find extraterrestrial beings? One reason is curiosity. Wouldn't you like to know whether we are truly alone in the universe? Other reasons exist too. Learning about other life-forms will help scientists understand how life came about on our planet and how our future might evolve. The Search for Extraterrestrial Intelligence Institute, or the SETI Institute, uses radio telescopes and other astronomy techniques to try to detect signals from *intelligent life* beyond Earth.

BE WISE

Wait a minute! What is meant by *intelligent life*? Are we calling some aliens smart and others dumb? Isn't it poor judgment to make assumptions? Shouldn't we avoid slapping labels on beings, including those from other worlds?

If these thoughts are tumbling about in your mind, you are truly in activism mode! For now, though, you can save your energy. *Intelligent life* simply refers to beings that can understand things and learn. That means you are an example of intelligent life, but microorganisms like bacteria are not.

SETI's goals include conducting research to help explain the origins and potential distribution of intelligent life in the universe as well as sharing the knowledge it gathers with the public. If you would like to get involved in the search for space signals, you can aid this nonprofit by fundraising or building awareness about its programs. You might also explore its activities that use *citizen science*. This is where members of the general public aid scientists by helping collect or analyze data.

One SETI Institute citizen science project is aimed at community college students in the United States and is called the Unistellar College Astronomy Network (UCAN). It is designed, in part, to train teachers how to use, and have their students use, special digital smart telescopes to help research planets outside our solar system, called *exoplanets*, which could potentially host life. In addition to contributing to exciting science, the program supports another SETI goal—to increase student and public interest in science.[10]

Like SETI, many other nonprofits devote some of their endeavors to *public outreach*—the effort to inspire and bring information to the everyday public. Unlike more formal education, outreach usually takes place on a one-time or short-term basis. If you're interested in activism that invites others to learn, look for outreach opportunities with the organizations you support.

NEAR-EARTH OBJECTS AND POLLUTION

Perhaps all this talk about outer space makes you curious. Suppose it inspires you to observe the Moon. Peering through binoculars, you examine the craters that formed when space rocks crashed into the lunar surface. Asteroids and comets don't strike as often as they did during our solar system's formation, but history shows that strikes can be deadly. The asteroid that smashed into Earth 66 million years ago created enough dust to block all of Earth's sunlight. It led to a global winter and extinction of the dinosaurs.

Space is so vast, the idea of *near* takes on new meaning.

Objects that pass within about 30 million miles (50 million kilometers) of Earth's orbit are called near-Earth objects (NEOs).

Scientists track NEOs with telescopes. So far, their observations show that Earth and its residents do not have to worry about a collision in the next hundred years. However, sometimes NEOs are only discovered when they're already close. If you want to tackle this challenge, educate decision-makers about the importance of finding ways to protect Earth from NEOs. Join the activists that work to make sure scientists have the resources and dark skies they need to observe approaching celestial objects.

Don't blame sunlight, moonlight, glowworms, or light reflecting off your teeth.

It's difficult to observe the night sky when *artificial light* takes away natural darkness. Artificial light includes lighting on buildings, signs, towers, bridges, and other objects.

Light pollution exists when too much artificial light is present and when light is used inappropriately, such as allowing indoor lights to shine out windows. If you've ever raised a hand to block bright headlights from your eyes, you've experienced a type of light pollution called *glare*.

As well as making it difficult to observe and explore the night sky, light pollution is a tremendous problem for wildlife. It interferes with the lives of animals who are adapted to being active at night. It also upsets the lives of those that are active in the day but in need of dark nights to sleep and avoid enemies. Imagine an owl that depends on dark nights to capture prey or a squirrel that needs darkness to hide from coyotes. The study of how darkness, or a lack of it, affects living organisms is called *scotobiology*.

It is easy to spot the effects of light pollution. You've probably noticed winged creatures circling light fixtures. Some insects, as well as other animals, are attracted to artificial light. It may seem harmless, but lights that draw insects away from their natural habitat leave less prey for birds, bats, amphibians, and other species seeking food. Lights that create *sky glow*—a glow in the night sky over a community—can affect ecosystems over a 3,861-square-mile (10,000-square-kilometer) area as well as interfere with night sky observations.[11]

Activists work to promote dark skies by educating others about the impacts of unwanted light at night. They provide information on ways to use light in responsible ways, such as making sure lights shine only where needed, rather than out across land and into the sky. Knowing how this issue affects animals and their use of habitat is a valuable tool. You can use it to reach people who are not especially interested in space. If you're having trouble convincing others that NEOs are an important matter, approach animal lovers about the effects of light pollution.

Lending your efforts to reduce light pollution helps the world in other ways too. When people reduce their use of light, less electrical energy is required, and fixtures need not be replaced as often. This cuts down landfill waste, lowers greenhouse gas emissions, and helps slow climate change. If you would like to help preserve the night, begin by visiting the DarkSky website (see page 163 to learn more about this organization). You can use their research and resources to promote the responsible use of light to businesses, industries, and government policy-makers.[12] Bring your message home to your family as well as to your school and community. Light pollution is an area where everyone can make an immediate difference. Unfortunately, it's not the only matter affecting the cosmos.

High overhead, our sky is littered with *space junk*—human-made objects in orbit around Earth. Most are items that no longer have a use. Think of broken satellites, nuts, bolts, flecks of paint, and *rocket stages*—sections of rockets that detach when their fuel is used up. Trash circling our planet is also created when astronauts lose items on space walks. As a result, we have plastic bags and pens, as well as a screwdriver and lens cap circling our planet! Objects zoom through space at 17,500 mph (28,164 kph), a speed many times faster than a bullet. About twenty-three thousand pieces of orbital debris are bigger than a softball. However, even tiny flecks of paint are a hazard to spacecrafts.[13] Larger objects cause even more damage. All this litter puts working satellites and orbiting telescopes at risk. It is a danger to astronauts and *space stations*—spacecrafts in orbit around the Earth, where people live and work on a continual basis. Beyond our atmosphere, trash adds to the danger of navigating the cosmos and impacts the sustainability of exploring the universe.

In 2006, a piece of space junk took a chip out of a window on the *International Space Station*—a space station in orbit where agencies from many different nations, along with their astronauts and cosmonauts, cooperate and conduct space exploration programs. In 2007, an anti-satellite device from China was used to deliberately destroy a weather satellite. The collision created thousands of debris fragments. In 2009, two satellites—one working and one inactive—collided by accident over Siberia. The smash-up created thousands of additional pieces of space junk.[14] In 2021, an uncontrolled Chinese rocket body hurtled toward Earth. The ninety-eight-foot-long (thirty-meter-long) object weighed twenty tons (eighteen tonnes). Scientists could not predict exactly where it would land. Most pieces of space debris burn up as they pass through Earth's atmosphere or disappear into the ocean. This time, however, experts calculated that the debris could fall on a populated area, with the possibilities including cities such as New York, Los Angeles, Beijing, and Madrid. Instead, the rocket became marine pollution in the Indian Ocean.[15]

SPREAD THE WORD!

Do you know how to grumble? If you're like most people, you've had a little practice. Put those skills to work by complaining to people who can make change.

Begin by jotting down some notes about what you want decision-makers to know about your cause. Next, telephone city/town administrators or elected officials. When you reach the correct person, introduce yourself using your full name and the name of your community. Describe your concerns, and then invite the person you're speaking with to share their opinion on the topic. Listen to the response and make notes before replying. Then request action, but be specific. You might ask, "Will you discuss space junk at your next meeting?" Let the person you're speaking with know you're not going away. Ask, "How long do you recommend I wait before calling back? Shall I try in a few weeks?" Write yourself a note to call back!

While nations use policies and laws to try to address these serious events, the space industry works together to promote responsible practices too. The Space Safety Coalition is a group of forty-nine organizations and stakeholders that advocate for safety in space. Since 2019, this nonprofit has encouraged the aerospace industry to follow existing safety rules and guidelines and to consider taking additional steps to keep space safe. Its recommendations encourage space program operators to consider sustainability when launching spacecrafts. It asks operators to design spacecrafts that are capable of maneuvering to avoid collisions and asks them to develop disposal plans as soon as possible after spacecrafts are no longer in use.[16]

Sometimes, space agencies are able to control the paths of dying spacecrafts. When this happens, they may choose to blast them upward into a *graveyard orbit*—an area two hundred miles higher than the region where active satellites work. This solution moves machinery out of the way but still contributes to sky trash. The other solution is to deliberately dump all that priceless technology into the waters of our oceans. The preferred location for a splashdown is Earth's most remote place—the Oceanic Pole of Inaccessibility.

Also known as the spacecraft cemetery and Point Nemo.

It is located in the South Pacific Ocean, about two thousand miles north of Antarctica. The dumping spot is thousands of miles from the nearest human civilization and is home to little shipping traffic. When the football-field-sized International Space Station needs to be retired, it will join more than 260 other spacecrafts in this part of the ocean. Objects that do not fully burn up when passing through Earth's atmosphere break into thousands of pieces. The debris spreads across the ocean floor, covering an area several hundred miles long. People and their property are protected from being hit, but your thoughts may rocket to these important questions: *How do falling space stations, and the hazardous materials they contain, impact marine mammals, fish, and other sea creatures? Can intelligent life find a better solution?*

One hurdle to removing solar system litter is politics. The Outer Space Treaty implies that space objects are the responsibility of the launching state. This makes it hard for others to clean up the mess.[17] In fact, the United States forbids anyone to touch its satellites, and interference may be seen as an act of war.[18] Governments around the world need to agree on rules for salvaging objects both in space and in the sea.

Activists needn't grow spaced-out, wondering where to start. You can begin by exploring the Space Surveillance Network (SSN). Operated by the US Department of Defense, the SSN tracks debris larger than approximately four inches (10.2 centimeters) across.[19] Another good source is the *European Code of Conduct for Space Debris Mitigation*, which outlines goals to prevent collisions and dispose of spacecrafts.[20] Be sure to also look up UNOOSA—the UN Office for Outer Space Affairs.[21] As well as promoting international cooperation and the peaceful use of the world beyond Earth, UNOOSA's work includes helping its members establish laws to govern space activities.

Your research will help you find the best ways to campaign for a clean universe. Maybe you'll be the one whose activism helps protect Earth's habitats and inhabitants from falling debris!

INTERNATIONAL COOPERATION

Can you imagine building a rocket and launching yourself into space without any help? Probably not. It takes many types of experts to solve space problems. It will take input from activists too!

Today, nations around the world work together to explore beyond Earth, but it wasn't always this way. In the late fifties, the United States and the USSR (Union of Soviet Socialist Republics, often called the Soviet Union) competed to be the first to put a human on the Moon. It wasn't until 1975 that the two countries began to cooperate. Now partnerships and joint missions are much more common. Governments know they can accomplish more alongside other nations. Their shared interests help build peaceful connections between countries.

Global organizations also foster cooperation in space and on Earth. One worldwide collaboration—the International Charter: Space and Major Disasters—combines satellite data from sixty-one satellites and 129 countries. Satellites, which provide information that cannot be gathered from the ground, can be used to help manage natural and human-caused disasters. With no cost to users, the charter shares information to assist with humanitarian aid and national disaster management.[22]

Satellite data makes it easier to manage emergency responses to cyclones, earthquakes, fires, floods, snow, ice, ocean waves, volcanoes, landslides, and sandstorms. It can be used to map areas impacted by oil spills, airplane crashes, train derailments, or accidents at large facilities, such as factories. Satellite data can even be combined with other information to show disease outbreaks and hospital locations in affected areas.

Established in 2000, the charter allows countries and disaster-relief organizations to quickly get the information they need—sometimes within hours or days—and plan the most effective responses. It was used to assist in 692 disasters, in 127 countries, in its first twenty years.[23]

GET CHATTY

Are you suspecting any bias as you read this chapter? It's true I've included plenty of examples showing support for exploring beyond Earth. Determined to be fair, I also sought groups and organizations against space travel. If there are any, I didn't find them. I did, however, discover arguments against leaving Earth's atmosphere (listed on the following page).

- Both animals and people have lost their lives traveling beyond Earth. We should only explore using robots and uncrewed spacecrafts. That way, missions can be money-saving one-way trips.

- Space exploration could result in encounters with beings that approach us with aggression. We should not search for signals from aliens.

- Before exploring the universe, we should deal with issues on Earth, such as crime, hunger, and war.

- Cosmic settlements will be dangerous. People living on the Moon or Mars will be too far away to rescue when emergencies occur.

- Exploration should be put on hold until solutions are found to prevent and eliminate space junk.

- Astronauts and others traveling beyond Earth could return carrying microbes that do not exist here. These organisms could threaten our environment and humanity.

- Taxpayers should not have to pay for exploring the cosmos.

- The race to dominate space will lead to unnecessary tensions between nations.

Invite friends to pick sides, either for or against space exploration, and research facts to support their positions. When you're ready, set a timer allowing five minutes of debate per point. Have fun sharing your viewpoints!

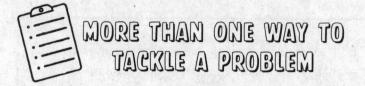

MORE THAN ONE WAY TO TACKLE A PROBLEM

Space: the final frontier. That's the ever-popular saying, and it can elicit either excitement or trepidation. But to get involved in an out-of-this-world sort of way doesn't have to be daunting. Remember, you don't have to become an astronaut to reach for the stars (though that would make you a pretty cool kid).

Adults recognize that children can be super creative and original problem solvers. Kids are good at dreaming up fresh ideas without getting hung up on details. Plenty of organizations know this too. NASA's Solve program, for example, issues student challenges and organizes competitions, complete with prizes, to help it solve issues that affect space missions.

HOW TO PROMOTE SPACE EXPLORATION

When it comes to looking for ways to excite people about getting up into space and seeing what's out there, you might look at joining the Mars Society, a group set on exploring the Red Planet. If globe-hopping isn't your scene, take part from the safety of Earth. You might enter a contest asking for space survival ideas or lobby governments to give property rights to future settlers of the cosmos. Finding ways to explore the universe may seem like something other people do, but as these organizations demonstrate, it doesn't have to be that way.

RUN EXPERIMENTS
{The Mars Society, Nonprofit, Colorado}

The Mars Society is a worldwide organization devoted to exploring the Red Planet and establishing a permanent settlement on Mars. It lobbies governments to pursue space exploration, but it's not waiting for others to take action.

The society has built two Earth-based research stations: one in Mars-like terrain in the Utah desert and one on an uninhabited island in the remote Canadian Arctic. The stations run simulation missions that allow crew members to work in environments that look and feel like Mars habitats. Crews live in isolation from other people, eat dehydrated food, and only go outside wearing space suits. Simulations last two to three weeks and help the society research challenges they will need to overcome on Mars.

With chapters and members around the world, the Mars Society also works to educate the public about Mars exploration and settlement. It invites the public to get involved![24]

ONE THING YOU CAN DO NOW

Explore the problems you might face as a space settler by conducting your own simulation. Choose one part of your home to be your habitat and plan to stay put for a day. Before starting, prepare for every possible need you might face. Don't forget exercise! You'll need to work out for 2.5 hours to prevent the bone and muscle loss that occurs when living far from Earth's gravity. (You can break your exercise time into chunks.)

Prepare to only eat canned or dehydrated foods. Also, expect to spend 20 minutes in the bathroom each time you visit. Without gravity, things tend to take longer. Record your experience in a journal and report your findings to a larger audience such as family, friends, and classmates.

Good news!

HOST A CONTEST
{National Space Society, Nonprofit, Washington, DC}

The National Space Society (NSS) believes that developing space settlements will better humanity and lead to new knowledge that will solve problems here on Earth. One of the ways it works toward its goals is through competitions. In one contest, participants can earn cash rewards for business plans that support humans living beyond Earth. They may explore any topic, from habitat technologies, to legal issues that could be faced by people who are *clones*—beings that are exact copies of other beings.

The NSS hosts art challenges, debates, and other contests that encourage young people to learn about our future in the cosmos. One competition invited high school students to design space cities large enough to house at least ten thousand people. Another called for students to take part in debate tournaments. The participants explored sustainability, military concerns, and the development of *space policy*—rules designed to guide future decisions about activities in space. With chapters around the world, the NSS also works toward finding ways to use mineral resources in space, make space solar energy accessible, and defend our planet from near-Earth objects.[25]

SUGGEST NEW LAWS

{The Space Settlement Institute, Nonprofit, New York}

The Space Settlement Institute (SSI) promotes establishing human communities beyond Earth. It doesn't believe, however, that government programs will be enough to get us there. Instead, it advocates for permitting private enterprises to invest in space for their own profit. The SSI feels that if laws allowed land ownership beyond Earth, private companies would be more willing to invest money to create the technologies needed to run settlements. It believes these companies would also spend money on activities like mining minerals from the Moon or asteroids, harvesting space solar power, and developing tourism beyond Earth's atmosphere.

To achieve its goal, the SSI has drafted legislation including the Space Settlement Prize Act. It would give rights to the first people to live permanently on the Moon or Mars. Settlers would be allowed to claim the land they live on and have the right to sell their property. If the act became law, investors would be required to build a fee-based transportation system for passengers between Earth and the settlement.

The SSI lobbies the US government to pass its proposed legislation. It encourages people in all nations to ask their elected officials for space settlement laws, and to bring the topic to the media.[26]

If all this seems far-fetched to you, consider that the cosmos have already inspired international cooperation. We see this in the work of the fifteen countries that came together to build the International Space Station.

The many organizations taking part in beyond-Earth activism show that the commercial use and settlement of space may become a growing part of our future. To ensure progress, it's essential to find ways to make sure that the cosmos are managed in ways that serve all of humanity.

> ## IMAGINE
> Imagine being a space pioneer. What challenges might you face living in a permanent off-Earth settlement? What benefits might you enjoy?

SPOTLIGHT ON . . .
DarkSky

Research shows that more than 99 percent of people in the United States and Europe cannot enjoy a natural, dark night. Elsewhere, light pollution is normal for 80 percent of the world's population.[27] DarkSky in Tucson, Arizona, is a nonprofit organization that fights for dark nights. It wants everyone to know the joy of being under a starry sky. It also wants to make sure scientists have dark to study the universe. *Astronomy*—the study of objects outside Earth's atmosphere—helps us better understand our planet and nearest star, the Sun. The science of astronomy helps scientists learn about threats to our planet including solar storms, asteroids or comets that get too close, and space junk, like old satellites, that could fall to Earth.

DarkSky works with volunteers around the world who aim to raise awareness about the impacts of light pollution. It has established more than two hundred Dark Sky Places to help preserve the night and protect habitat from light. DarkSky also set up a lighting "seal of approval" program, which makes it easier for people to choose *sky-friendly lighting*—lights that shine where needed rather than into the sky or surrounding habitat.[28]

ONE THING YOU CAN DO NOW

Examine how much light escapes from your home. Do you keep curtains and blinds closed at night, or is light allowed to leak? Are outdoor lights on even when everyone's inside? Instead of using outdoor holiday lights, can you find other ways to decorate? Discuss ways everyone in the family can help use light in responsible ways.

MEET YOUNG ACTIVISTS
HARP

In 2018, a group of five motivated students at Bioscience High School in Phoenix, Arizona, set out to tackle light pollution. They started a project they called Helping Achieve a Renewable Planet (HARP). Its goal was to make it possible for people in their city to experience the joy of a natural, dark sky. The students broke the issue into five areas: how excessive light impacts astronomy, human health, wildlife, ecosystems, and the economy. After researching their topics, the students decided they could make the most difference by raising awareness about how unwanted light impacts people and the environment. They built a website to share information and invite change. They also arranged meetings with *light pollution stakeholders*—individuals or businesses with an interest in solving the problem. The students asked for advice on how to best handle challenges they might face in raising awareness. One of the conclusions they reached is that with small efforts, everyone can help ensure dark skies—from choosing to use less light in their personal lives to talking to neighbors about choosing dark-sky-friendly lighting.

As the author of the children's book *Dark Matters: Nature's Reaction to Light Pollution*, I was invited to participate in a stakeholder meeting.

I was able to help the Bioscience High School students in Arizona cross the miles to a small northern town in Alberta, Canada. HARP shared its research with a student astronomy club, run by a middle school librarian and aurora photographer. Armed with HARP's research, her students encouraged their town council to reduce light pollution.[29]

See how I'm up-front about my own involvement? It's okay to have a bias for a cause. Revealing it builds credibility.

SATISFY YOUR CURIOSITY

Check out the websites of these stellar organizations for more super-galactic information:

- Committee on the Peaceful Uses of Outer Space (COPUOS)
- DarkSky
- The Mars Society
- The Moon Society
- National Space Society
- National Air and Space Intelligence Center
- Space Safety Coalition
- The Space Settlement Institute
- The Space Surveillance Network
- United Nations Office for Outer Space Affairs (UNOOSA)

PART III

PEOPLE ISSUES

7

THREATS AND VIOLENCE

BRINGING PEACE TO OUR WORLD

"Fight for the things that you care about,
but do it in a way that will lead others to join you."

Ruth Bader Ginsburg, Supreme Court justice, United States

Have you ever wished—even for a moment—you were a dog? Imagine the perks! You'd never have to do homework. Your life could be all about lazing in the sunshine and rolling over for a treat. You would never, ever stay awake at night thinking and worrying about world events. Why? Because canines only react to incidents they directly experience. They live with all four paws firmly planted in the present. Their brains are, however, capable of yearning for things they want.

Like you, pooches can dream, and this raises another interesting question. Is it possible dogs might wish to be human? After all, they see

WOOF!

us doing things they can't. Dogs may view your abilities—such as being able to grab a meat loaf from the fridge or draw water from a faucet—as superpowers. What canines don't know is the source of your real strength: being able to react to circumstances even if you don't experience them firsthand. You're able to imagine how others feel and dream up ways to help. A dog's ability to focus on the present is useful, but it's the human capacity for compassion that feeds the urge to ease suffering. Being able to imagine or understand another person's suffering as if it were your own experience is what will help you find ways to be an effective activist. It all begins with ensuring the basic universal right for all beings: protection from harm.

Each year, violence causes the deaths of more than 1.6 million people worldwide.[1] Threats and violence appear in many forms. Some are world events, such as wars between two or more nations. These large-scale conflicts are enormous, complicated problems that cause intense human suffering. People who survive may endure loss of loved ones, poverty, food shortages, interrupted education, economic loss, and *displacement*—being forced to flee from home. They may face *oppression*—unfair or cruel treatment from public officials who abuse their power. They may also endure environmental damage. Discharged weapons harm land, sea, and freshwater habitats, while the construction of military weapons, aircraft, vehicles, and training sites uses energy and creates CO_2 (carbon dioxide) emissions.

The abundance of weapons in our world is one of many factors that threaten world peace. Others include *transnational crime*—unlawful activities that cross international borders, such as drug and weapons smuggling,[2] and the horrendous offense of *human trafficking*—when individuals are forced to do things against their will, such as donate organs, work without pay, or provide sexual services.[3]

Climate change, which can upset people's abilities to meet their needs, also impacts peace. The shifting climate can affect the

ONE THING YOU CAN DO NOW

Say no to violence. Injustice can make people feel so helpless and frustrated that revenge starts to seem like a solution. Never give in to angry impulses. Instead, make a personal commitment to only channel your energy into *nonviolent resistance*–actions that use peaceful methods to effect change.

availability of water and other vital natural resources.[4] People who farm, fish, and herd animals to support themselves face difficulties when rising temperatures affect animal health and meat production. Climate change can also make it hard for people to access healthcare and can contribute to poverty. When people can't get what they need, the result is *instability*—a state of being in which life is unpredictable. People who are unsure whether they will have the food, water, and shelter they require will seek new ways to survive. They may migrate to another region or country or break the law to obtain money. This instability increases the risk of conflict.[5]

Another threat to world peace is *extremism*—when individuals or groups promote political, religious, or cultural positions outside what is normal within a society. Violent extremism can lead to *terrorism*—the use of fear and violent acts to draw attention to political or social demands. Hunger, injustice, and inequality allow terrorism and extremism to blossom.[6] Hostile groups and nations may further threaten world peace through cyber warfare. This can involve using the internet to spread misinformation or launch electronic attacks against critical banking, energy, and healthcare service structures.[7]

Some hostilities occur much closer to home, even in our own neighborhoods. Gang wars, shootings at schools, and other bloodshed upsets peace within communities. In towns, cities, and rural regions, racism, discrimination, and inequality frequently lead to violence. Sometimes police act irresponsibly and cause bloodshed instead of upholding peace. From 2015 to 2021, Black Americans made up more than half the victims of fatal police shootings.[8] The excessive use of police force against unarmed Black people sparked a movement called Black Lives Matter (BLM). Supporters began using the hashtag #blacklivesmatter to spread their message and highlight the need to stop racism, mistreatment, and other injustices.

IMAGINE

Can you picture liking someone more or less because of their eye color? Brown is the most common eye pigment in the world, followed by blue. Human peepers may also be amber, hazel, gray, green, or even red. Imagine if people discriminated against each other because of eye color. What would your life be like if you had the wrong shade under your lids? If everyone in your family had a different color than you, would you feel differently about them?

Some tough issues are less obvious or are deliberately hidden such as *family violence*— when a family member uses abusive behavior to harm or control another person in their household. Violence may be *physical*—when someone is intentionally harmed or killed. It may involve activity that is *sexual*—touching,

Wait!
Did I just describe
the eyes in your
family?

kissing, or *intercourse*—physical contact with another person's *genitalia*, such as the penis or vulva. *Molestation* occurs when someone makes unwanted or improper sexual advances towards someone, including forcing physical and usually sexual contact on someone. Sexual abuse also takes place when a person forces sexual acts upon someone who has not provided *consent*—freely given permission for the sexual activity to take place.

Activists fighting sexual assault want everyone to understand that consent is reversible and that any person who agrees to a sexual activity has the right to change their mind at any point.

How can social action help people who experience behind-closed-doors brutality? You can run awareness campaigns to help survivors understand that violence is never okay and certainly not the fault of the person being hurt. You can share information on prevention, publicize help line numbers, and raise funds for shelters. Improving awareness is an important part of fighting this tragedy.

Thinking about the violence in our world can fill your heart with pain, but there is an effective solution. Aim to keep your thoughts positive by looking to the child activists you're about to meet and focusing on their accomplishments. These remarkable individuals have found success in speaking up about the matters they care about.

ACTIVISTS AND THEIR ISSUES

Malala Yousafzai: calls for equal education for both girls and boys

Greta Thunberg: demands meaningful climate change action

ACTIVISTS AND THEIR ISSUES (CONTINUED)

Thandiwe Abdullah: successfully advocated to end random searches of students in her school district and cofounded the Black Lives Matter Youth Vanguard

Desmond Napoles: speaks out on LGBTQ issues and works to inspire others to be themselves[9]

Bana Alabed: used Twitter to bring attention to the siege in Aleppo, Syria[10]

Jaylen Arnold: educates kids about bullying[11]

David Hogg: demands gun law reform[12]

Naomi Wadler: brings attention to family violence and gun violence[13]

SPREAD THE WORD!

One of the best ways to influence others is face-to-face. A person who can see the expression on your face and hear the emotion in your voice (and frankly can't escape too easily) will be more likely to appreciate your important cause. Phone calls and emails are easy to ignore, but the person in front of you may feel obliged to hear you out. It's true you will probably need to prearrange face-to-face meetings with *VIPs*—very important people—but if that doesn't work, you still have options. Try walking into a newspaper office and asking to speak to a reporter or editor. Another approach is to ask permission to give a short presentation at a town or city hall meeting. Bring one or more friends, plan what you will say, and include reasons for the changes you want to see. It may take more than one try, but returning again and again can be what it takes to get the attention your cause needs.

LET'S GET STARTED

Around the world people are finding ways to shrink violence-related concerns into parts they can manage. You might engage in a campaign that draws attention to a cause and educates people about its consequences. You might get involved in activities that pursue solutions or ones that aim to prevent bloodshed in the first place. Your activism could take the form of providing support to victims of war, local crimes, and other unwanted behaviors, including bullying. It could even involve demanding that governments take action. Choices abound when it comes to nurturing peace and reducing human suffering. Here's a sampling of approaches and issues to help you brainstorm the many directions you could pursue.

PROMOTE

Common-sense gun reform

Nuclear weapons bans

Equal education opportunities for all people

International action on climate change

PREVENT

Hunger

Youths from joining gangs

The spread of misinformation

Discrimination based on ethnicity, sexuality, religion, political opinions, or beliefs

SUPPORT

Refugees trying to reach safety

Efforts to distribute free school supplies

Actions to harness solar energy

Immigrants living in your community

EDUCATE

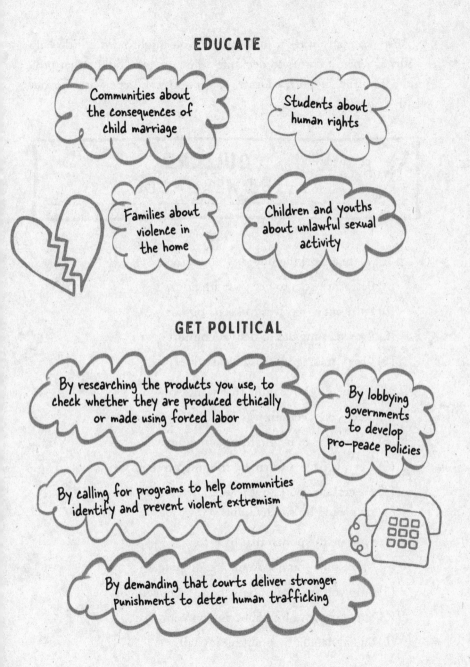

Communities about the consequences of child marriage

Students about human rights

Families about violence in the home

Children and youths about unlawful sexual activity

GET POLITICAL

By researching the products you use, to check whether they are produced ethically or made using forced labor

By lobbying governments to develop pro-peace policies

By calling for programs to help communities identify and prevent violent extremism

By demanding that courts deliver stronger punishments to deter human trafficking

With so many ways to help others, you might need a little help yourself when it comes to deciding whether you would rather promote, prevent, support, educate, or get political. Let's work this out with a quizard.

QUIZARD
IF I WERE A DOG

1. If I were a working dog, I would rather:

(A) Perform tricks to get your attention

(B) Sniff out explosives to keep you safe

(C) Provide snuggles to deliver comfort

(D) Carry messages across a war zone

2. I'd be the kind of canine that wants to:

(A) Steer you a certain way by pulling my leash

(B) Deter thieves by guarding buildings

(C) Keep your feet warm by sleeping on them

(D) Be certain you know where my territory lies by peeing on fire hydrants

3. I might be the pooch that likes to:

(A) Make sure you notice me by jumping up

(B) Stop you from taking my bone by burying it

(C) Show my love by slobbering on your face

(D) Signal danger by pointing my tail

4. If I were a dog, I would probably:

(A) Tell you what I want by tugging your sleeve

(B) Protect your family from danger by herding you together

(C) Stop you from feeling alone by keeping close

(D) Stick my head out the car window to gather information

5. If I were a hound, I would:

(A) Make you look by zooming in circles

(B) Prevent my freedom from being restricted by digging a hole under the fence

(C) Distract you by putting a toy in your lap

(D) Signal that change is needed by howling

6. If I were a dog, I might:

(A) Bark until you give me what I want

(B) Sniff out illegal drugs

(C) Rescue people buried under snow or rock

(D) Communicate "problem solved" by wagging my tail

QUIZARD RESULTS

If you answered mostly:

A, you have all kinds of tricks to draw attention to your cause. You lean toward promotion.

B, you aim to take direct action. Your style is to prevent things from getting worse.

C, the thing that brings the most satisfaction is providing face-to-face help. You thrive on offering direct support.

D, you're inclined to impart useful information. Education is your thing.

Are your answers all over the place? If that's the case, you may just be a multitalented breed. Or you might lean toward getting political, a possibility the quizard doesn't cover. Dogs do a lot of cool things, but none of their actions quite match creating new laws!

MAKE PEACE SUCCEED

Throughout history, people have worried about their safety and security. Today's modern world delivers constant access to news on conflict within and among nations and the suffering that people struggle to escape. Whether you live in a region untouched by violence or one much less secure, you can still work to promote peace.

Let's start with a look at what peace really means. Maybe you've heard an adult in your life demand peace and quiet, and not in the softest tone! You know what's expected. No arguments. No physical violence. No nasty words. They want to see cooperation, kindness, patience, and forgiveness. The dictionary tells us *peace* is a state of quiet or tranquility.

When your mind feels calm rather than disturbed.

Peace is also freedom from war or violence. In other words, you can leave your home without fear of being harmed. No one is trying to overthrow the government. Airplanes are not dropping bombs. Guns are not going off around you. Girls and women are not forced to follow extreme rules about how they dress. Enemies are not trying to control your community or country.

The opposite of peace is war, and it was violence that led to the formation of the United Nations (UN). When the Second World War ended, fifty nations came together to address their shared goal—maintaining international peace. Knowing that truces can be fragile and temporary, the UN chooses to go further in its definition of peace. It describes *a culture of peace*—an entire way of living based on factors that include respect for life and all human rights. This definition of a culture of peace includes a commitment to settle conflicts peacefully and a determination to use education, cooperation, and dialogue to promote nonviolence.

The UN puts actions behind its words. It works to prevent conflict and bring opposing countries together to exist in harmony. One of the ways it does this is by deploying peacekeepers—soldiers, police, and civilians who work together to maintain or restore peace.[14] The UN encourages countries to create conditions where citizens can live free from war and violence, as described in its *Declaration and Programme of Action on a Culture of Peace*. This important document is detailed! It tells us what needs to be done to go about making the world a safer place.[15] The declaration's *Programme of Action* gets specific with advice you can follow. Here are some of its goals, along with ideas on ways to get started.

KEEP THE PEACE

THE GOAL	ORGANIZE A PROJECT	AID A GROUP INVOLVED IN THESE ACTIVITIES
End violence	○ Ask your school to host a speaker who survived gun violence. ○ Organize a poster project on the theme of ending discrimination. ○ Raise funds to support orgs that promote peace.	○ Help prevent school violence by installing panic buttons or other early warning systems. ○ Help captive child soldiers return home. ○ Clear land mines and educate children on how to identify and avoid mines.
Eliminate poverty	○ Arrange for your school to collect canned goods for your local food bank. ○ Encourage others to only support companies that pay workers fair wages. ○ Ask your local government to provide community gardens where families can grow their own vegetables.	○ Teach skills that allow learners to earn an income. ○ Provide microfinancing to help people start small businesses. ○ Make housing affordable to people with low incomes.

THE GOAL	ORGANIZE A PROJECT	AID A GROUP INVOLVED IN THESE ACTIVITIES
Eradicate illiteracy	○ Run a school-wide "Caught with a Book" week to promote reading. ○ Ask your public library to start a book buddy program where students read to one another. ○ Invite an author to promote literacy at your school.	○ Work to provide education during conflicts. ○ Raise funds to purchase school supplies for students in need. ○ Provide free tutoring to students.
Promote *social development*— the growth of well-being for all individuals in a society	○ Start an anti-bullying campaign to make school a place where all students feel accepted. ○ Ask your principal to set up a student government to address school issues. ○ Write letters to law makers to demand equal healthcare access.	○ Help people with disabilities escape conflict. ○ Assist vulnerable refugees, such as children and pregnant women. ○ Teach kids about physical, verbal, and cyber bullying.

You can even host the author of the book you're holding!

THE GOAL	ORGANIZE A PROJECT	AID A GROUP INVOLVED IN THESE ACTIVITIES
Use education to foster peace	○ Organize a school art or poetry festival on the theme of peace. ○ Create a survey asking classmates questions about equal rights, and share your results. ○ Gather up your pals and volunteer with a local community service group that promotes peace.	○ Help both girls and boys attend school. ○ Bring books to children in remote locations. ○ Assist people facing violence at home.

THE GOAL	ORGANIZE A PROJECT	AID A GROUP INVOLVED IN THESE ACTIVITIES
Encourage respect for human rights	• Organize a sticky note wall where students share ways to show kindness. • Ask your public library to set up a display of kid-friendly books about human rights and activism. • Arrange for students to research and share inspirational messages each day on the school's public address (PA) system.	• Lobby to change local, national, or international laws. • Ensure citizens have the right to vote for their representatives in government. • Assist children at risk of experiencing female *genital mutilation*—a procedure that, for nonmedical reasons, injures or removes female genital organs.

THE GOAL	ORGANIZE A PROJECT	AID A GROUP INVOLVED IN THESE ACTIVITIES
Support the role of media in promoting a culture of peace	○ Write a peace-promoting article for your school or local newspaper. ○ Ask television news directors to produce more stories demonstrating kindness and cooperation. ○ Provide local radio stations with *public service announcements*, called PSAs, that raise awareness about family violence, bullying, and other important topics.	○ Promote ethical reporting. ○ Fight fake news. ○ Help consumers identify misinformation on social media.

A SIMPLE APPROACH

Sometimes the first step toward activism is as simple as expressing your concerns to the right person, even if it takes more than one try. You might follow the example of Samantha Smith, a ten-year-old fifth grader who, in 1982, took her mother's advice to write to Soviet Union Leader Yuri Andropov about her wish for peace. Samantha mailed him a letter that included these words:

I have been worrying about Russia and the United States getting into a nuclear war. Are you going to vote to have a war or not? . . . I would like to know why you want to conquer the world or at least our country.

Excerpts of her letter were published in the Soviet newspaper *Pravda*, with comments from the Soviet leader. This led Samantha to write again, now asking why Andropov did not reply to her directly. This time the Soviet leader not only wrote back but he also invited Samantha and her parents to visit. Her family spent two weeks in the Soviet Union in 1983, where Samantha became an ambassador for peace. The press in both the Soviet Union and the United States gave Samantha a great amount of attention, which helped citizens of each country to see each other as individuals instead of enemies. Welcomed home with a parade, Samantha earned the nickname America's Littlest Diplomat.

Just a few years later, tragedy struck when Samantha and her father died in a plane crash in August 1985. Samantha's mother, Jane, continued her daughter's mission to promote peace by establishing the Samantha Smith Foundation (later called the Samantha Smith Center) to organize activities such as Soviet-American youth exchanges.[16]

A CULTURE OF PEACE

Peacekeepers have the job of creating conditions where harmony can succeed. As well as running justice systems that ensure equality, nations must provide citizens with the ability to meet their basic needs and earn a living. These sound like government jobs; however, the *Declaration and Programme of Action on a Culture of Peace* makes it clear that maintaining peace is not only up to politicians.

Article 8 says this role "belongs to parents, teachers, politicians, journalists, religious bodies and groups, intellectuals, those engaged in scientific, philosophical and creative and artistic activities, health and humanitarian workers, social workers, managers at various levels as well as to non-governmental organizations."[17]

Look at the roles of these community members, consider your issue, and see who might be able to help you achieve your peacekeeping goals. For starters, parents, teachers, and journalists can help influence others when it comes to supporting a cause. Some concerns, like nuclear weapons treaties, clearly call for politicians to take a stand. Your personal peacekeeping team can help them along, though, by working to keep the subject in the news. You might want to also raise controversial topics like capital punishment (also called the death penalty), along with fair trials and just sentencing when children commit crimes. Governments must uphold prisoner rights, and activists can get involved by advocating to stop overcrowding and violence in prisons, improve medical care, and provide better treatment for children, women, and men in solitary confinement. It's necessary to remember that the penalty of imprisonment is about taking away lawbreakers' freedoms. Guards and others in authority do not have the right to inflict additional punishment through cruelty, violence, or other mistreatments that abuse basic human rights. Families of prisoners, intellectuals, and religious groups might join you in stepping up to raise awareness about why this is important.

Slavery is a matter that needs both government and community involvement to make change and promote peace. Modern slavery can include forced labor as well as *debt slavery* or *bondage*—when a person is forced to work to pay off money owed, under threat of punishment. It may involve *descent-based slavery*—when a child becomes a slave because a parent is a slave. Child slavery can involve forced marriages, trafficking, soldiers, and *domestic slavery*—where a victim is forced to cook, clean, and manage other household tasks without pay, safety, or freedom. Nongovernmental organizations, humanitarian workers, and social workers are good choices to approach for these peacekeeping missions. You can seek ways to

BE THE CHANGE!

The United Nations declared September 21 the International Day of Peace. It asks those in conflict to mark the day with nonviolence and twenty-four-hour cease-fires, and for all people to help build a culture of peace.[18] Show your support by devoting a day (any day) to promoting peace. A school peace party is a fun way to get started. Kick off activities with an announcement describing how the peace symbol came to be. (You'll want to research the full details, but the quick explanation is that it combines symbols that represent an *N* for *nuclear* and *D* for *disarmament*, surrounded by a circle representing Earth.)[19]

Next, plan activities that promote unity:

- Arrange students in the shape of a peace symbol or dove.

- Create posters, paragraphs, or poetry on the theme "I create harmony by . . ."

- Host a "hippie day" where everyone dresses as members of the sixties and seventies movement that promoted nonviolence.

- Encourage students to march in a parade of nations.

- Ask for school choirs and bands to learn and perform peace-promoting tunes.

support them in assisting refugees, migrants, and *asylum seekers*—those fleeing a country to escape harm, usually due to their ethnicity, religion, sexuality, opinions, or beliefs.

The threats and violence that affect humankind are daunting and disturbing. Remember that you don't need to tackle these things alone. Take the UN's advice and bring others together to help you build a *culture of peace*. And if any of this starts to bring you down, take a pointer from the quizard. There's more than one way to solve a problem. Sometimes you need to set your worries aside for a little while and live in the moment like our doggie pals. You're sure to emerge refreshed!

SPOTLIGHT ON . . .
Black Lives Matter
Global Network Foundation

The Black Lives Matter (BLM) movement began when a jury found George Zimmerman not guilty of the murder of Trayvon Martin, a seventeen-year-old Black teen in Florida killed by Zimmerman in 2012. (To find Zimmerman guilty, the jury would have needed to reject his self-defense claim.) Nationwide protests took place, and Patrisse Cullors, Alicia Garza, and Opal Tometi came together to try to stop the violence Black communities face. They launched an international organization called the Black Lives Matter Global Network Foundation (BLMGNF). The organization aims to end *white supremacy*—the belief that white people are superior—and *systemic racism*—the social and political systems that give lighter-skinned people advantages over other races. It is committed to supporting all Black people, including those who are *marginalized*—discriminated against or made to feel less important. Marginalized populations include women, the LGBTQ community, disabled people, people with criminal records, and those who are *undocumented*—without legal papers to show they are lawfully entitled to be in a country.[20]

Alleged means accused of a crime or offense but not proven guilty.

A BLM breaking point occurred when a Black man named George Floyd was killed by a police officer in Minneapolis, Minnesota, on May 25, 2020. It happened during an arrest for a minor *alleged* offense.

Seventeen-year-old Darnella Frazier used her cell phone to record the murder. It later served as key evidence, which led to the arresting police officer being found guilty.

Darnella was recognized with a journalism award—a Pulitzer Prize Special Citation—for the role of citizens seeking truth and justice.

She posted the video on Facebook, and viewers around the world felt shocked. The recording triggered massive protests against police violence and racism.[21] On June 6, 2020, half a million supporters gathered in 550 locations. BLM may be the largest protest movement in American history.[22]

The movement spread around the world, and the BLMGNF received $90 million in donations in 2020. The foundation's activism takes many forms. The organization funds other Black-led organizations working on the same goals. It speaks out, calling for those who enable police violence to accept responsibility for their actions. It releases statements demanding change, comments on government plans for racial justice, and hosts webinars to promote healing. It also recognizes that arts and culture are a privilege not everyone can afford and works to provide opportunities for Black writers, artists, dancers, musicians, filmmakers, podcasters, and other creatives to improve their crafts and use their talents to express joy.

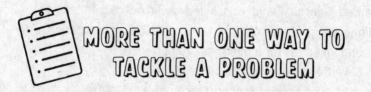

MORE THAN ONE WAY TO TACKLE A PROBLEM

Private American citizens own more guns than civilians in any other country, and more school and mass shootings occur in the United States than in any other nation. Many Americans want stronger gun laws. Others feel that restrictions would go against the right to own and bear arms as described in the US Constitution's Second Amendment. School shootings, however, are not an issue only in America. They occur around the globe and are a worldwide crisis that needs attention.

STOP THE VIOLENCE

A mass shooting is categorized as a crime in which at least three people are injured or killed by an attacker using a firearm. Whether the violent act takes place at a school, synagogue, concert, or other location it is an act of terror. Often, mass shootings are committed by individuals who feel marginalized or are victims of bullying, mental illness, or other problems and need help. School shootings are particularly complicated, but that's not stopping the groups mentioned in the following pages from trying to stop gun violence.[23]

ORGANIZE A PROTEST

{March for Our Lives, Nonprofit, New York and Florida}

On February 14, 2018, an expelled student fired a legally purchased semiautomatic rifle inside Marjory Stoneman Douglas High School in Parkland, Florida. Seventeen people lost their lives in this tragedy. Another seventeen were injured. Devastated student survivors came together and made a plan. They would demand a stop to gun violence by *demonstrating*—engaging in a protest or public display to support a cause and call for change.

The students shared their plan with national media and invited students across America to walk out of school on March 24, 2018. They raised millions of dollars through crowdfunding and private donations and used the funds to organize the rally, pay for expenses (such as travel), and make a toolkit for other kids, showing how to organize a march in their own towns. Their efforts led more than eight hundred groups from across the country and around the world to take part in March for Our Lives demonstrations in their communities. Tens of thousands also gathered in Washington, DC. David Hogg, X González, Alex Wind, and other leaders and founders of March for Our Lives, along with other student speakers, spoke about how gun violence had affected their lives, and they demanded change. Nine-year-old Yolanda Renee King, granddaughter of assassinated civil rights activist Martin Luther King Jr., also spoke to the crowd about her dream for a gun-free world. March for Our Lives is described as America's biggest student protest.[24]

ORGANIZE A PROTEST (CONTINUED)

Three weeks later, Florida passed new gun restrictions. It was a welcome start, but the students knew more work was needed. Others agreed, and now members in more than three hundred chapters across the nation fight for tighter gun regulations. When March for Our Lives organized another march in June 2022 to protest the mass shootings that continue to occur, protest events took place in more than 450 worldwide locations.[25]

DONATE AN HOUR A WEEK
{Everytown for Gun Safety, Nonprofit, New York}

Everytown for Gun Safety is the largest American organization working to prevent gun violence. More than ten million people support its efforts, including gun violence survivors, gun owners, and these advocacy networks: Moms Demand Action, Students Demand Action, and Mayors Against Illegal Guns. One of the ways Everytown encourages members to get involved is by joining the Gun Sense Action Network. Participants are invited to donate an hour a week to phone politicians and ask them to pass safety legislation. The volunteers share information with voters on upcoming elections and ask them to choose candidates who support common sense gun policies. Reaching out to the membership is another important role. Callers ask new members and former volunteers to get involved in the organization's anti-violence activities and help the movement grow. Volunteers make a difference, one conversation at a time.[26]

USE TECHNOLOGY
{Protecting Our Students, Nonprofit, Missouri}

Protecting Our Students (POS) is devoted to ending shootings in K-12 schools. POS believes that the quickest way to ensure student safety is to use state-of-the-art technology and security to prevent shooters from entering schools. It offers an app called POSSafetyNet, which guides users in identifying how a gun could be brought inside and how to use security to prevent active shooter incidents. POS provides schools with the app on a device, and then retrieves the results to create a report and an emergency operating plan, which includes steps to take if an incident does occur. It advocates for America to adopt a national K-12 security program, and it works with schools, consultants, safety professionals, law enforcement, and other agencies to make schools safe.[27]

ONE THING YOU CAN DO NOW

Help support victims of bullying. With a little creativity, you can find simple ways to help others feel less alone. Start by saying hi when you cross paths. Greet them by name. Issue invitations to join you in a sport or other activity. Sit next to them on the bus or at lunch. Encourage your friends to find ways to be considerate too. Remember, you don't need to wait for others to get picked on to brighten their day. Consider what might happen if you also treated bullies with extra kindness.

MEET A YOUNG ACTIVIST
Bana Alabed

When the city of Aleppo in Syria was under siege in 2016, eight-year-old Bana Alabed began to tweet about her experience of living during wartime. With help from her mother, Fatemah, she wrote about bombs falling in her neighborhood and on her school. Bana also wrote about the death of her best friend in an air attack, and she described her fear of losing her family and her own life.

When soldiers blocked roads in and out of the city, preventing the transport of food and supplies, Bana tweeted about having only rice and macaroni to eat. She used Twitter to ask government leaders from around the world for peace, including Syrian president Bashar al-Assad, Russian president Vladimir Putin, US president Barack Obama, and UK prime minister Theresa May.[28] Bana called for an end to all wars, and her messages for peace made people pay attention. Hundreds of thousands of people began to follow Bana's now famous Twitter account (on the social media platform now called X).

In December of 2017, Bana and her family escaped the war, moving to Türkiye as refugees. She wrote a book about her wartime experiences and living through war. Simon & Schuster published her book—*Dear World: A Syrian Girl's Story of War and Plea for Peace*—in 2017. By sharing her firsthand experiences, Bana raised awareness about a country in crisis. In a statement issued through her publisher, Bana said, "I hope my book will make the world do something for the children and people of Syria and bring peace to children all over the world who are living in war."[29] Bana later went on to write *My Name Is Bana* (Simon & Schuster, 2021), a picture book on living through war and finding hope.

SATISFY YOUR CURIOSITY

Gather the facts you need to tackle threats and violence by using these keywords in an internet search:

- Samantha Smith, America's Littlest Diplomat
- Black Lives Matter
- Malala Yousafzai
- March for Our Lives
- Never Again movement
- Everytown for Gun Safety
- Systemic racism
- Nonviolent resistance
- Bana Alabed

8

COMMUNITIES

ENSURING EQUALITY

"Everybody can be great because everybody can serve.
You don't have to have a college degree to serve. . . .
You only need a heart full of grace, a soul generated by love."

Martin Luther King Jr., civil rights leader, United States

Have you ever played the word-association game? To begin, a player says a word, and then the next person says the first word that comes to mind. Two or more can take part, and anyone who doesn't see a logical connection between paired words can demand an explanation. Challenges often lead to glee as participants present their logic and defend their word choices.

Where do weird word chains come from? Look no further than each players' personal life. Our unique experiences in the communities where our lives unfold lead us to view the world in a particular manner. *Communities* are made up of people with common characteristics. Members might live in the same place, share interests, practice the same customs, or live similar experiences. They might endure the same social condition, such as living in poverty or being undocumented. They might work toward shared goals, such as winning a sports championship or making school bus rides shorter. They might have a common faith, ethnicity, language, age, gender, or sexual orientation. Sometimes, when people challenge one another during the word association game, it's because they are encountering details of a community outside their experience.

LIKE THIS, SEE?

AMY: Soldier.

JOAN: Child.

AMY: Night-light.

JOAN: Pollution.

AMY: What? Explain that!

JOAN: Lights can create light pollution.

> Joan is an advocate for dark skies.

AMY: Ha! Let's try again. Music.

JOAN: Piano.

AMY: Trumpet.

JOAN: Bells.

> Amy wins this round.

AMY: Kettle.

JOAN: What? No way!

AMY: At Christmastime, members of the Salvation Army ring bells and collect cash in kettles to raise funds for people in need.

TYPES OF COMMUNITIES

Well-established organizations like the Salvation Army are formal communities. They clearly and publicly state their goals. A group of friends selling hot dogs to raise money for cancer research or neighbors teaming up to demand safer roads are informal groups. Just as important as formal communities, informal groups can accomplish valuable work.

One reason community members unite is to ensure they are treated with equality. Women, children, LGBTQ people, individuals with disabilities, and Indigenous peoples are some of the groups that work to defend their rights.

We all belong to multiple communities, and we move in and out of some of them on a regular basis. You might be part of the soccer community one year but get involved in a different after-school program the following year. Communities are handy things for activists because they can connect people who want the same changes.

How many communities are part of your life? Can you think of any to add here and on the next page?

Country | City | Town | Rural area | Neighborhood

Family | Friends

Club | Hobby
Sports team
Fan club
Arts

School | Homeschool cooperative
Study group

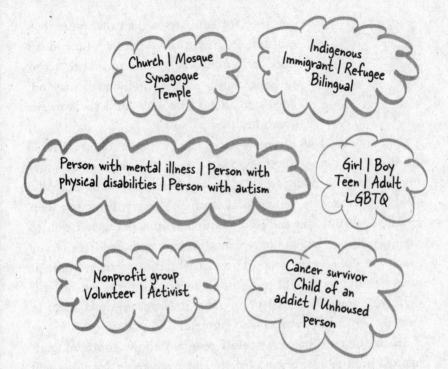

COMMUNITIES HELPING COMMUNITIES

Whether the group is formal or informal, members typically enjoy a sense of belonging and feel a willingness to help one another. Some people, however, do not legally belong to what seems like the most basic community—a country. Those who are not recognized as a citizen of any nation are called *stateless*. Many circumstances can lead to this situation. Children can be stateless if born outside the country where their parents hold citizenship. Members of minorities can experience this problem when governments discriminate against them. Sometimes, citizens lose their status when laws or borders change.[1] In 2019, the United Nations counted 4.2 million stateless people. However, collecting accurate data is not easy,

These are commonly called papers.

and the UN estimates suggest that more than ten million are actually affected.[2] Individuals need citizenship documents to ensure access to basic rights. Stateless individuals may not be able to attend school, obtain legal work, or access healthcare.

A great many laws dictate who can legally enter a country. People fleeing their home countries due to poverty, violence, or other matters become undocumented in countries they enter illegally. Without documents, refugees are unable to marry or register their children's births, and the issue continues from one generation to the next. People without papers may become separated from family members. Police may detain refugees while trying to verify their identities and their right to be in a country. Government officials may place undocumented immigrants in *detention*—hold them in custody while they await court judgment.

In the United States, a special program allows some undocumented immigrants to work legally and avoid being *deported*—sent out of the country.[3] Deferred Action for Childhood Arrivals (DACA) gives rights to people who meet certain criteria. One is that the person must have arrived in the United States before their sixteenth birthday. DACA has enabled hundreds of thousands to obtain work, attend school, and contribute to the economy. DACA has been a positive step toward humane immigration policies, but it's not a perfect solution. Every two years, recipients must pay to renew their status in the program. At several hundred dollars, plus legal fees, it's not cheap. Furthermore, people in the program—called *Dreamers*—still need laws allowing them to obtain citizenship. Activism to aid undocumented and stateless communities can take many forms. You might lobby governments to ensure human rights, work with agencies to directly aid those affected, or address related problems such as poverty and access to education and healthcare.[4]

ONE THING YOU CAN DO NOW

Inclusivity—including everyone, especially those who may historically have been left out because of race, ability, or other characteristics—helps builds safe and caring communities. Help your school become a place where everyone feels welcome. Ask if a friend bench can be added to the playground. Include a sign that reads, "Sit here if you would like someone to invite you to play." You might need to raise funds to pay for the bench, installation, and sign. Once it's set up, make sure everyone knows how to use the spot and why it's important to treat all people with kindness.

CHIPPING IN

You've probably noticed there is *strength in numbers*. This means groups of like-minded people enjoy more power than individuals. When communities face complicated challenges, their members can take advantage of this phenomenon. They may work together to ensure that their rights are respected, to advocate for important new laws, or to create opportunities for disadvantaged members. When Russia invaded Ukraine on February 24, 2022, a great many people were forced to flee their homes. In the first four months of the war, nearly five million escaped to other countries, and another eight million became displaced within Ukraine.[5] Many members of the *international community*—countries around the world

acting together—took action. Their efforts included providing defense weapons, humanitarian aid, and financial assistance. They also imposed on Russia certain *sanctions*—government orders to stop trade, or other measures designed to encourage a nation to obey international law. Working together allowed the international community to have a stronger impact than any one country could have on its own.

Informal communities also found ways to support Ukraine's freedom and democracy. Some used special skills to make a difference—like coding, cooking, or music. Two Harvard students set up a website called Ukraine Take Shelter to allow refugees to connect with people who are willing to host them in their homes.[6] Chefs and restaurant owners raised funds by offering special suppers. They served traditional *pierogi*—small dumplings filled with mashed potatoes, cheese, or other fillings— along with other Ukrainian foods. Musicians collected donations through concerts and paid downloads.

It can feel exciting to help people in distant countries, but providing aid close to home is just as important. Community activism can be as simple as seeing a local need and trying to fill it. That's how it worked for nine-year-old Hana Fatima.

Hana was living in Ontario, Canada, when the COVID-19 pandemic began in early 2020. She visited a grocery store with her father and had to wait an hour to get inside the door. People were stocking up on food and other necessities in fear that shops might run out of needed items. Many were buying toilet paper.

Hana noticed someone having trouble managing her purchases. It was a senior, which made her think of her grandparents. Hana and her father—Tariq Syed—helped the elderly woman carry her items to her car.

No one wants to go without this!

Her grateful reaction gave them an idea: to shop for seniors. This would help some of the most vulnerable people in the population avoid COVID-19 exposure in busy stores.

Tariq set up a Facebook page, and the Good Neighbour Project was born. They invited single parents, people with disabilities, health-care workers, and those in quarantine to also call their hotline for help. In its second year, the delivery network grew to include more

BE THE CHANGE!

When you undertake activism, aim to create environments where everyone can feel included.

- Incorporate local languages when making posters or pamphlets.
- Acknowledge the needs of the elderly. Show seniors consideration and respect.
- When you want to speak to someone accompanied by a caregiver, direct your conversation to the individual, not the attendant.
- Avoid making assumptions about what people with disabilities can or cannot do.
- Consider the needs of mothers with infants and small children.
- Use the pronouns people prefer to use to refer to themselves.
- Understand that it takes time and practice to change habits, and forgive yourself and others for making mistakes.

than six thousand volunteers in thirty cities.[7] That is strength in numbers in action! Looking past the needs triggered by the COVID-19 pandemic, the Good Neighbour Project became a registered charity and is widening its work to aid those experiencing poverty.

MATTERS FOR ALL CITIZENS

Gender equality—equal rights for all genders—should concern every person. The term is inclusive, but the discrimination that girls and women face leads many to think of them first when discussing gender equality. It is common for females to earn lower pay for equal work. Girls and women may experience forced marriage or endure sexual and domestic violence. In some countries, women are not allowed to drive, vote, obtain a passport, or leave home without their husband's approval. Discrimination based on sex is called *sexism*. It can affect the ability of females to access education and healthcare. Sexism is not just a matter for girls and women to confront. Boys and men must also boost and empower this population. They must support the rights of their grandmothers, mothers, aunts, and sisters, as well as all other communities facing discrimination.

Gender can take many forms, including agender, bigender, cisgender, gender fluid, nonbinary, transgender, and Two Spirit.

Boys and men can also be victims of gender equality issues. New fathers may not have access to *parental leave*—time off from work when a new baby is born. They may feel pressure to be the main income earner or appear emotionally strong. Men may face sexual harassment or discrimination based on appearance, sexuality, or behaviors that do not match the ways people expect males to behave.

Sexual orientation is commonly used as grounds for harassment, exclusion, and violence. Same-sex sexual activity is a crime in seventy countries. In some nations, it is punishable by death.[8] One way to get involved is by joining a gay-straight alliance, also called a GSA or *genders and sexualities alliance*. As student-led organizations, GSAs build community by bringing LGBTQ youths and their allies together. GSAs provide places where members can safely be themselves, along with the opportunity to explore and respond to situations members face. Also, alliances welcome anyone who wants to take part—some students use them as safe places to explore their own identity, while other students attend to show support for the LGBTQ community. GSAs provide safe and welcoming places when any factor—including disability, ethnicity, and religion—causes students to feel excluded. If your school doesn't have a GSA, think about asking for permission to start one.

Pride Month offers more opportunities to get involved. Every June, events build awareness, celebrate LGBTQ culture and rights, and promote the LGBTQ community's positive impacts on society. You might join a parade or demonstrate support by organizing a team to create and showcase rainbow-themed art. Used as a pride symbol, the rainbow reflects LGBTQ diversity and unity and is used in the brightly striped flag as a common symbol. Other versions of the flag use wavy lines and other symbols to celebrate specific identities within the LGBTQ community.[9]

Another way to support the LGBTQ community is to watch for *stereotypes*—commonly held, often unfair beliefs about a group that suggest all members are the same. It is believing in a stereotype to assume:

o   Lesbians always have extremely short hair.

o   All women with strong, masculine traits are lesbians.

- Only gay men dress with style.
- All men who are emotionally sensitive are gay.

If you observe such generalizations in television shows, films, music, or books, write to production companies or publishers. Ask them to reconsider how they portray characters.

Stereotyping occurs in all communities, and you don't need to look far to find examples. It is stereotyping, for example, to think boys are better at math, girls are stronger in language arts, firefighters are all men, and nurses are always women. It is unfair to believe that females are bad drivers, people who wear glasses are smart, everyone who is blind can't detect or see light of any kind (known as complete blindness, a condition that is very rare), all people in wheelchairs are ill, or that people with autism look different. Immigrants are often labeled with broad statements. They may be unjustly called criminals, terrorists, or drug dealers simply because of the country where they were born. They may even be put down as people who don't work or people who take jobs from citizens by birth!

We are all guilty of expressing stereotypes. It is part of being human. Even though we have values, we also have habits, and we *all* make mistakes. For example, if you automatically refer to a doctor as *he*, does it mean you are stereotyping? Yes. Does it mean you are a bad person? No. It just means you have a bias to correct. Not every bias is hurtful, but labeling people does not allow us to see and appreciate individuals as they really are.

One way to be an activist is to help squash stereotypes. It's easy to do, just one conversation at a time. For example, if you heard someone say, "Deaf people can read lips," you could ask, "Do you know anyone who is deaf? Are you sure that's true for all deaf people?" By encouraging others to question their own statements, you help them to realize their *prejudices*—irrational attitudes against a person, group, or race based on characteristics they suppose exist. Prejudice, which leads to discrimination, is damaging in any community.

Before tackling gender issues, explore how others do it. Search the Malala Fund, MenEngage Alliance, the National Center for Transgender Equality, and CenterLink: The Community of LGBTQ Centers. As you research, look for organizations that share your values.

TRY THIS AT HOME

One way to support gender equality is by beginning with your immediate circles. Check out the list of tasks below, and think about who usually does them in your home:

- Set the table
- Wash the dishes
- Empty the dishwasher
- Take out compost or garbage
- Do laundry
- Maintain the vehicle
- Pay bills
- Drive children to activities
- Help with homework
- Shovel snow
- Shop for groceries
- Answer the door
- Deal with home repair
- Take recyclables to the depot

- Mow the lawn
- Weed the garden

(chat)

SPREAD THE WORD!

One way to get people to think about your message is to tie it to a fun activity. Arrange to set up this special display at a community event, such as International Day of the Girl Child on October 11, National Son and Daughter Day on August 11, or during Women's History Month in March. You'll need a large whiteboard, marker, Hula-Hoop, nonslip rubber bath mat, and a kiddie pool containing bubble solution. Better include a towel too!

Step 1: List household chores on a large whiteboard.

Step 2: Ask people who walk by to examine the list and consider whether housework is shared equally among the genders in their home.

Step 3: Invite them to remove their socks and shoes and carefully step onto the rubber bathmat in the kiddie pool filled with bubble solution (it may take some convincing).

Step 4: Use a Hula-Hoop to draw a giant bubble up and around your visitor.

Step 5: Tell them the bubble represents bias. Ask them to pop the bias bubble and bring the conversation about gender stereotypes home.

Does a gender bias exist? Consider whether household responsibilities could be shared more equally. How does sharing different types of work break down gender barriers? What benefits do members gain when they take on new tasks? It's also important to ask, if everyone chips in more or less equally, does it matter which gender does what? These are interesting questions to explore as a group. You could bring it up at suppertime or call a family meeting. Just remember—keep your discussion relaxed and be sure to choose your time wisely. If you raise the topic right after being asked to complete a chore, you might not have the friendly conversation you want!

THE DREADED *DO-GOODER* LABEL

In the strongest communities, people support one another, feel valued, and live with dignity. But our world is complicated. It takes work to create change, and there are always ways to improve. Communities grow stronger when their members—people like you—seek ways to make fairness, equality, and justice a reality for all citizens. After all, that's what activism is all about—making things better. Why is it, then, that some activists are labeled *do-gooders*?

Even activists can face stereotypes!

The word is usually uttered in a tone that suggests a do-gooder, or someone helping out, is *not* always a good thing. The word describes those who are keen to make a difference but are not fully informed about the issue at hand. People labeled do-gooders surely think they are doing the right thing. Unfortunately, the ones receiving aid can be left feeling that outsiders are interfering in their lives.

Suppose staff at a day care in the United States decide to undertake a project to support literacy in another country. Families collect gently used books, a sponsor pays for shipping, and boxes of books are dispatched to a small library in Afghanistan. The day care's intentions are good, but a big *oops* has occurred. Patrons at the library cannot read English. The books go to waste, and everyone is disappointed. Here's another scenario. Suppose a group of teachers notice that visitors to your school who use wheelchairs struggle to enter the building. They notice jagged cracks on the concrete ramp and assume they trap the wheels. The teachers arrange for the cracks to be filled and smoothed, but wheelchair users still stay away. It turns out that the ramp is too steep.

Fortunately, these types of scenarios are easy to avoid. Instead of diving straight into problem-solving, begin your activism by talking to communities affected by the matter you want to tackle. If the day care had asked the Afghanistan library what it needed, they would have learned what language readers understood. If the teachers had asked wheelchair users what stopped them from using the ramp, they would also have been in a better position to help.

In your activism, ask for feedback by using *open-ended questions*— ones that cannot be answered with a yes or no. You might ask, "What does your library need to help children and the rest of the community?" or "How can the school make it easier for you to visit?" People living with physical disabilities may raise worries about *accessibility*—whether those individuals will be able to use doors, bathrooms, elevators, and other things. Or they might surprise you with a concern that has not occurred to you, such as difficulty seeing over the counter in the school's office. Asking for opinions and advice is called *consultation*. It's an important tool!

Consulting demonstrates respect to communities by showing you are not claiming to be an expert on their lives. The public is more likely to support your work when they see you've invited others into the decision-making process. As you consider the many possible ways to create change, keep in mind that if you are viewed as a do-gooder, it will be harder to make the changes you want to see. Think about your own communities and where you will be most readily accepted.

TRADITIONAL RIGHTS

Some societies are bound by customs, beliefs, language, and *land ties*—spiritual connections to land, which are part of one's identity. Outsiders may not be readily welcomed, particularly if they are associated with *colonialism*—when a foreign nation takes political control over people, settles in their land, and claims the territory for their own country.

Members of *Indigenous*—relating to the earliest known people to live in a place—cultures share rights and traditions. Around the globe, they seek recognition for their unique identities and rights lost through colonialism. The United Nations Declaration on the Rights of Indigenous Peoples (UNDRIP) recognizes that Indigenous peoples have historically suffered injustices. These communities are often discriminated against and marginalized. Adopted on September 13, 2007, UNDRIP acknowledges that Indigenous peoples have the right to occupy and use traditional lands and the right to *self-determination*—to make their own choices and control their future.[10]

The world's 370 million Indigenous peoples live in more than ninety countries.[11] Activists can support these communities by finding particular issues to focus on, such as safe drinking water on reserves, protection for sacred sites, or better access to healthcare in remote communities. One of the best ways to be a respectful ally is to support Indigenous organizations and charities. You might start by researching Spirit of the Sun, which has a special interest in supporting youths and young

adults in Native American communities, or Indspire, which supports Indigenous education in Canada. Another approach is to organize letter-writing campaigns to government officials, asking them to create laws that honor the UN Declaration on the Rights of Indigenous Peoples.

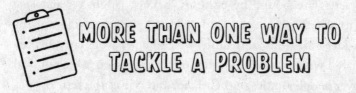

MORE THAN ONE WAY TO TACKLE A PROBLEM

Learning opportunities give children the tools they need to navigate daily life. Education improves gender equality and can help kids escape poverty and achieve independence. Critical thinking and empathy are also key skills to develop and practice in school. Honing such habits helps children grow into productive young adults who will be better able to function independently in the world at large and add their voices and skills to create change.

THE FUTURE IS YOUNG

Organizations around the world are finding ways to ensure children have opportunities to learn. Some provide preschool support. Others set up temporary schools in war zones or publish books in local languages. Education provides children with hope for a better future. The programs below highlight some of the super ways activists are inspiring brighter tomorrows.

HELP KIDS CATCH UP
{Save the Children, Nonprofit, International}

A global organization supporting young people in 117 nations, Save the Children works to remove barriers that prevent learning. It puts the most vulnerable first—children that experience discrimination, poverty, war, natural disasters, or other crises. The organization sets up temporary learning spaces during emergencies and helps kids who have dropped out of school catch up with learning. By making it possible for kids to attend school, the nonprofit helps provide protection from child marriage and human trafficking. Save the Children consults directly with children, their families, and community leaders, and then creates programs that address the specific obstacles kids face. Projects may support preschool education, nutrition, health, and distance learning.

Save the Children chapters exist in thirty countries. In the United States, kids get help with the goals to enter school ready for kindergarten and to read by third grade. In Canada, work includes efforts to help First Nations, Indigenous children, and *Métis*—descendants of people born to an Indigenous parent and a parent with European ancestry—reach their potential. Since being founded in 1919, Save the Children has improved the lives of more than one billion children.[12]

PROVIDE DIVERSE BOOKS
{Room to Read, NGO, International}

Room to Read is a global volunteer network that works in twenty-one countries to promote literacy and gender equality. It strives to help children in historically low-income communities learn to read, and then takes its program even further by working to build the important habit of reading.

One of Room to Read's approaches involves setting up child-friendly libraries with diverse books in local languages. It recognizes that literature coming from developed countries does not always reflect local experiences.

To address this, Room to Read partners with local publishers, authors, and illustrators to create and distribute local-language children's books that reflect the people and places it serves. The NGO also maintains an online education platform called Literacy Cloud. It includes a robust library, story time videos, training videos for educators, and the ability to search books by language, theme, and grade. Room to Read trains teachers and hires locals to run its programs, and it part-

It's not enough to know how to read; you must do it on a regular basis to experience the benefits.

Developed countries, also known as industrialized countries, have mature economies, advanced technology, and diverse services and industries. Residents can usually access healthcare and opportunities for higher education.

PROVIDE DIVERSE BOOKS (CONTINUED)

ners with local governments to integrate its programming across the countries it serves. It ensures access to education for girls, who may be discouraged from learning due to discrimination, cultural bias, and safety issues. Room to Read programs have aided more than thirty-two million children in over forty-nine thousand communities.[13]

TRAIN TEACHERS
{Justice Rising, Nonprofit, California}

Justice Rising provides education to children and support to adults in communities affected by war. Its projects range from building and operating schools to setting up community programs. Every year, the nonprofit teaches more than 2,500 students at its schools across three countries (Democratic Republic of Congo, Iraq, and Syria), and it has trained more than 140 teachers and support staff.

One of its community programs—the Leadership League—invites child soldiers, and those at risk of becoming soldiers, to lay down their weapons and play soccer. It encourages mothers from ages thirteen to twenty-seven to access counseling and enjoy friendships built around playing volleyball.

Justice Rising also helps adults cope with and recover from the pain of war through a special program called the Storytelling Movement. Participants are given the opportunity to share their experiences in a supportive environment.[14]

SPOTLIGHT ON . . .
Theirworld Global Youth Ambassadors

Around the world, 244 million children and youths from ages six to eighteen do not go to school.[15] An international charity called Theirworld is determined to fight this education crisis. One of its approaches is to harness the power of young people with its Global Youth Ambassador (GYA) program, which is made up of young people, ages eighteen to thirty. Over a two-year period, the participants access virtual training opportunities that show them how to try to change policies that prevent marginalized children from attending class. By the time they are fully trained ambassadors, they have gained communication, networking, and leadership skills, which they can use to campaign both in their communities and globally.

Theirworld supports its ambassadors by sharing advocacy opportunities and providing publicity through its newsletter and social media. It offers opportunities to take part in awareness campaigns, meet with high-level officials, and participate in other events that can influence change. In 2022, Theirworld challenged people to walk twenty-six miles to raise funds for the more than 200 million children not in school, directly supporting its mission to give children safe places to learn.

Over the past two decades, the charity's network has grown to about two thousand global youth ambassadors from over ninety countries. Every year, more young people sign up to add their voices to its efforts to ensure that every child can access education. Theirworld has helped more than 4.5 million children attend school.[16]

IMAGINE

Imagine not being able to attend school because you:

- Are a girl
- Live too far from a school
- Need to work to help support yourself and your family
- Live with physical disabilities that make it impossible to enter the building
- Do not have a teacher
- Need bathroom facilities that offer privacy
- Cannot pay school fees
- Do not have pencils, paper, books, rulers, protractors, computers, or other learning materials
- Live with disabilities or conditions that call for extra support
- Are too hungry to leave home
- Are so malnourished that your ability to clearly think, understand, and learn is affected
- Spend so much time hauling water for your family, no time is left for school
- Do not have a school building
- Had to flee your home due to war
- No longer have a school because an environmental problem, such as a flood, destroyed your school

MEET A YOUNG ACTIVIST
Malala Yousafzai

Imagine being told you're not allowed to go to school. That's what happened to Malala Yousafzai in 2009. She was eleven years old and living in Mingora, Pakistan. An extremist militant group called the Taliban was making rules that restricted the freedoms and human rights of girls and women. Malala loved learning and attending school. She understood that education is the best way for individuals to rise from poverty. Unable to accept the Taliban's actions, Malala began to make speeches about girls' right to education. She appeared on television and wrote a diary-style blog published by the British Broadcasting Corporation (BBC).

Malala was not alone in her fight. She was lucky to have parents who valued education. Malala's father, a teacher and school administrator, did not accept the extremists' views either. Not only did he encourage Malala to speak out but he also made the dangerous decision to allow both girls and boys to attend his schools.

As the Taliban grew stronger, they started banning books and the use of computers. They even destroyed schools. Eventually, the Taliban relaxed their rules and allowed girls ages ten and under to return to class, so Malala pretended she was younger and kept her books hidden to attend. When Malala was thirteen, the Pakistani army regained control from the extremist group, and girls ten years and older, including Malala, were able to return to school, but the Taliban was still active. Even while back in school, Malala continued her activism, being an outspoken advocate for educating all children, including girls, and this drew Taliban leaders' attention, angering them. In 2012, as she rode the school bus, the driver was forced to stop, and two men with guns climbed inside. She remembers them boarding, but she does not remember being shot.

Malala regained consciousness in a hospital in England. She had been shot in the head by the Taliban soldiers— targeted because of her continued activism. But no bullet would stop her cause.

Malala had a serious brain injury, which meant having part of a skull bone removed and later replaced with a titanium plate. Malala needed a cochlear device to allow her to hear with her left ear, and she had to relearn how to talk and walk. In the years since the attack, Malala has endured multiple procedures and surgeries to repair the damage.

After Malala was shot, doctors guided her recovery far from the dangers of Pakistan, and her story continued to spread across the world. This violent crime put a spotlight on her experience, and the international community received a disturbing picture of the injustices happening within her country. Malala received thousands of cards and other signs of support, including many from politicians and other prominent people.

It took time to regain her strength, but Malala was able to return to classes and her activism by attending high school in Birmingham in England because the Taliban was still a threat to her safety in Pakistan. Malala continued to inspire others, and in 2013, at the age of sixteen, she was invited by the United Nations to speak. Malala used this tremendous opportunity to ask the world's leaders to ensure that all children have access to education. At seventeen, Malala was recognized for her work to bring attention to girls' education issues in Pakistan and was awarded the *Nobel Peace Prize*—a distinction given to those who most strongly aid humankind. It is regarded as the world's most respected honor, and Malala is the youngest person to receive it.

Now an adult, Malala continues her powerful activism. She started a charitable foundation—the Malala Fund—which works to break down the barriers that prevent girls from attending school and being able to choose their own futures. Malala writes books, appears on television, makes speeches, and continues to lend her powerful voice to the discussion—at local, national, and international levels—about the importance of education.[17]

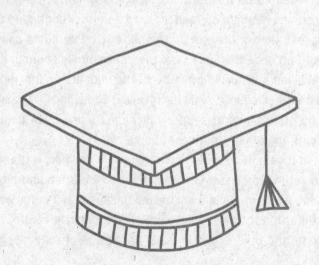

SATISFY YOUR CURIOSITY

Ready to meet new people and explore communities?
Pull a chair up to a computer and enter these words
into a search engine:

- United Nations Declaration on the Rights of
  Indigenous Peoples (UNDRIP)
- DACA
- Stereotypes
- MenEngage Alliance
- National Center for Transgender Equality
- CenterLink: The Community of LGBTQ Centers
- The Good Neighbour Project
- Spirit of the Sun
- Indspire
- Save the Children
- Room to Read
- Justice Rising
- Theirworld
- Malala Fund

9

POVERTY AND ITS PARTNERS

BOOSTING INCOME, SUPPORTING HEALTH, AND ENSURING EDUCATION

"The older generation has a lot of experience, but we have ideas, we have energy, and we have solutions."

Natasha Wang Mwansa, women's and girls' rights activist, Zambia

Can you wake up at the same time every day without using an alarm? If your eyes automatically pop open at the same moment each morning, it's because you've developed a habit. Routines make it easier to manage the things you need to do. Daily patterns free your mind to focus on more difficult tasks. While it may not sound exciting, this secret weapon—undertaking the same activities on a regular basis—makes you get better at them.

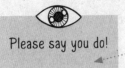

Please say you do!

Try it!

Try this too!

If you brush your teeth after breakfast each day, you will become so skilled, you can do it with your eyes closed.

If you make a new poster promoting your favorite cause once a week, your art, lettering, and sentence structure will improve with each new effort.

People reading your first posters might say, "Hmm, that's nice." A month later, they might go, "Wow!" Most of us stick to our routines until something forces us to change. Let's get into how that happens.

NATURAL AND HUMAN-MADE DISASTERS

Our daily routines can be interrupted by something fun, like a vacation, but sometimes it's more serious, like a ferocious storm or an event that creates an emergency situation. A *calamity* is a disaster that causes misfortune, suffering, or loss of life. Large natural events cause calamities around the globe—about four hundred natural disasters strike our planet each year.[1] Earthquakes, mudslides, tsunamis, volcanoes, hurricanes, floods, wildfires, and other unstoppable events disrupt people's normal, day-to-day routines.

Survivors may find it difficult or impossible to meet their needs for food, water, clothing, and shelter. Disasters can disrupt people's education, ability to work and support themselves, and access to healthcare. People may lose their homes and other possessions and even be forced to abandon their pets. Disasters make it hard to care for animals on farms and in zoos and aquariums. Aiding wild creatures affected by fire, flooding, and other calamities is also a tremendous challenge.

Not all disasters are natural. Some are caused by human activities. Think of war and other violent conflict. Picture pandemics that occur when conditions allow viruses to jump from animals to humans. Consider oil spills, nuclear plants that leak radiation, mines that collapse, and other accidents set off by human development.

As well as causing physical injury, calamities can trigger mental health problems. One of these, *post-traumatic stress disorder (PTSD)*, is a psychological reaction to highly stressful events. PTSD may cause anxiety, recurring nightmares, and other responses.

Social activism can aid people suffering from both the mental and physical effects of disasters, and there are many ways to help. You could raise funds to support rescue efforts and aid for survivors. You can publicize disaster distress *helplines*—special phone numbers set up to help people during emergencies. Another approach is to uncover human decisions that lead to calamities, and advocate for better laws and protections. Earthquake-prone regions, for example, may need activists to fight for building codes that only allow earthquake-resistant buildings. People at risk from wildfires may need laws to require the use of fire-resistant materials in building construction.

The United Nations Office for Disaster Risk Reduction (UNDRR) encourages UN members to look at ways to protect people and infrastructure from natural disasters. They would like to improve *resilience*—the ability to recover from or adjust to misfortune—and see communities do more than respond to disasters after they take place.

One way to reduce threats is to arrange for infrastructure, such as signage, sirens, radios, and towers, that can be used to deliver warnings to populations in at-risk regions. Helping could take the form of educating adults about the importance of keeping insurance to replace lost possessions. Activists might get involved by showing people how to make a *personal emergency plan*—a document that outlines what a family will do if a crisis occurs. It might include details such as the fire extinguisher location, how to turn off electrical breakers, the best route for leaving the neighborhood, health and insurance information, a place for family members to meet if everyone's not together, and other details needed to ensure safety. Activists might also provide directions on how to prepare

SPREAD THE WORD!

Why not try your hand at making an activist video? Videos can make issues more personal and influence how viewers feel. You might ask people to spread the word, donate funds, change a behavior, or take on a challenge. This approach was successful for the ALS Association, which wanted to raise awareness about amyotrophic lateral sclerosis, also called Lou Gehrig's disease. The organization asked people to film themselves dumping a bucket of ice water over their head, or the head of another person, and to nominate others to do the same. Nominees that didn't take the challenge were asked to donate to the ALS Association. The association received $115 million within the first six weeks of the challenge and went on to fund new treatment centers and conduct important research.[2]

an emergency kit with water, food that won't spoil, flashlights, batteries, a first aid kit, medications, cash, important family documents, and other essential items.

POVERTY

Climate change is leading to more frequent and violent natural disasters, and society's poorest populations are the most affected.[3] During a flood, for example, water collects on the lowest land first, which is often the more affordable land. This means less desirable, less expensive building occurs on these lowland locations, where low-income earners are more likely to live in poor-quality homes. Houses without storm windows or solid foundations are less able to survive typhoons or other weather that brings heavy rain. People with low incomes, which often includes seniors or individuals living with disabilities, may not have access to the internet or other technology commonly used to deliver warnings. They may be unable to pay for transportation, shelter, or other costs that arise when escaping danger zones.[4] Disasters are hard for everyone affected, but they make life even more difficult for those who already struggle to pay for the things they need. One way to reduce long-lasting damage from natural disasters is to improve people's abilities to support themselves.

Poverty is linked to numerous social issues. Think of hunger, poor nutrition, living in unsafe neighborhoods, homelessness, education, and healthcare.

Imagine needing glasses but not being able to afford an eye exam.

Money-related hardships occur for a variety of reasons. *Situational poverty* is the result of an incident or set of circumstances. It might occur when illness makes it hard to hold a job, a death or divorce occurs in a family, or all possessions are lost during a natural or human-caused disaster. Situational poverty can be temporary. Other times it is difficult to escape.

Generational poverty occurs when individuals are born into a poverty cycle that lasts two or more generations. Breaking free is complicated. People trapped in this situation often don't have access to education, funds to start a business, or other resources that could help. A child trapped in generational poverty may not have role models who escaped being poor. It is hard to know how to go about improving your circumstances if you have never seen anyone try and succeed.

Absolute poverty—common in developing nations—occurs when people struggle to meet basic daily needs for food, water, and shelter. A life-threatening situation, absolute poverty describes the minimum amount of income needed to survive. This is unlike *relative poverty*, which occurs when people can meet their basic needs but do not have anything left to spend on the extras that others take for granted. Picture a family with enough to eat but not enough money to pay for home internet access, movies, or sporting events. Relative poverty is not life threatening, but it is still an obstacle because it creates  exclusion. Living without fun extras prevents people from experiencing normal daily life within their communities.

The International Poverty Line is used to describe how many people around the world live in poverty. It is based on how much it costs to sustain one adult in each country. In 2022, the line was set at $2.15 US dollars per day.[5] Anyone living on less than this daily amount is viewed as living in extreme poverty.

The ten highest poverty rates in the world are found in:

- South Sudan
- Equatorial Guinea
- Madagascar
- Guinea-Bissau
- Eritrea
- Sao Tome and Principe
- Burundi
- Democratic Republic of the Congo
- Central African Republic
- Guatemala[6]

Poverty exists in every nation in the world. In 2020, 37.2 million people in the United States fit into this category.[7] In 2021, 2.8 million in Canada suffered the same hardship.[8] Around the world,

EXPLORE MORE

A haircut makes you feel fresh, clean, and presentable. It's also a luxury people experiencing homelessness can't usually afford. To help, explore the events that volunteer barbers and stylists have organized to offer free hair care to people who cannot afford to pay. If you decide to try this, you'll need to invite hair stylists, pick a date and location, gather shampoo and other supplies, and find a way to let people know about the event. Partner with a salon, shelter, or other nonprofit who would like to help those in need.

about one billion kids do not have access to basic nutrition, clean water, housing, education, or healthcare.[9] It can be so overwhelming to see these statistics and see how widespread help is needed. So, what now?

FIND YOUR PATH

How can you work to bring poverty numbers down? Begin by narrowing where you want to focus your energy. Do you want to tackle the problem close to home or in a distant country? Also consider where your interests lie and how you can do the most good. You might choose to aid children, youths, families, or single mothers with babies. Perhaps you'd prefer to support the elderly, people living with disabilities, those facing discrimination, or another marginalized group. After choosing a focus, select an approach.

One of the best solutions is to support learning. Job training and education help people raise themselves from poor living conditions, no matter where they live. If you feel drawn to aiding developing nations, you might ask your teacher or principal about entering a process called *international school partnerships*. This approach offers a personal way for students to learn about other cultures, traditions, and global issues. Educators in both locations may work together to plan and teach a joint subject and share teaching practices, a process that helps boost education in developing nations. Teachers and students learn how social issues affect real individuals and their families. International school partnerships also support language learning, grow tolerance, and may even lead to lifelong friendships. As you learn about your partner school's needs, you could engage in activism or fundraising to support a specific project, such as building a well or buying school supplies. In the end, both schools benefit from international school partnerships.

No matter what type of poverty you tackle, you can always help by lobbying decision-makers at local, national, and global levels. One way to narrow the problem is to start with the need for shelter. Call for governments to ensure that every person has a safe place to live. Children, youths, and adults can experience homelessness. People without a permanent residence can find it extremely difficult to acquire food, get adequate sleep, hold jobs, maintain good health, avoid violence and harassment, or care for their personal needs. For some, homelessness is a temporary setback. Others may live without a permanent residence for decades, which we often see is the case in war-torn countries where people become refugees when escaping violence.

Deadly natural disasters also lead to homelessness. The massive earthquakes in Türkiye and Syria on February 6, 2023, flattened tens of thousands of buildings, killed more than forty-one thousand people, and left millions without permanent shelter. The disaster forced victims in these developing nations to live either out in the open or in tents, train cars, greenhouses, and other places with little protection from icy winter temperatures, and no way to meet their basic needs. Whether people in other countries become homeless due to war, natural disasters, or other circumstances, the fastest way to help is to raise funds for reputable organizations with experience in helping in these situations. The International Committee of the Red Cross, for example, works in more than 90 countries, while Doctors without Borders works in more than 65 countries. For a set period during a crisis, some federal governments will even match donations to an approved organization.[10]

Within developed nations, mental illness and illegal drugs can be the leading cause of homelessness. In 2022, more than half a million people in the United States endured homelessness. These states had the highest homeless populations:

- California
- New York
- Florida
- Texas
- Washington
- Massachusetts
- Oregon
- Pennsylvania
- Arizona
- Ohio[11]

It will take input from affected communities, elected officials, and nonprofits to find long-term solutions to homelessness. You can dive in by sharing your concerns with every level of government. Ask them to tackle the leading causes in the most affected locations and provide jobs, decent wages, and affordable housing. Lobby for laws to ensure *living wages*—payment high enough for workers to support themselves. You can also call for improved social service programs to help people living on the street. Ask city officials to assist *vulnerable populations*—people with higher risks of poor health due to limitations from illness, disability, or lack of resources. Vulnerable individuals include those suffering from substance abuse and other addictions, including mental health issues, and those escaping family violence or abuse.

Another way to help is to support *emergency shelters*—facilities that provide people who have nowhere else to go with a temporary place to sleep for the night.

You could raise funds or get directly involved by volunteering. Shelters, soup kitchens that provide meals, and other charities that help homeless populations need hands-on help. You could sign up to distribute clothes, meals, or water; chop vegetables; sort donations; or take on other behind-the-scenes work. Shelters for women and children might welcome help with story time sessions or other children's activities. They may appreciate donations of toys, books, laptops, and other devices. You could organize a collection event, but before you get started, make contact and find out what is needed. Sometimes relief agencies become bogged down with inappropriate donations. There's no point, for example, in giving a men's shelter clothes for kids or dropping off broken appliances at a thrift store. Unsuitable donations create work for relief agencies and add to their costs when they have to pay for disposal.

Emergency shelters provide a much-needed temporary solution. Affordable housing, however, provides a new way of living. One way to help is to get involved with Habitat for Humanity. This global nonprofit based in Georgia, USA, helps families obtain

BE WISE

Help your activism along by being aware of the language you use to describe people. If you're talking about those living on the street, choose *people experiencing homelessness*. If you're talking about those addicted to drugs, refer to *people living with addictions*. These terms reflect the fact that humans are more than the situations they experience. They are more helpful than unkind terms, such as *bums* or *drug addicts*.

affordable housing in all fifty American states and approximately seventy countries. Those approved for housing work with volunteers to help build their own homes or renovate existing homes.[12]

Training is provided!

No matter how you get involved in tackling poverty and homelessness, invite others to join you! It's a great habit, and every time you bring another person on board, your activism footprint grows larger.

GIVE POVERTY A KICK

Let's return to a topic I've been itching to write more about—activism through books. Good reading material can offer a much-needed escape to children and adults in shelters. In fact, reading is a solution for anyone in need of a break from the chaos around them. Stories bring us to new places and help us understand people who think and behave differently than we do. Nonfiction helps us explore topics we're curious about, find answers to our questions, and solve problems.

Do you see a bias here?

The issue is, not everyone learns to read. In fact, there are children in the world who have never seen a book and wouldn't know what it was if you handed one over. The ability to read and write is called *literacy*. Almost 130 million adults in the United States read below a sixth-grade level, and only about a third of students in grades four, eight, and twelve are skilled readers.[13] We could also say it like this: in the United States, 21 percent of adults are *illiterate*—unable to read or write—and 54 percent of adults have a literacy rate below the sixth-grade level.[14] This is a worldwide tragedy. In 2015, 14 percent of the world's population over age fifteen could not read. For comparison, more than two hundred years ago in 1820, only 12 percent of the world's population *could* read and write.[15]

Those struggling to read may not be able to:

Pass a driver's test

Read danger warnings

Help children with schoolwork

Do homework

Understand road signs

Calculate how much change to expect when paying with cash

Follow instructions on medicine bottles

Read a menu

Apply for financial aid

Fill out a job application

People without literacy skills typically earn lower incomes. They are more likely to drop out of school and depend on government aid.[16] Literacy provides the quickest path to learning and gives people access to the information they need to make daily decisions. It makes it easier to solve problems, manage finances, get job training, and access opportunities to earn money. As a reading and writing activist, you can help people build skills that will help them take control of their lives, escape poverty, and improve their health and safety. Your support can help girls and women in developing nations grow more independent.

Promoting literacy can be as straightforward as fostering a love of reading. Chapter 8 included a few ideas (see page 216) on how to turn the page on this challenge, but many more approaches exist. You could start by getting involved in the movement to share books. Little Free Library is a nonprofit organization that encourages individuals to set up small libraries in their yards or other spaces. It has registered more than one hundred thousand little libraries worldwide. They share library locations on their website and offer premade little libraries for purchase or building plans and setup tips if you like the idea of getting your hands sawdusty.[17] Visitors are invited to take a book or leave one for others to read. If you've spotted a weatherproof book box, perhaps with a glass front and a hinged door, you've seen an example of this global book-sharing movement.

Not into building or don't have a spot to place a little library? Try this approach: invite coffee shops or other businesses to set up book-sharing spots in their spaces. Ask municipal leaders to allow bookshelves in the lobbies of local hockey rinks, swimming pools, recreational centers, or other locations where people gather. If they're not keen on the idea, persevere with details on why literacy is important and what leadership means!

IMAGINE

Think about what your day would be like if you did not know how to write. For starters—you would not be able to mark a special day on the calendar, label your belongings, or create a to-do list. You would need to remember everything! What other challenges would you face?

Now spread your activism net even wider. Challenge schools in your district to join you in a friendly literacy-building competition. Invite them to set up shelves with free books, organize book-buddy reading programs, or raise funds to ensure that all students have writing supplies. Keep track of your progress, share ideas with one another, and celebrate your efforts at year-end.

Another way to promote literacy is to use social media to recommend books and demonstrate this important fact: reading is cool! Get started by observing how other kids use video, art, and words to promote books online, and then develop your own original style.

MEET A YOUNG ACTIVIST
Madeline Weber

Madeline Weber was eight years old when she set out to share her love of books and encourage other kids to enjoy reading. With help from family, she erected a little library in Yamhill, Oregon. This small farming community, nearly a twenty-minute drive from the nearest public library, was also once home to acclaimed children's author Beverly Cleary. Madeline's Library is located a few blocks from where Cleary lived.

Visitors are invited to keep books from the top shelf—titles recently reviewed on Madeline's website. If borrowing from the bottom shelf, though, they are asked to return the books so others may enjoy them too. Madeline wants everyone in Yamhill to have access to books, but she would especially like local kids to be able to enjoy the pleasure of being able to walk to a library.

To help raise money for a local library, Madeline created a Read-a-Thon, complete with the chance to win prizes. Students are challenged to set a reading goal for the school year, record the titles they read, rate them from one to five stars, and ask family and friends to donate a set amount of money per book. The Yamhill Downtown Association supports Madeline's efforts by collecting donations for Madeline's Library, a nonprofit organization. Her parents and other family members help with video production, website updates, and ensuring a safe online presence.[18]

When Beverly Cleary was a young girl, her mother, Mable, wrote to the State Library of Oregon and requested books to be sent to their small town of Yamhill (which did not have its own library). Her mother worked as the librarian after setting up the library in an upstairs room over a bank.[19]

The internet plays a sizable role in our lives, but it's not the only way to communicate. Most important, it may not be

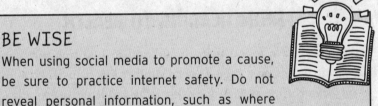

BE WISE

When using social media to promote a cause, be sure to practice internet safety. Do not reveal personal information, such as where you live or go to school. Don't wear school colors or stand in front of objects that give away details that could be used to locate you. Ask your parents or guardians if you may post publicly, and get their feedback on your videos and posts before going live.

accessible to the people you most want to reach. Challenge yourself to find other ways to share book recommendations. Here are a few ideas to get you started:

- When you enjoy a book, think of others who might like it too, and tell them about it.

- Ask your school librarian if students can put a gold star on the spines of their favorite books.

- Draw pictures that represent the different categories of books in the nonfiction section of your school library, and ask your librarian to post the drawings in each section to help learning readers find books.

- Make bookmarks with a sentence that begins with "You might like this book because . . ." Ask school and public librarians to give the bookmarks away.

- Use sidewalk chalk to draw arrows on sidewalks pointing to library and bookstore entrances. Share messages like "Libraries are your friends," "Books are fun," and "Everyone welcome."

FROM READING TO HEALTH

Researchers have found that, in addition to boosting intelligence, exploring words on a page delivers another key benefit. It promotes good health. One way it does this is by reducing stress, a leading factor in about 60 percent of diseases. Reading may even slow and help prevent *cognitive decline*—the reduced ability to think, remember, and make judgments during aging.[20] A Yale University study on reading determined that readers live longer lives. Regardless of education factors, wealth, race, or gender, the

study determined that people reading books for more than three and a half hours per week lived twenty-three months longer than nonreaders.[21]

The average age a person is expected to live to varies throughout the world. This age is described as *life expectancy*. In 2022, Hong Kong had the highest expectancy at 87.8 years for females and 82 years for males. The lowest expectancy was in the Central African Republic, where the average was 57 for females and 53 for males in 2020.[22]

Life expectancy depends on access to healthcare as well as gender, genetics, crime rates, and lifestyle choices, such as diet, exercise, hygiene, smoking, and *substance abuse*—the repeated use of drugs, alcohol, or other harmful substances. Substance abuse is like a direct attack on the mind and body, and people living with addictions often endure one or more health issues. Inhaled substances can damage nerve cells in the brain. The drug methamphetamine causes dental problems seen as broken, black, and rotting teeth, and known as meth mouth.[23] Other consequences include loss of self-control and poor decision-making, such as driving while under the influence, which can lead to injuries and death. Substance abuse and other types of addictions harm family relationships and the person's ability to learn and work. Addictions can lead to expensive legal and treatment costs, and impact communities. This is seen through child abuse and neglect, family violence, increased crime rates, hospitalizations, and the spread of the human immunodeficiency virus (HIV), which causes AIDS. The World Health Organization has found that almost half the world's population does not have access to needed health services. Others live where health services are available, but the cost is not affordable. The WHO reports that one hundred million people each year enter extreme poverty because of the money they spend on healthcare.[24]

Activists interested in health might work to improve access to services, reduce harm from substance abuse, or promote *wellness*—a state of good health based on factors that include physical and mental health. To get started, consider these examples, and see where your interests lie.

IMPROVE ACCESS TO HEALTH SERVICES

Promote blood, plasma, and organ donation.

Demand rights for refugees and undocumented persons.

Call for better access in rural and remote regions.

Raise funds for hospital equipment.

Lobby governments to make health services available to all citizens.

REDUCE HARM

Create a presentation on how to reduce risks from disease-spreading mosquitoes and ticks.

Promote the use of clean needles by IV drug users to prevent the spread of HIV.

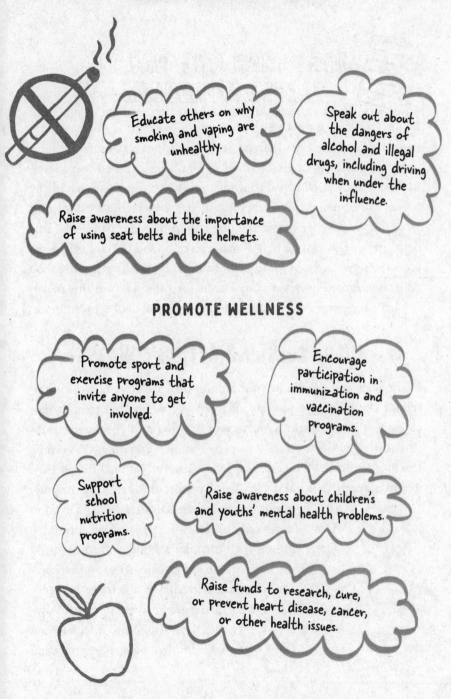

Educate others on why smoking and vaping are unhealthy.

Speak out about the dangers of alcohol and illegal drugs, including driving when under the influence.

Raise awareness about the importance of using seat belts and bike helmets.

PROMOTE WELLNESS

Promote sport and exercise programs that invite anyone to get involved.

Encourage participation in immunization and vaccination programs.

Support school nutrition programs.

Raise awareness about children's and youths' mental health problems.

Raise funds to research, cure, or prevent heart disease, cancer, or other health issues.

MORE THAN ONE WAY TO TACKLE A PROBLEM

Poverty touches everyone in one way or another. If you've always had your needs met, you might wonder how poverty touches everyone, but think about times when you've been exposed to poverty. Maybe you saw it while vacationing in another country or driving by a long line of people outside a local shelter. Maybe your school runs an annual fundraiser before the holidays to help the families of students in need (it can be that close). You're bound to have witnessed it on the news or been reminded of the problem when passing food collection bins. Poverty and its effects surround us, and this makes it hard to ignore. Maybe this cause is one you'd like to embrace.

EVERY COIN AND ACTION COUNTS

Individuals and groups in your community are already working to reduce the effects of poverty. Perhaps you've spotted them. Signs at grocery stores ask for contributions to *food banks*—organizations that distribute donated food to people in need. People wear poppy lapel pins around Remembrance, Veterans, or National Poppy Day. Their donated coins and bills help support the needs of the military community and their families. The Salvation Army sets up red collection kettles at store entrances. Their ringing bells are like a holiday carol inviting passersby to give cash at Christmastime, with donations used locally to aid those in need. The organizations listed in the following pages have also found distinct ways to help combat poverty—providing

244

kids with computers, stopping food waste, and making it easier to pay for energy to heat or cool homes.

REFURBISH COMPUTERS
{Computers for Kids, Nonprofit, Idaho}

Technology plays a key role in our day-to-day lives. We use it to access information, track money, and manage a multitude of other tasks. Kids who know how to use computers gain skills that will help them learn and one day get jobs, but those without devices are at a disadvantage.

Computers for Kids (CFK) is a charitable organization that wants to make sure all kids have equal access to the technology needed to learn and compete in today's world. It upgrades donated computers with current technology and distributes them to K–12 students in need in Idaho, Oregon, Washington, and Utah. Students in the first two years of college or university can take advantage of the program too. CFK also offers devices to schools and other nonprofits. Since 2002, CFK has distributed more than fifty thousand computers.[25]

STOP FOOD WASTE
{Feeding America, Nonprofit, Chicago}

In the United States, Feeding America is the largest organization to assist those experiencing hunger. It works with partners—grocery stores, food manufacturers, restaurants, caterers, and farmers—to collect good quality, healthy food that would otherwise be thrown away, and delivers it to people in need. Feeding America also provides food, water, and relief supplies to people during disasters. The organization operates a website and app called MealConnect, which links donors with volunteers who can pick up surplus food from local businesses. In 2022, Feeding America prevented 3.6 billion pounds of groceries from going to waste and provided 5.2 billion meals. It also distributed $239 million in grants to food banks.[26]

TACKLE ENERGY POVERTY
{Renewable Energy Transition Initiative, Nonprofit, North Carolina}

Some low-income households in the United States pay up to 30 percent of their income to manage the temperature in their homes.[27] An energy bill that adds up to more than 6 percent of a family's income is considered unaffordable. This *energy burden* is a frustration for millions of American families. DeAndrea Salvador founded the Renewable Energy Transition Initiative (RETI) to tackle *energy poverty*—having trouble paying the cost to heat your home. This nonprofit undertakes research and advocacy, offers educational programs, and works to make renewable energy easier to access. One project involved helping a family reduce its energy costs by providing them with a rooftop solar array. RETI offers training for individuals who would like to learn about energy issues and bring solutions to their own communities.[28]

WE CAN FIX THIS!

Poverty, hunger, and human suffering all feel like huge monster problems that are beyond your control—what could one kid do to help? But the organizations above show that if you focus on one aspect of a situation, you can find ways to make things better. And small improvements do add up! The strongest solutions give people the tools and information they need to regain control over their own lives. Use your activism to help others reach for solutions.

ONE THING YOU CAN DO NOW

Researchers estimate that one third of all food in the United States is wasted.[29] When food is discarded, the energy to produce, process, transport, and store it is also squandered. Processing more food than we need increases greenhouse gases and contributes to global warming. Do your share to prevent food waste by preparing smaller portions. Ask your family to participate by choosing produce that is considered ugly, such as crooked carrots or imperfect pineapples. Some companies market "ugly produce" to reduce waste. Find out which fruits and vegetables should be stored at room temperature and which need to be refrigerated. Research other ways to prevent waste, and spread the word!

SPOTLIGHT ON . . .
IBBY

The International Board on Books for Young People (IBBY) promotes the belief that every child has the right to become a reader in the fullest sense. This means being able to access books and enjoy the benefits of reading, which include being able to think critically, take part in society, understand the world, and be *empowered*—have the power to control your life or situations you face.

IBBY was founded in 1953 in Switzerland by Jella Lepman. She "believed books could build bridges of understanding and peace between people."[30] Following World War II, she could see that German children's need for books was as great as their need for food and other necessities. She wanted children to know that they were not alone and that there was a whole world to discover.

IBBY's activities include providing funding to establish new libraries, awarding literary prizes, training educators, and supporting other projects that promote reading. One of the nonprofit's many projects is the IBBY Children in Crisis program, which aids children affected by natural disasters, war, and other conflicts. With the belief that books can change and save lives, the program helps provide therapeutic storytelling and *bibliotherapy*—the use of books to help solve personal problems. IBBY also works to replace libraries and book collections that have been damaged by civil unrest, war, and natural disasters, making sure the replacement books are in local languages. Its members in eighty nations work to bring books and children together to foster change.[31]

BRAIN NUGGET

Accepting others shows respect and is essential to effective activism, yet we all have the habit of looking at people and making on-the-spot judgments. Our brains process information by putting people into categories, which are often stereotypes. Make a decision to avoid judging people based on outward appearances, such as their hairstyle or the clothes or jewelry they wear.

MEET A YOUNG ACTIVIST
Alexandra (Alex) Scott

Four-year-old Alexandra (Alex) Scott was fighting cancer when she set up a lemonade stand in her front yard in Connecticut. Her goal was to raise funds to help find cures for all children living with this disease. She sold the drink for twenty-five cents, along with snacks, and the first stand raised $2,000!

With family and friends pitching in, Alex continued to hold yearly lemonade stands in front of her new home in Pennsylvania. She continued to spread the word about her personal battle and her cause by appearing on local and national television, including popular shows such as *Good Morning America* and *The Oprah Winfrey Show*. Through this dedication and bravery, Alex inspired people around the world to take action. They responded by setting up lemonade stands too, and donating the money they raised to Alex's cause.

In 2004, at the age of eight, Alex lost her battle with cancer and died. In those four short years before her death, Alex and her supporters—spanning more than ten countries and all fifty US states—had raised more than $1 million. Her family continues the work Alex started. By 2023, the nonprofit Alex's Lemonade Stand Foundation had raised over $250 million and funded more than 1,500 research projects.[32]

SATISFY YOUR CURIOSITY

Use these internet search terms to get familiar with the problems people face and possible solutions:

- United Nations Office for Disaster Risk Reduction (UNDRR)
- International poverty line
- Little Free Library
- Madeline's Library
- International school partnerships
- Computers for Kids
- Feeding America
- Imperfect Foods
- Renewable Energy Transition Initiative (RETI)

PART IV

CHANGE IS
EVERYWHERE

10

CHANGE THROUGH THE ARTS

USING CREATIVITY TO SPOTLIGHT ISSUES

"Gentleness can be a great strength, and quiet action can sometimes speak as powerfully amid the noise as the loudest voice."

Sarah Corbett, founder of the Craftivist Collective,
United Kingdom

When you hear the words *artistic talent*, your mind might jump to famous painters, legendary musicians, film stars, or other fancy folk. These stars are indeed inspiring examples of creativity. It is not necessary, however, to produce a masterpiece, achieve a hit single, or star in a movie to be considered an artist. Anyone can express themselves in creative ways, and people in every community take part in *the arts*—activities that require imagination and skill to create objects, experiences, or environments.

In their many forms, the arts inspire us to feel grounded and connected to the world. They reveal the experience of being human and offer ways to explore ideas. These remarkable traits put arts and activism on the same team. It's a powerful partnership because both those who create art forms and those who consume them reap great

benefits. Creators gain the unique joy of making something where nothing existed before. They find satisfaction in using their imagination and creative talents to communicate messages. Audiences that encounter these messages may react with strong emotions, an experience that also brings fulfillment. They might feel joy, understanding, sorrow, anger, pain, or other powerful sentiments.

Works of art can inspire people to ponder how they feel about a topic and may even lead them to reexamine their views, reflect on social issues presented, and debate how change can be achieved. As an activist harnessing the power of the arts, that's exactly what you want to do—help others picture better ways of managing our world. Artists use many forms or mediums to deliver their magic, and some artworks fall into more than one category. What favorites might you add to these bubbles?

LITERATURE
{arts that are read}

biography, drama, essays, fables, fairy tales, fantasy, fiction, folklore, historical fiction, horror, mystery, mythology, nonfiction, poetry, science fiction, short stories, speeches

PERFORMING ARTS
{arts delivered as a live presentation or event}

circus arts, dance, improvisation, marching band, mime, music, musical theater, opera, painting, poetry, poi, spoken word, stand-up comedy, stilt walking, storytelling, street performance, theater

MEDIA ARTS
{arts created by recording visual images and/or sounds that change along a timeline}

animation, 3D products, audio, cinema, computer-generated art, film, graphics, interactive media, internet productions, photography, radio, television, video, video games, virtual reality, web design[1]

VISUAL ARTS
{two- or three-dimensional creations that can be seen}

cartoons, carvings, ceramics, computer art, dolls, drawings, flower arranging, graffiti, lace designs, mosaics, murals, needlework, paintings, photographs, posters, printmaking, relief models, stained-glass designs

FINE ARTS
{arts created primarily for the sake of beauty}

collage, architecture, drawing, filmmaking, graffiti, music, painting, photography, pottery, printmaking, sculpture, videography

Wait a minute! Architecture can be pleasing, but buildings have practical purposes. Does it really belong under *fine arts*? Hard to define and categorize, art is often a matter of opinion. When it comes to architecture, think of the artistic elements of noteworthy structures, especially historic buildings. Consider what makes them beautiful or interesting, such as the use of color, texture, and light. Look for decorative aspects—fountains, domes, columns, or carved figures called gargoyles—and you will recognize fine arts.

DECORATIVE ARTS
{arts handmade by a skilled craftsperson}

carpentry, carpet making, crafts, fashion design, furniture making, glassblowing, jewelry design, knitting, macramé, metalworking, needlework, pottery, quilting, stained glass, woodworking

COMMERCIAL ART
{images or labels designed to sell a product}

billboards, book covers, greeting card art, illustrations, logos, magazine ads, photographs on restaurant menus, posters, product packaging, propaganda

ONE THING YOU CAN DO NOW

Using items you have around the home, create a sculpture that makes a statement about a cause you care about. Think about how you might use clay, bags of leaves, pasta, play dough, recycling, snow, tires, or other interesting objects to make your point.

ARTS FOR CHANGE

If you enjoy the arts, you're not alone. A 2020 arts participation survey measured how many adults in the United States took part in different types of arts and cultural activities during the one-year period immediately before the COVID-19 pandemic. It found that 80.2 million (32.2 percent) attended events such as dance, live music, or theatrical performances, while 97 million (40 percent) also participated by reading literature and consuming art though electronic media. Performing or creating art was also popular with 23.7 million people (almost 10 percent) who played a musical instrument, 19.5 million (close to 8 percent) who chose singing for practice or performance, and 25.6 million (10.4 percent) who spent time taking photos for artistic purposes. Other activities included drawing, painting, sculpting, weaving, woodwork, metalwork, leatherwork, visiting sites with historic or architectural value, and creative writing.[2]

My personal favorite!

All this adds up to tons of people enjoying creativity, and that's useful for activists. Art can move people to think beyond what is presented. You've surely had feelings triggered by art. Let's check.

Have you ever:

- Cried during a movie?
- Laughed out loud in a theater?
- Hidden beneath a blanket to avoid seeing a scene on television?
- Felt tears well up or gasped in shock when reading?
- Cringed at a photograph?
- Longed for characters in a movie to behave a certain way?

- Sung or danced with joy while listening to music?
- Felt serious upon seeing stained-glass images?
- Giggled and clapped during a street performance?
- Cheered at a circus?
- Rolled your eyes at a picture on a billboard?
- Felt amazed or in awe by a castle or other mind-boggling structure?

The arts certainly have the power to trigger an outpouring of emotion, and this helps us connect to ideas, experiences, and one another. The arts can lead us to focus on things we do not normally spend time thinking about. They open our minds to the ways others see and experience the world.

We live in an age in which information is constantly communicated to us, especially online. It's easy to feel bombarded by messages. Art provides participants with ways to experience knowledge without feeling numbed. It can deliver an escape from daily life and at the same time motivate people to consider community needs.

As an activist, you can take advantage of this energy and use it to make change. One of the best ways to do this is by harnessing the power of story. Chapter 3 touched on the value of storytelling, but as you'll see, there's much more to explore!

Story in its written form—literature—is a direct route to sharing information. If you think back for a moment, I bet you can recall a time someone shared a tale with you that deliberately communicated a lesson. Parents, teachers, and other caregivers are particularly famous for this. If you've been introduced to the story of "The Tortoise and the Hare," for example, you've been encouraged to learn a moral through literature. This legendary Aesop fable is about two very different creatures competing in a race. When the too-confident hare stops for a nap, the tortoise plods on and wins the competition. The yarn imparts a message— *slow and steady wins the race.*

This is good advice for you and any volunteers helping with your cause!

Like adults, you can use literature to encourage people to make wise choices and avoid risky behaviors. In other words, you can let stories do some of the work for you!

To begin, look for both fiction and true tales that match your cause, and then use them to raise awareness and encourage change. Talking about books and recommending ones that spotlight your concerns shows that you are a well-informed activist. This is sure to help you attract supporters.

Storytelling in literature—or any other form—offers other benefits too, such as the ability to communicate events that have already occurred and those that might happen. Suppose you want to draw attention to the matter of bullying. You might produce a *skit*—a brief dramatic performance—or a *monologue*—a dramatic speech by one actor. The performance could show how victims have reacted to cruelty in the past as well as how bystanders can respond in the future. You might consider performing poetry, like students in the Get Lit program. Founded in Los Angeles in 2006, Get Lit teaches students how to express themselves through classic poetry, original writing, and spoken word performances. The nonprofit, which offers a curriculum to middle schools and high schools in California and online fellowships for students around the world, inspires social awareness and transforms participants into activists. It also builds vital literacy skills. Teens in the program can audition for the Get Lit Players, an award-winning performance troupe that has brought social messages to the United Nations, the White House, and other important venues.[3]

Think about how you might promote your cause through a performance, song, dance, painting, sculpture, poem, or other art form. You can use creations that already exist or create your own. Either way, you'll find that storytelling through the arts has the power to truly lock in viewers' attention.

SPREAD THE WORD!
Wear a Sandwich Board Sign

Step 1: Take two large sheets of foam board or cardboard, position them vertically, and use scissors to cut rope holes near the top corners of each sheet.

Step 2: Using a pencil and sheet of paper, make a rough copy of a message you'd like to share.

Step 3: Use markers to write your message on the foam board. Add some art! Remember to keep the message short and catchy, and make the lettering as large as you are able so your cause is easy to read and understand from a distance.

Step 4: Pull a rope (or bathrobe sash) through the holes to connect the boards. Leave the boards loose enough to pull over your head, and allow room for your arms to come out the sides. Adjust it to fit comfortably before knotting.

Consult with a parent or other adult in your home to figure out the safest place to stand or walk while wearing your sandwich board sign.

ARTS INVITE CONVERSATION

When it comes to demonstrating the importance of human rights and ways to overcome challenges, the arts have muscle. Their ability to provide starting points for conversations on social issues is a major strength.

Arts encourage people to explore their opinions, ideas, and emotions, but sometimes a work leaves consumers feeling puzzled. They may look at a painting, for example, and say, "I don't get it. What's it supposed to mean?" Understanding artistic expression sometimes means knowing the views of the artist or the historical period during which an object was created. You do not, however, need to know an artist's worldview to take something away from a creation. In many cases, the story or message is deliberately left to consumers to figure out. This is one of the reasons why diverse individuals can find the same art meaningful. They find their own value and significance in it.

Artistic works might highlight messages that express:

As well as creating empathy, which is so important in breaking down bias, the arts can be used to spark protest. Activists may create or share *protest art*—works designed to create awareness about injustices. This might include graffiti, printed materials, live performances, music, or other artistic forms.

If you know the song "Yankee Doodle," you've heard lyrics tied to a social issue. A British doctor named Richard Shuckburgh is generally credited with composing the words to belittle patriot fighters during the *American Revolution*—the fight for independence from Great Britain (1775–83).[4] The lyrics describe Yankee Doodle as riding a mere pony, rather than a horse, and suggest he thinks it takes only a feather in his hat to make him as stylish as some Europeans. The insult backfired, and the song became a rallying song for the colonists.[5]

Songs focused on social change might call for political change or draw attention to bullying, racism, inequality, police brutality, war, or other matters. In 1861, during the American Civil War, Julia Ward Howe wrote the lyrics for "The Battle Hymn of the Republic." It became a protest song calling for freedom for all people. The hymn is still part of US culture, and the lyric "Mine eyes have seen the glory of the coming of the Lord" completed the last speech that American civil rights activist Martin Luther King Jr. delivered before his assassination the following day.[6]

Modern musicians continue the tradition of using music to make a point. Lee Greenwood's song "God Bless the U.S.A." became an anthem during Operation Desert Storm (also known as the Persian Gulf War), which began when Iraq invaded Kuwait in 1990. The song is also popular at American Independence Day events.

After George Floyd was murdered in 2020, rapper Lil Baby wrote and recorded the protest anthem "The Bigger Picture" about police and the Black community. In 2021, singer-songwriter Chris

Pierce released the folk song "American Silence" to comment on not acting in the face of violence.[7]

Memorable songs can be long-lasting, and live performances and recordings help social messages grow even more powerful. If you've got the know-how to create original tunes and lyrics, you've got a super way to promote your cause. However, you don't need to be a singer or songwriter to harness the clout of music. You can promote existing tunes and other forms of protest art. Just make sure any creations you promote fully line up with your values and that you respect copyright and give credit to creators when legally using works.

When it comes to using art as a tool, the only limit is your imagination. This handy quizard will help you figure out places to start.

QUIZARD
FIND THE CREATIVE GENIUS IN YOU

1. If a mysterious gift with my name on it was going to land at my door, I'd prefer:

(A) Drawing software

(B) A snazzy journal and pen set

(C) Face paint

(D) A harmonica

(E) New pencil crayons

(F) A computer printer

2. On a Saturday, I would rather:

(A) Make animation using an app

(B) Write poetry

(C) Go to drama practice

(D) Compose a song

(E) Attend art class

(F) Hand out art exhibition flyers

3. If receiving an award, I'd like it to be for:

(A) Most views

(B) Greatest screenwriter

(C) Most convincing performance

(D) Highest number of downloads

(E) Best portrait

(F) Behind-the-scenes excellence

4. When it's time to relax, I like to:

(A) Write code

(B) Dive into a book

(C) See a stage show

(D) Listen to tunes

(E) Take photos

(F) Look up media contacts

5. My arts activism club would be called:

(A) Star Techies

(B) Pen Warriors

(C) Pure Drama

(D) Listen Up

(E) Picture This

(F) Big Mouth Publicity

QUIZARD RESULTS

If you answered mostly with the letter:

A, you lean toward digital creativity.

B, you favor writing.

C, live performance is your stage.

D, music is your high note.

E, visual arts appeal to you.

F, promotion is under the spotlight.

If it was hard to make selections or your answers jumped around too much to slap a label on, don't worry. More types of artistic expression exist than can fit in a quizard. Advances in technology frequently inspire new creative art forms, and some artists are using their imaginations to create all-out original techniques.

Haisu Tian, for example, attaches ink to her inline skates and glides across rice paper to create landscapes. John Bramblitt, who began to lose his sight at age eleven, uses fabric paint with raised edges to create portraits and other visual creations. Ben Tre carves images on chicken eggshells using a dentist drill.[8] No matter what medium artists use to get creative, they find that communicating through art is a useful tool for promoting social change.

REACH SUPPORTERS WITHOUT SCARING THEM

If someone you don't know approaches you while you're walking down the street and tries to hand you a flyer about a social issue or tries to start a conversation with you so you'll sign a petition, how do you react? After all, you've surely been warned to be cautious of strangers. Perhaps you avoid eye contact and hurry along. Arts activism, on the other hand, offers a less aggressive way to connect with possible supporters. People enjoying the arts are likely to feel relaxed, entertained, and open to new ideas. Like the activists profiled below, seek ways to use creativity to draw people willingly to your project.

TUNE IN!
{Individual, Grassroots Approach, Kenya}

South Sudan was at war when Emmanuel Jal was born. At the age of eight, he became a child soldier. Aided by a British aid worker, Emmanuel escaped the war and attended school in Kenya. Now a peace activist, recording artist, and international hip-hop star, he uses performance and public speaking to build empathy and support for war victims and to deliver messages of peace and forgiveness. Emmanuel has spoken at the UN, to the US Congress, and at gatherings with other high-level government representatives. In 2009, he set up a charity called Gua Africa, which aids those affected by poverty and war in East Africa, especially Kenya. His activism has been recognized with numerous prestigious honors, including the Vaclav Havel International Prize for Creative Dissent award. If your school hosts a Gua Africa fundraiser, Emmanuel might connect with your school via the internet and personally share his story with you and your classmates.[9]

SLAM SOME POETRY!
{Individual, Grassroots Approach, South Africa}

Black, transgender, South African Lee Mokobe is confident language can fuel change. They often share their powerful writing through *slam poetry*—a spoken-word performance where writers present poetry—at competitions that call for audiences to serve as judges. At age nineteen, they gave a TED Talk in which they performed a poem about how it feels to be transgender. It has attracted more than 1.6 million online views. As well as exploring LGBTQ identities, Lee's writing explores African and immigrant rights and other social justice issues. They have presented their work across the globe and founded Vocal Revolutionaries, an award-winning youth arts education organization. It teaches South African youths how to use poetry and art to express themselves and provides mentoring, motivational talks, and opportunities to perform.[10]

ILLUSTRATE A MESSAGE!
{Individual, Grassroots Approach, England}

Banksy is an anonymous England-based graffiti artist, painter, filmmaker, and activist. His distinctive style of art, which communicates political messages, has been spotted around the world. It brings attention to gang violence, homelessness, war, and other serious matters. Banksy's art has become famous, but painting on private walls and erecting art in public spaces is illegal. The artist protects himself from getting arrested by keeping his real identity and name a secret and using the pseudonym "Banksy." The mystery of who the artist is makes people pay even more attention to the work. Many debate whether Banksy's work should be celebrated when others face punishment for vandalism. Some argue about who owns the art left behind and whether the creations should remain public, as that appears to be the intention. At auction, Banksy's art has sold for well over a million pounds. One piece sold in 2021 for £16.8 million ($23.2 million), with funds going to support a UK hospital. Estimates suggest Banksy's art has resulted in nearly £30 million being donated to charity.[11]

WRITE IT DOWN
{Individual, Grassroot Approaches, Canada and Yemen}

Deborah Ellis is an anti-war activist and award-winning author in Canada. Her books include the Breadwinner trilogy (Oxford University Press), which highlights challenges faced by children around the world. Some of her books enable kids to share their experiences, such as *Looks Like Daylight: Voices of Indigenous Kids* and *Three Wishes* (Groundwood Books), which spotlight Israeli and Palestinian children in war-torn regions. Deborah gives most of her royalty income to charitable causes, and the Breadwinner series has triggered more than $1 million in donations.[12]

Another author, Nujood Ali, promotes change by writing about her own experience. Her book, *I Am Nujood, Age 10 and Divorced* (Three Rivers Press), written with Delphine Minoui, tells how she was forced to marry a man three times her age when she was only nine years old. Nujood fled to a court-house and found a lawyer to help her fight against the system that allows child marriage. Her experience sparked change in Yemen and other Middle Eastern countries. Her book shines an important light on the need to enforce children's human rights.[13]

HIT THE STAGE!
{Theatre of the Oppressed, Nonprofit, New York}

Have you ever watched a show and found yourself wanting characters to make a certain choice or behave in a specific way? Theatre of the Oppressed is a form of theater that aims to inspire audiences to do more than wish for a happy ending. Instead, it calls for participants to actively examine problems and rehearse solutions. The style combines education, activism, and performance. It is meant to motivate players to find ways to tackle social obstacles rather than sit back and watch characters sort them out onstage. Theatre of the Oppressed NYC (TONYC) organizes community members from local organizations into sets of theatrical performers, called *troupes*. They create and perform plays based on topics that relate to social, health, and human rights injustices, including racism and economic inequality. After a performance, the actors and audience brainstorm about how to make change on community and political levels as well as personally. TONYC collaborations involve more than sixty performances a year.[14]

BUST A MOVE!

{Individual, Grassroots Approach, Los Angeles, California}

Shamell Bell is a dancer and choreographer. She uses movement to express her political concerns and teaches others how to create change through street dance activism. Shamell wants to transform protest by calling people of all dance abilities to unite in bringing attention to social issues. Dancing is used to build empathy for protestors and the difficulties they face. It provides an opening that makes it easier for protestors to discuss their interests and be heard. One dance protest—about the deaths of unarmed Black people—was held outside the Los Angeles Police Department headquarters. Shamell and LA street dancer Dashawn "Day Day" Blanks taught moves to anyone

who walked by. They wanted dancing to express "Living Is Resisting." An original member of the Black Lives Matter movement, Shamell is also a scholar who studies the intersection of arts and activism.[15]

TAKE A PHOTO!

{Individual, Grassroots Approach, New York}

Builder Levy studied art at Brooklyn College and worked as a public schoolteacher in New York City for thirty-four years. During this time, he became frustrated with the way media portrayed the Black and Hispanic neighborhoods where he worked. To counter racism, Builder began to capture pictures that showed the rich family life and culture he witnessed.

Over a photography career lasting more than fifty years, Builder took photos aimed at highlighting social problems. His images depict civil rights marches, anti-war rallies, under-privileged children, and difficult conditions faced by coal miners. He also photographed social troubles in Mongolia and other developing nations. Builder's photos appear in more than fifty public collections worldwide as well as in books. They are effective in bringing attention to poverty, war, labor conditions, and other struggles.[16]

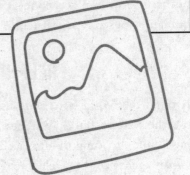

IMAGINE

Imagine your life without photography. You would never see pictures in news stories, advertisements, books, or family albums. You would not know what you looked like when you were younger or how your community looked before you were born. How might a lack of photos change what you know about the world?

MORE THAN ONE WAY TO SOLVE A PROBLEM

Across the globe, war, violence, human rights abuses, and other issues had forced 89.3 million people to flee their homes by the end of 2021. Since this calculation, millions more have escaped Ukraine or been displaced within the country since the war broke out in February 2022, raising the number of refugees to more than 100 million. How can we counter the pain and suffering our fellow human beings are experiencing?[17]

HELP REFUGEES

Around the world, artists are using their talents to respond. Some use their art to build awareness, provide comfort and therapy, or raise funds to support displaced peoples. Others have worked to encourage citizens to welcome refugees and recognize them as individuals whose rights must be respected. These are just a few of the many ways creative people are tackling the refugee crisis.

PUT ON A PLAY
{AnomalousCo, Performance Collective, New York}

AnomalousCo is a queer/woman-led theater company in New York City that creates performances designed to portray urgent social matters. In 2022, it brought together actors and activists from eleven countries to bring attention to the Russian invasion of Ukraine. The company performed its show *(beyond) Doomsday Scrolling*, which references the practice of repeatedly scrolling through bad news when online. Using music and documentary drama, it reveals the experience of war and being forced to flee your home. It also examines the difficulties faced by Russians against the war. The show's unique approach includes sharing the exact words of people impacted by the conflict. At the end of the performance, a journalist-led discussion invited the audience to explore ways to address the crisis.

Rather than setting a ticket price, organizers advertised the event as *pay-what-you-can*. They raised $11,500 for Ukraine refugee relief. As well as going toward medical supplies, funds were used to assist artists and cultural NGOs in Ukraine and to help give Ukrainians opportunities to make themselves heard.[18]

MAKE A FLOATING SCULPTURE
{Schellekens & Peleman,
Visual-Artists Collective, Belgium}

In Belgium, a visual-artists collective wanted to draw attention to refugee crises around the world. Schellekens & Peleman created a twenty-foot-tall (six-meter-tall) inflatable sculpture of a man in a life jacket sitting on the deck of a wooden boat, his arms clasped around his knees. The sculpture was symbolically made of stuff too flimsy to withstand waves, such as low-quality inflatable rafts—the same material human traffickers use to transport passengers across the Mediterranean Sea, when they load more passengers than the boats are designed to safely carry. Displayed on a boat and towed, the sculpture shows how refugees are *dehumanized*—subjected to conditions or treatment that take away human dignity. The artwork was designed to inspire spectators to think about refugees' needs and human rights.[19]

To further break down barriers between the local community and refugees, the collective initiated a letter-writing campaign called Moving Stories. Migrants were asked to handwrite letters explaining how they became refugees. Their messages were translated and copied 166 times—once for each nationality in Belgium. While walking around the Belgium capital region of Antwerp, the refugees chose mailboxes at apartments and houses and posted their letters, which included postcards inviting recipients to mail back a reply. Planners hoped that communicating with migrants would help citizens develop more informed opinions. The project, which saw fifty postcards returned, enabled important conversations.[20]

HELP PEOPLE TELL THEIR STORIES
{Child and Youth Refugee Research Coalition;
Alliance of Academics, Community Groups,
and Government Agencies; Canada}

The Child and Youth Refugee Research Coalition (CYRRC) assists refugee children and youths in Canada. This alliance of academics, community groups, and government agencies accomplishes its goals through arts-based research and by working directly with kids at events that invite participants to use creativity to express their ideas and experiences. One CYRRC project involved inviting youths to take part in activism and social justice workshops and create art in different forms, including painting, poetry, photography, and storytelling. Participants gained empowering artistic skills. They also benefited from the chance to be around others with similar backgrounds and challenges, such as living in temporary camps and moving to new countries.

The coalition found that engaging in the arts helped kids cope with difficulties and offered them ways to communicate even when they did not speak local languages. Art consumers got to witness immigrant stories, not only when refugees first arrived, but also as they continued to build lives in their new home country. This gave members of the public an opportunity to see beyond stereotypes associated with young refugees.[21]

EXPLORE MORE

One way of connecting with newcomers is by speaking to them in their native language. While mastering a language could take years, learning a few words and phrases is doable. Find out what languages people in your community speak. Access a translator app, and practice a set of words and phrases, such as "hello," "good-bye," "how are you," "have a nice day," and "thank you." You'll discover how it feels to try to learn and speak a new language. This is going to trigger some serious empathy! It will also show newcomers important things: you're friendly, you see them as individuals, and you're making an effort to connect.

SPOTLIGHT ON . . .

The Center for Artistic Activism

In 2009, the Center for Artistic Activism (C4AA) in New York recognized that activists were growing frustrated. Petitions, marches, and other traditional ways of seeking change didn't seem effective enough. The organization also noticed that artists wanted to use their skills to bring about social change but didn't know how. It decided to offer programs to help marginalized individuals share their unique perspectives and use their creativity to gain power and build change. Since then, thousands of people from hundreds of organizations around the United States and in nearly forty other countries have taken part in training.

C4AA has helped them brainstorm and develop strategies for matters relating to undocumented youths, mothers of imprisoned youths, LGBTQ communities, war veterans, and life under oppressive and corrupt governments.

The not-for-profit shares its research through methods that include lectures, webinars, podcasts, and a database that shows how others have combined arts and activism to improve democracy and further human rights. C4AA has published a book called *The Art of Activism: Your All-Purpose Guide to Making the Impossible Possible*. It guides readers on how to make strategic plans that harness the emotional appeal of the arts.[22]

MEET A YOUNG ACTIVIST
Sonita Alizadeh

To escape Taliban rule, Sonita Alizadeh and her family fled from Afghanistan to a camp in Iran, where they lived as undocumented refugees. She learned to read and write through an NGO and became interested in poetry and music. Her parents tried to sell her as a bride at age ten, but the contract was not completed. Sonita was not forced to marry, but the issue was not dropped or forgotten. When Sonita was sixteen, her parents tried to sell her once more, hoping to get enough money to purchase a bride for her brother in Afghanistan. Sonita protested against their plans again, but this time she did something more public. She wrote and recorded a rap song called "Daughters for Sale." The video went viral and brought attention to the demeaning tradition of selling daughters for money. In Afghanistan, $500-$2,000 often buys a bride, with prices depending on a girl's beauty, reputation, and age (parents are paid more for younger daughters.) A family's status along with price trends in their community also affect price.[23] At first, Sonita's parents were angry with her for rebelling against their marriage plans. Eventually, though, her success in music and at school helped them realize girls can be strong, make decisions about their futures, and support themselves. Finally, Sonita's parents stopped pressuring her to marry, and when her sister also refused a marriage prospect, they did not force her to comply.

Sonita realized that if she could change the way her family thought, she could also influence other people to see girls as more than future wives and mothers. She now advocates for other people to lead the change in their own countries because they are in the best position to understand how traditions, poverty, and lack of education can lead to forced child marriages.

A powerful role model, Sonita continues activism to end child marriage around the world. She uses music to encourage others to rethink destructive traditions that turn children into sexual and domestic slaves. She calls for families, politicians, traditional leaders, and communities to change the way girls are treated.

Sonita is involved with a UK charity called Girls Not Brides: The Global Partnership to End Child Marriage. It has more than 1,600 member organizations in over one hundred countries, and 40 percent of these organizations are youth-led. Along with other champions and international human rights activists including the late Archbishop Desmond Tutu and Mrs. Graça Machel, Sonita amplifies the voices of girls at risk. She defends girls' rights to stay in school, be healthy, and live lives of their own choosing.

In 2015, a film called *Sonita* was released. It tells the story of how she responded to finding out she was worth $9,000 as a bride. The awareness her music and film generated led to an invitation for her to attend school in the United States, where Sonita continues her work to help girls.[24]

SATISFY YOUR CURIOSITY

It's fascinating to see how activists use the arts to champion change. Check out these terms and creators online, and think about how you might get involved:

- Arts and activism
- Emmanuel Jal
- Banksy
- Shamell Bell
- AnomalousCo
- Nujood Ali and Delphine Minoui
- Theatre of the Oppressed
- *Inflatable Refugee* by Schellekens & Peleman
- Child and Youth Refugee Research Coalition
- Get Lit, Los Angeles
- Lee Mokobe
- Deborah Ellis
- Builder Levy
- Sonita Alizadeh

11

KEEP GOING

ACCEPTING THE PACE OF PROGRESS AND STAYING POSITIVE

"At such moments I don't think about all the misery, but about the beauty that still remains."

Anne Frank, author of *The Diary of a Young Girl*,
Germany/the Netherlands

ow! You have marched through a pile of social issues. It's been an eye-opening human rights journey through violence, poverty, and community crises. We've talked about frogs and dogs and performing animals as well as habitat loss, pollution, and climate change. In fact, we've rocketed all the way to outer space with a look at Moon ownership, weapons in space, and asteroid mining. All that, and you're still here! It's clear that caring and compassion are part of your makeup. I think you've stuck around for another reason too. The activists you've met here—from the boy promoting motorcycle helmet safety to the teen rapping about child marriage—have shown you how to take action and what can result. They each demonstrate inspiring ways to build the world you want to see—a place where people live in peace, animals do not suffer, and the environment is sustainable. It's plain to see that when young people tackle serious concerns, others pay attention. Like the changemakers spotlighted in each chapter, you have the ability to inspire and make change. You have the grit and imagination to take problems and make them smaller. Your intellect recognizes that achieving change in this complicated world can be more than a dream; it can be a realistic goal.

Including adults!

When you research activists and examine their progress, look for clues on how long they've been at it. Keep in mind that a single paragraph can piece together work, events, and successes that took months or years to complete. It's not often that achievements are as quick as we hope. You might think of activism as a *quest*—a long and challenging effort to do something. One important truth, though, is that it's more satisfying to succeed when you've worked hard to overcome difficulties. Consider, for example, the emotion you would feel picking up a pencil compared to how you would feel raising a hundred-pound weight.

Forgettable.

As an activist, perseverance is one of the most important characteristics you can develop. Your ability to keep going will help

Thrilling!

you make the most headway, even when setbacks make you want to vent some steam. Fortunately, there are at least as many ways to deal with your frustration as there are letters in the English alphabet.

When you need a little break to help you keep things in perspective, try one of these aggravation blasters:

A) Hug a tree.

B) Pet an animal.

C) Make art.

D) Recite a tongue twister.

E) Turn up the tunes and dance.

F) Dash around a park.

G) Learn a yoga pose.

H) Splash water on your face.

I) Shout into a cushion.

J) Stargaze.

K) Write a limerick.

L) Relax in a bathtub.

M) Clean something.

N) Play a beat using chopsticks.

O) Watch a sunrise or sunset.

P) Make a list.

Q) Stand on your head.

R) Doodle on some paper.

S) Belt out a song.

T) Take a nature walk.

U) Count to ten in another language.

V) Organize something.

W) Enjoy a good cry.

> Kids on quests quietly quash chaos.

> Like the bathtub!

> If that's too easy, try it backward.

X) Feel the sun upon your face.

Y) Stretch to be as tall as you can.

Z) Smell flowers.

BEWARE OF THE BOTTLENECK

Why does progress sometimes take so long? What kind of hold-ups are we talking about? For starters, elements of your project may depend on others agreeing to take action or to share relevant data with you. You can't control when people will get back to you with the information it takes to move forward. Everyone has different habits and ways of behaving. Some act quickly. Others *procrastinate*—intentionally put off actions that should be done. You might find yourself waiting for someone in authority to answer your questions, make a decision, or schedule meetings. Volunteers might fail to complete what they agreed to do. Perhaps you can't take certain steps until you raise funds. Sometimes the problem is closer to home. For example, you might be forced to wait for your sister to get off the computer or for an adult to drive you across town. It can go on and on, making you feel frustrated and impatient, but don't give up on people. It takes persistence to make great change, and it's hard to make progress alone. Just remember your end goal, and how important it is, as you strike up the resolve to reach out to the slowpokes on your list one more time.

Other delays to your cause can come in the form of natural elements. Suppose your project depends on seasonal activities, like frogs migrating, and you need to wait for winter to turn to spring. A snowstorm could force your school to cancel classes on the day of your special event, or a lightning strike could cause a power outage that stops you from printing your posters and other promo materials when you need them most. Holdups can come out of nowhere! Try to accept that delays and interruptions are normal. At times, things will work out exactly as you planned. But not always.

A bottleneck is something that slows progress.

Right?

Suppose you list a *to do* item on your calendar and find you must keep moving it forward. Occasionally, the *bottleneck* isn't other people—it's you! It can be tricky to find as much time as you like for your goals. Let's face it, you have other things to do, like homework and helping around the house. Your days might include music lessons, drama club, sports, babysitting, or other obligations. Sometimes, too, you're going to just want to hang around with your buddies.

News alert! It's 100 percent okay to take the breaks you need. In fact, it's essential. Downtime is important, and you must enjoy it guilt-free. *Wait a minute* (I hear you thinking). *How could this be? Isn't activism the most important thing?* In fact, downtime can help your activism.

Scientists report that the human brain is still active during idle time, and taking time to daydream can even help you overcome frustrations. It's as if relaxing takes your mind to a special place where worries untangle without direct effort on your part. While there's no guarantee a break will solve a problem, a useful idea may very well come to you.

Taking breaks will help you:

Be more productive

Stay motivated

Make sense of things you've just learned

See what happens if you simply sit and daydream, but if that's too much stillness for you, try a mindless activity like walking or picking lint off your clothes or picking lint while you walk. You might think video games or television count as mindless pastimes, but these activities do call for focus and won't free your thoughts in the same way.[1] Too bad!

BRAIN NUGGET

The paragraph above is based on *scientific evidence*—facts collected by testing predictions and analyzing data in a process called the scientific method. The paragraph below is *anecdotal evidence*—information based on individual observation or experience. An *anecdote* is a personal story, and you already know about the power they can hold. In this case, the story supports the scientific evidence. Sometimes, though, anecdotes present unproven claims as fact. Remember to always consider the source of any information you use to support your cause.

Now to my story—a true confession. After several hours of writing, I get stuck. My sentences won't work. They're stubborn. I just can't wrestle them into shape. (Is it possible the office parakeet has pointed a wing at my keyboard and delivered a curse?) I try to persevere until a glance at the clock makes me realize it's the time each day when my brain says stop. Luckily, I've found a solution. I haul myself outside for a walk. It's like a magic wand on my problem. My brain gets its break, and my body gets a stretch. When my hands return to the keyboard, I can rearrange my disastrous compilation into usable sentences with much less effort. In fact, I can't believe the passage was ever a puzzle.

I could have said *masterpieces,* but then my story would contain an unproven claim.

Now you have both scientific and anecdotal evidence for how taking breaks, instead of relentlessly pursuing your goals, can help you achieve more.[2]

To ensure progress and reduce frustration, keep your goals clear. Ask yourself, What's the most important thing I can do this week to move my project forward? What do I want to have done after one, three, and six months? Where do I want to be at this time next year? If progress is slower than expected, how should I adjust my approach?

When out-of-your-control delays interrupt your main goals, creep forward with other activities. Look for ways to build awareness, make your communications stand out, and bring others to your cause.

What would you add to this list?

Look up *how to build a simple website* and create a place where you can share information about your activities.

Turn a pet into a mascot for your cause. Make a promo sign, and photograph your animal cheerleader next to it. Arrange to share the images on social media.

Make a vision board. Cut words and pictures from old magazines, and glue them on a poster board to help visualize the future you want to see.

Bring attention to the good work other activists are doing. Tell their stories, one conversation at a time.

Organize a scavenger hunt. Make a list of rules, such as where participants can go and the time limit. Charge teams a fee, and offer winners 30 percent of the profits. Connect the hunt to your cause by making sure everyone knows how the funds will be used.

Design a quizard game show to test knowledge of your topic. Make cards with "yes" on one side and "no" on the other, and instruct players to hold up their answers. Play at family gatherings, and arrange to bring it to classes at your school.

Research how to create an effective logo. Design an image to represent your cause, and use it on letters, posters, and other communications.

Research nonprofits in your community. Find one you admire, and schedule a visit to its headquarters for you and an adult family member. Bring a list of questions.

Write a letter or email to a VIP. Describe what you're trying to accomplish, and then respectfully ask for help promoting your activities.

Create a board game that teaches important facts about your issue. Ask your school library to lend it out to teachers and other students.

Set up spare-change jars to collect coins for your cause. Label them with details about how the money will be used, and ask family members to take a jar to work, or ask local businesses to keep one near the register.

Ask your school to host a superhero day. Students can create original costumes or dress up as a superhero they admire. Tie the event to your theme by asking participants to donate to your super cause in exchange for taking part.

THE WHISPERED WORD

As well as delays, you may experience something people don't always want to talk about. I'm talking about what happens when you try to do something and it doesn't work out. It's usually called f-a-i-l-u-r-e. Is this a word that should be spelled out in a shameful whisper? No! Let me say it in all its glory: FAILURE! Prepare yourself to now read an amazing truth. Stand up. Hold the book tightly. Snap your heels together, and read the next paragraph out loud.

Failure is not a bad word. It is not fatal, nor a permanent condition. In fact, it can be an important experience that steers you toward higher achievement. Just as good activists know better than to slap labels on other people, don't tag yourself a failure if things don't go as planned. Instead, view upsets as opportunities that steer you toward better ways to rock your goals.

> Actually, animals go through trial and error too. Have you ever watched a bird learn to fly?

Humans learn by making mistakes. Maybe you can't remember your tiny tot years, but you did not learn to walk without falling or speak clearly without first mispronouncing words.

> Smaghetti, anyone?

You had to try again and again to get better, just as you will need to practice at being an activist. Accept that fumbles are normal and expected parts of the process. Take pride in the fact that you keep going, even when things fall apart. Activism will help you grow comfortable with struggle. Setbacks will help you become adaptable, creative, and skilled at making decisions. Obstacles will help you learn how to develop work-around solutions and move forward. There are always times when we need to manage disappointments, but with practice, it becomes easier to take events in stride and maintain *optimism*—the tendency to bring a positive outlook to things that happen and expect the best possible result. An optimistic outlook, for example, might see barriers simply as temporary delays. This attitude worked for Thomas Alva Edison, inventor of the light bulb and holder of more than one thousand patents. Edison was not afraid to fail. In fact, he once said, "I have not failed 10,000 times—I've successfully found 10,000 ways that will not work."[3]

BENEFITS OF FAILURE

You discover how to:

Identify skills you need to learn

Find better ways to do things

Anticipate difficulties in advance

Get comfortable with discomfort

Judge others less harshly

Accept struggles as challenges you can manage

Look at problems from more than one angle

Choose when it makes the most sense to take risks

One way to manage your workflow and line yourself up for success is by following Anna DeVolld's example. Anna became a changemaker in Alaska after getting curious about the bees she saw gathering on sunflowers. She discovered that habitat loss and pesticides are serious issues for pollinating species and that food production and plant sustainability depend on pollinators. Anna realized that the most effective way to help would be to start small and move on to bigger goals after she built a solid foundation. Step by step, the high school senior grew an award-winning education program called Promote Our Pollinators (POP).[4]

HELP! I DON'T KNOW HOW TO BE A LEADER

Picture this: You've found a cause you want to pursue and chosen a strategy to make change. You've even got a team of people who want to help you. Suddenly you're a leader! People are looking to you for direction. They're asking things like "What's next?" "What should we do?" and "How should we do it?" You may know some of the answers. Others, you're going to have to think about. When you're not sure, be honest. You can say:

- "I don't know, but I'll answer you once I have more info."
- "Let's talk about this as a group. Many minds are better than one!"
- "What do you think is the best approach?"
- "Let's pick three solutions and then narrow it down to one."
- "I'm not ready to give you a definite answer. Let's talk about this soon."

Leaders are people who motivate others. They understand that others may do things differently than they would, but that can be okay. Rather than bossing everyone around, they find ways to bring out the best in their teams. Leadership skills grow with practice.

BE THE CHANGE

Intolerance occurs when people don't approve of views, beliefs, or behaviors that are different than their own. Help promote peace by acting and leading with *tolerance*. This means treating everyone with respect, even if their opinions or behaviors upset or annoy you. Trying to understand others, rather than judging them, is one way to reduce prejudice. Be the change by being curious!

MAKE YOUR ACTIVISM HAPPY

One way to keep yourself and volunteers motivated is to add elements of fun. Taking part in activism should make participants happy and build a sense of community, not create a weighty burden—even when dealing with a serious issue. Remember the old saying "You catch more flies with honey than with vinegar."

In this case, flies are a good thing! You get that, right?

Here are some tips to help you get started.

○ Give genuine compliments when you see good work. Say thank you, and let helpers know you value them. Find creative ways to show appreciation like:

→ Play the name game with your fellow volunteers. Choose complimentary adjectives that start with the first letter of their name, and then post them somewhere visible, along with their photos—*Amazing Amelia, Clever Clarke, Notable Nujood, Terrific Toni, Marvelous Mae, Stupendous Sonita, Jazzy James, Mighty Michael, Edward Eagle-Eyes.*

→ Choose a song with meaningful lyrics, and dedicate it to your group at the start of a meeting or event. You never know, it may end up becoming your theme song.

→ Use sidewalk chalk to write decorative thank-you messages where volunteers will be arriving.

→ Give your team something to look forward to by planning potluck cookie parties after milestones are reached.

→ Write a personal note reminding helpers that you're thankful for their contributions.

○ Help your team learn from one another. Create a wall space where participants post comments written on sticky paper. Ask them to share successes as well as the obstacles they face. Invite the group to offer solutions.

Problem: No one returns my calls.
The Fix: After three tries, I send a handwritten note.

Problem: People act like this isn't a serious issue.
The Fix: Try firing off a bunch of statistics and quoting the source.

Problem: I feel funny asking
for donations.
The Fix: I remind myself that I'm not
asking for money for me. It's for an
important cause and for people who can't
ask for themselves. I even say this when
asking for donations.

Problem: I've never done this before.
The Fix: Ask if you can start by helping
someone with experience.

Problem: There's so much to do. I don't
know where to start.
The Fix: I make a list and alternate between one
easy item and one trickier item.

Another way to build happy experiences is with leadership that creates atmospheres where everyone can feel they belong. Remember the importance of having a sense of community? Try these approaches to keep things upbeat and to smooth your way when working with others:

○ Lead by example. Work alongside your squad, and show them how it's done. There are times when you need to delegate, but if you don't put in the work you ask of others, they may not follow you.

- Give clear directions, followed by questions such as, "Is there anything you're not sure about?" or "Is there something you'd like to ask?"

- Be careful not to desert your volunteers. Keep in touch to ask how it's going. Expect that some people will ask questions or share ideas when you're one-on-one, but not in front of a group.

- Ask for help when you need it. Find people with leadership experience, and ask them for advice when you feel stuck. Parents, teachers, coaches, or other mentors may have helpful solutions.

NIMBY AND BANANA

Suppose you've worked hard to highlight a situation such as homelessness. Your contacts share the opinion that this situation must be improved and affordable housing is the answer. Unfortunately, not everyone agrees on the best location for housing.

Residents often believe high-density housing developments in their neighborhood will lead to unwanted consequences, fearing increased traffic, that property values will fall, and that crime levels will go up. Homeowners claim that housing complexes in their neighborhoods make it difficult for residents to resell their homes. They may also worry that newcomers will have different values and *social norms*—the informal rules we perceive that guide acceptable behavior within a social group or culture.

Social norms include personal habits such as how close to stand to someone you're speaking to or whether to take your shoes off before entering a home.

Not wanting certain infrastructure close to home is an outlook commonly called *NIMBY*. It stands for *not in my backyard*. Activists may encounter the NIMBY attitude when discussing where to locate different types of infrastructure, including:

- Affordable housing
- Homeless shelters
- Wind turbines
- Power lines
- Pipelines
- Landfill sites
- Nursing homes
- Firearms stores
- Nuclear waste storage facilities
- Accommodation for refugees

Another acronym—*BANANA*—stands for *building absolutely nothing anywhere near anything* (or *anyone*). If you encounter these stances, don't despair. Instead, pull out the best tools at your disposal: education and consultation. Find out what residents are saying about the proposed project, and correct any misunderstandings. They may not have all the facts. If their concerns are valid, ask them to offer solutions.

You might arrange consultation through an *open house*—an informal gathering that allows people to meet and talk. Residents who speak directly with city or town planners, architects, and builders may feel reassured, especially if planners can showcase similar projects they have completed. You might even get some residents to change their outlook to *YIMBY*—*yes, in my backyard.*

GET CHATTY

Activism teaches you to adapt to change, make decisions, and manage emotions. Instead of dwelling on your own problems, you shift your focus outside yourself and put your effort into something worthwhile. As well as helping you discover your own abilities, volunteering is good for mental health. Ask the people around you, what other benefits do activism and volunteering bring?

THE FUTURE

The issues that capture your interest today may hold your attention for many years to come. You might continue to promote the causes you care about as you attend high school, college, or university. Perhaps you'll decide to carry on with advocacy while working full-time, or choose to make tackling social causes a full-time career. The activities you take on now will expose you to many different activism-related jobs. You may meet politicians, reporters, nonprofit directors, scientists, and others who use their roles to promote or make change. Some of their activities and tasks are sure to pop out as extra interesting to you. Perhaps they get to work with elephants; travel to interesting places; or speak to government leaders, famous people, or other VIPs. You might find yourself thinking, *Wow, I can't believe people get paid for this. I wouldn't mind that job.* If that happens, pay attention. This period of your life is the perfect time to ask questions, think about what you might like to learn more about, and explore where you might fit.

IMAGINE

If you could change one thing in the world today, what would it be? Imagine how the future would look if enough people worked together to shrink this problem.

JOBS WITH ACTIVISM ROLES

Whether or not you choose to make activism a career, the experience you gain now can help you inch toward your employment goals. The smallest thing may turn out to be important. As a twelve-year-old, I volunteered at a nature center where I learned how to use a film projector.

> A film projector is a type of tech that was once the go-to way to show movies.

Fast-forward to early adulthood when I applied for a job in an audio-visual department at a vocational school. My interviewer wanted to know if I'd be comfortable learning how to run a projector, and I was able to say that I already knew how. I later learned that this skill got me the job. He didn't want the hassle of training a *technophobe*—someone scared of technology.

Imagine how your advocacy abilities might make you stand out when it comes to applying for a job or post-secondary program. What skills, you ask? Activism can help you learn how to be a leader, organize a project, raise funds, and communicate information.

You might learn to:

- Use helpful apps or computer programs
- Make spreadsheets

- Write and send effective emails and letters
- Reach and speak to people by telephone
- Write and deliver speeches
- Excel at debate
- Take messages
- Manage time
- Organize people
- Conduct research
- Stick to a budget
- Keep financial records
- Speak to media

You may even become an expert on your favorite topic, like Dessi Sieburth, who knows a lot about birds; Josiah Utsch, who supports nautilus research; or Duncan Jurman, who shares butterfly facts.

Many of the jobs described here will require a university education. In some cases, experience will be especially valued.

Fundraisers manage campaigns to raise money for charities, political candidates, events, and activities. People in this role must demonstrate perseverance, money management, and communication skills.

Legal professionals including lawyers and *paralegals* (professionals who assist lawyers) provide legal advice to people encountering injustice and hardship, such as people experiencing family violence or immigrants seeking citizenship. They also help organizations trying to bring about change.

Victim advocates guide crime victims through the court system. They help survivors cope with challenges by sharing their knowledge of the justice process. Police, nonprofits, and prosecutor offices may employ victim advocates.

Social workers help individuals and families manage and overcome personal challenges including addiction, homelessness, poverty, family violence, and other problems. They often work with vulnerable populations.

Project managers use communication and organization skills to manage project tasks and find solutions that help organizations, such as nonprofits, achieve their goals.

Researchers provide the information and evidence that activists need to support the claims they make and the solutions they propose. Researchers gather and analyze information, create statistics, and communicate their findings in clear language.

Communications jobs cover a lot of territory. Charities and other organizations aimed at activism may need writers, editors, publicity and social media experts, photographers, illustrators, or translators to help communicate their messages. They may employ communicators in-house or hire freelance experts to work about specific projects.[5]

Journalists gather information and report on it in print, digital, and broadcast media. They use their communication skills to raise awareness about important issues.

Policy analysts conduct research on topics such as climate change, criminal justice, the environment, food security, health, national security, and other challenges. They analyze situations, raise awareness, and form policies used by governments and other organizations.

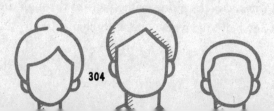

Sustainability specialists guide organizations on how to best operate in ways that meet current needs without upsetting the ability to meet future needs. This might include finding ways to reduce waste, save energy, reduce emissions, and meet environmental regulations.

SUSTAINABLE ACTIVISM

Do you remember the two families with peach trees? The first chopped down their tree and burned its wood. The second one practiced sustainability, allowing future generations to enjoy both fruit and shade. If you want your activism to deliver benefits into the future, you'll need to practice personal sustainability. That means not allowing your devotion to lead to *burnout*—stress and exhaustion that comes from trying to do too much.

If you're constantly frustrated, take a break. If you feel overwhelmed or discouraged, take time out. If you're juggling too many activities and they are affecting your ability to meet other obligations in your life, step away for a while. Trying to do too much, too fast, can wear you out. Prevent overfatigue by taking time to be kind to yourself. If you don't, the vision and excitement you bring to your projects might fade. You might struggle to do your best work, and begin to feel like giving up.

Instead, remember that you are one individual. Do what you can to the best of your abilities, and celebrate your progress along the way. When things get tough, repeat this: "Saving the world is not solely my responsibility or my sole responsibility."

The world is made up of many communities, and when you feel overburdened and take a break, others will be working and making progress. When you feel recharged, society will welcome you back.

You have the qualities to succeed, and I know this because you're reading this book, and that reveals more about you than a psychic could ever guess. If you're interested in activism, it's safe to say that you are curious, compassionate, thoughtful, energetic, and open to new ideas. Take the time to enjoy new experiences. Look for goodness, as well as problems to solve. Taking the time to observe and examine qualities like honor, kindness, and justice will inspire your efforts. Most of all, take pleasure and pride in using your zest and sense of right to help create the world you want to live in.

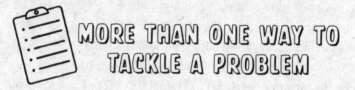

MORE THAN ONE WAY TO TACKLE A PROBLEM

One way to help others understand a cause and support solutions is to provide clear facts backed by evidence. It's tough to win people over when conflicting claims or misleading data get in the way. When evidence is scarce, people find it easier to walk away than make decisions. For this reason, effective activism organizations make a point of letting the public know where their data comes from. Steering clear of false claims, they use science-based evidence to tackle important issues.

PROVE YOUR POINT

The organizations below use effective communication to encourage change. They release position statements, produce educational materials, and remind people to pay attention to evidence-based science. Their approaches make it easier for people to understand their work and make informed decisions.

MAKE DEMANDS
{Fridays for Future, Global Movement, Sweden}

Every day, for three weeks in 2018, Greta Thunberg skipped school to protest outside the Swedish parliament to demand action on the climate crisis. Other strikers joined the fifteen-year-old activist, and they decided to continue striking on Fridays. The hashtag #FridaysForFuture came to represent their message. The Fridays for Future (FFF) movement spread around the world as students and other activists called for governments to take climate change science seriously and commit to change.

FFF organized the Summer Meeting in Lausanne Europe (SMILE) and issued a joint statement by four hundred activists from thirty-eight countries. It outlined their purpose and goals as well as their approach as a nonviolent movement. The statement lists clear demands, including a call to leaders to pay attention to the best science available and follow the historic Paris Agreement, which sets long-term goals to guide nations in tackling the climate crisis.[6] FFF strikes have taken place all over the world. In just three years of reporting, over sixteen thousand events were held.[7]

In addition to inspiring international climate activism, Greta is a role model to those also living with a form of autism spectrum disorder often still called by its former name: *Asperger's syndrome*—a condition that includes finding it difficult to relate to others socially. Being open about her diagnosis and calling it her "superpower" has empowered others to better appreciate themselves.[8]

PRODUCE EDUCATIONAL MATERIALS
{Masks4Canada, Grassroots Approach, Canada}

Masks4Canada formed during the COVID-19 pandemic. Its members are all volunteers who share a goal—to help people in Canada protect themselves from the virus by making health and safety decisions based on scientifically proven facts. Made up of medical doctors, scientists, academics, lawyers, teachers, other professionals, and students and parents, the organization shares information with the public and all levels of government. It sends decision-makers *open letters*—correspondences that are published so that anyone may read them. The letters urge governments to create fair, evidence-based public health guidelines.

The initiative provides scientific evidence that supports mask wearing, physical distancing, hand hygiene, and room ventilation and filtration. Masks4Canada suggests safety protocols for healthcare workers and offers tips for keeping safe at school and at holiday gatherings and events like those held at Halloween. As well as producing videos, infographics, and other educational materials, the organization invited students to assist by creating graphics aimed at helping people manage their mental health during the pandemic.[9]

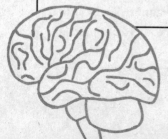

DEFEND SCIENCE

{Union of Concerned Scientists, Nonprofit, Massachusetts}

The Union of Concerned Scientists uses evidence-based research to tackle urgent global problems. Think climate change, nuclear war, and sustainable ways to provide food, power, and transportation. The union's members—nearly 250 scientists, analysts, policy experts, and other professionals—seek practical solutions to ensure a safe world. They make it easy for others to get involved by providing wording for letters that can be sent directly from their website to the US president's administration, members of Congress, and others in authority. The union battles misinformation and works to make sure the US government makes decisions based on facts. It surveys scientists to gather data on harassment and works to expose political leaders who pressure scientists to distort or suppress scientific findings. With an impressive scope of work over more than fifty years and more than five hundred thousand supporters, the union focuses on advocacy that serves the common good. It wants all people to enjoy the same advantages.[10]

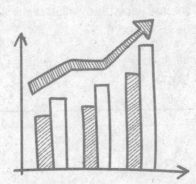

EXPLORE MORE

Find your way to a bookstore or library and explore these books about how other activists have found ways to shake things up.

You Are Mighty: A Guide to Changing the World by Caroline Paul (Bloomsbury Children's Books, 2018)

Count Me In by Varsha Bajaj (Nancy Paulsen Books, 2020)

It's Your World: Get Informed, Get Inspired & Get Going! by Chelsea Clinton (Puffin Books, 2017)

I Am Malala: How One Girl Stood Up for Education and Changed the World (Young Readers Edition) by Malala Yousafzai and Patricia McCormick (Little, Brown Books for Young Readers, 2016)

I Will Always Write Back: How One Letter Changed Two Lives by Martin Ganda, Caitlin Alifirenka, and Liz Welch (Little, Brown Books for Young Readers, 2016)

Anti-Racist Art Activities for Kids: 30+ Creative Projects that Celebrate Diversity and Inspire Change by Anti-Racist Art Teachers: Abigail Birhanu, Khadesia Latimer, Paula Liz, Lori Santos, Tamara Slade, and Anjali Wells (Quarto Publishing Group USA, 2023)

Momentus: Small Acts, Big Change by Hannah Alper (Nelson Trade, 2017)

MEET A YOUNG ACTIVIST
Hannah Alper

Hannah Alper believes in the power of young people. She was nine years old in 2013 when she decided to write a blog. Her parents told her it should not be a diary of her day-to-day life. Instead, they encouraged her to write about something she felt passionate about.

Thinking through what that meant, Hannah asked herself questions like, *What do I care most about? What do I want to tell the world?* She decided to highlight environmental problems, blogging about how small actions can trigger change, and encouraging others to act too. Hannah received feedback on her posts, and eventually her interests expanded into anti-bullying, clean water, education, hunger, poverty, and other social concerns. She became involved with organizations focused on activism, and this resulted in her first public speaking engagement. At age ten, Hannah spoke to an audience of twenty thousand other young activists. It left her feeling energized!

Hannah continued to accept speaking opportunities, including a TEDx Talk. At age thirteen, she began to amplify her messages using social media. It enabled her to reach even more people with her original formula: issue + gift = change. The formula encourages matching the issue you care about with your gift—the approach you'll take to improve the world.

Hannah went on to write a book called *Momentus: Small Acts, Big Change*. Creating it involved personally interviewing nineteen inspiring social activists.

While continuing to use her voice for change on many different issues, Hannah entered a university journalism program in 2021.[11]

Including celebrities!

SPOTLIGHT ON . . .
DoSomething.org

The nonprofit DoSomething.org makes it easy for youths to strengthen their own communities. It invites people to get involved in making change by signing up for one of its civic actions, social-change movements, or other efforts. With more than three hundred research-backed campaigns on the DoSomething.org website, it's easy for participants to research different causes and ways to help. Participants can perform either in-person or online volunteering and choose from more than a dozen causes including animal welfare, education, mental health, racial injustice, gun safety, and sexual harassment.

One popular project, Teens for Jeans, invited youths to collect gently used jeans for their peers in homeless shelters. The organization advised students on how to run denim drives, and 4,990 schools got involved. Aéropostale partnered on the scheme and placed drop-off bins at its US retail stores. As well as collecting 132,295 pairs of jeans and empowering youths to act, the campaign taught participants about the struggles of youths experiencing homelessness.

DoSomething.org gives participants certificates recognizing their work, enabling them to gain volunteer credit hours for school. It also offers volunteers who are US citizens the chance to win scholarships. Based in New York, DoSomething.org is active in every US state and 131 countries.[12]

BE A CHAMPION OF CHANGE

As you pursue your quest for an ideal world—one that respects human rights, treats all species with compassion, and supports a sustainable planet—remember the image of a long string connecting one social issue to another (see page 18). Finding solutions will mean both zeroing in on dilemmas and taking a giant step back to look at them from every angle. Taking the time to "circle" your concerns will help you find the best way to grab hold of that string, unsnarl the tangles, and loosen the knots. Return to this book as you take on new challenges, and use it to spark ideas and help you build the communities and world you want to see. With patience and perseverance, you will grow your natural strengths and build new talents to be an effective and important champion of change.

SATISFY YOUR CURIOSITY

Use these search terms on the internet to add to your knowledge and be an activism ace:

- NIMBY
- YIMBY
- Activism jobs
- Fridays for Future
- Greta Thunberg superpower
- Masks4Canada
- Union of Concerned Scientists
- Anna DeVolld
- Hannah Alper
- DoSomething.org

CONCLUSION

> "A change is brought about because ordinary people
> do extraordinary things."
>
> Barack Obama, 44th president, United States

Around the world, kids just like you are standing up for human rights. They're also raising their voices about rights for animals, our planet, and even outer space! Their experiences reveal the many ways to work either individually or with others to achieve change. Every one of the success stories shared within these pages proves it doesn't matter how old you are if you want to make a difference.

If at any point you feel stuck in your efforts, turn to the tales of others who devote themselves to a cause. Their creative approaches are sure to motivate and inspire you. Look for activism stories in books, in newspapers, in magazines, and online. I know that I would have been in a better position to guide my daughter, Amy, when she first came to me

Watch out! If you ask me a question like Amy did, I might answer with an entire book!

with her concern for child soldiers, if I'd had a book like this as a reference.

Since that time, we've both found ways to contribute to the world we want to see. In junior high, Amy and some like-minded classmates created a PowerPoint presentation about children experiencing poverty in Myanmar and shared what they'd learned with the other grade-nine classes in her school. They collected donations and gave the money they raised to an organization that helped children in Myanmar who were in need. When refugees fled the civil war in Syria and came to Canada in 2016, my father, Amy, and I volunteered to spend time with a family of newcomers and help them adjust to living in a new country. The father and two of the children had a growing grasp of English, but the mother did not. My father, fluent in Arabic, was able to bring them the comfort of communication in their own language.

Helping them meant trying to imagine the day-to-day experiences they might face. For example, Halloween is not celebrated in Syria. We were able to warn them that children wearing costumes would be coming to their door shouting "trick or treat" and expecting candy. It may sound like a minor matter, but imagine not knowing about October 31st traditions and finding children—some dressed in gory costumes or even as soldiers—pounding at your door shortly after your escape from a war zone.

Our growing friendship with this immigrant family made us better value the opportunities available to us in a country at peace. This is one of the interesting things about activism. Even though you provide help, you also benefit. Each experience gives you greater perspective and makes you more compassionate, knowledgeable, and skilled at responding. You come to learn about existing support services, where to turn for guidance, and how to help others grow their independence. These skills are important tools that build on your power to make change.

Can you guess how I use my own abilities to raise awareness about issues I care about?

You get three tries!

I use my passion for writing and opportunities for public speaking to raise awareness about topics that matter to me, including the issues revealed here in *Make Your Mark, Make a Difference.* I've written other books that highlight topics I care about too. *Dark Matters: Nature's Reaction to Light Pollution* draws attention to how artificial light at night harms wildlife and makes it hard for scientists to study the universe. *The Story of Malala Yousafzai: A Biography Book for New Readers* shares the story of Malala's work to ensure that both girls and boys are allowed to attend school. I wrote *Too Much Trash: How Litter Is Hurting Animals* in the hope that readers will join efforts to clean up our world and protect wildlife, pets, and farm animals from the hazards of garbage on the ground and in bodies of water. I'm working on another book about road ecology that spotlights how roads dissect habitats and what we can do to help affected wildlife. These are varied topics! Remember that you don't need to limit yourself to one issue or cause, and that activism can take many forms.

Find the style that fits your best self. Go out and **make your mark and make a difference**. Uncover ways to highlight issues and bring others to activism. You'll be glad you did!

NOTES

CHAPTER 1

1. S. Prasad, "Please Wear Helmet, Insists Five-Year-Old Aakaash," *The Hindu*, April 5, 2015, https://www.thehindu.com/news/cities/puducherry/please-wear-helmet-insists-fiveyearold-aakaash/article7070195.ece.

2. Akshaya Asokan, "This 8-Year-Old Chennai Boy Leads Protest on the Streets Against Liquor Shops, Helmet-less Riding," *The New Indian Express Edex Live*, May 18, 2018, https://www.edexlive.com/beinspired/2018/may/18/how-eight-year-old-aakaash-a-is-changing-society-in-little-way-he-could-2894.html.

3. *Encyclopaedia Britannica*, s.v. "Jackie Coogan," accessed February 25, 2021, https://www.britannica.com/biography/Jackie-Coogan.

4. "Coogan Law: Full Text," Screen Actors Guild: American Federation of Television and Radio Artists (SAG AFTRA), accessed October 2020, https://www.sagaftra.org/membership-benefits/young-performers/coogan-law/coogan-law-full-text.

5. United Nations, "Universal Declaration of Human Rights," accessed October 2020, https://www.un.org/en/about-us/universal-declaration-of-human-rights.

6. UNICEF, "Convention on the Rights of the Child: The Children's Version," accessed July 16, 2021, https://www.unicef.org/child-rights-convention/convention-text-childrens-version.

7. Jason Shvili, "Is China a Developing Country?" WorldAtlas, January 18, 2021, https://www.worldatlas.com/articles/is-china-a-developing-country.html.

8. United Nations Economic Analysis and Policy Division, Department of Economic and Social Affairs of the United Nations Secretariat, World Economic Situation and Prospects 2022, "Statistical Annex," accessed October 16, 2022, https://www.un.org/development/desa/dpad/wp-content/uploads/sites/45/WESP2022_ANNEX.pdf.

9. We-Cycle-USA, accessed October 2020, www.we-cycle-usa.com.

10. Wish for Wheels, accessed October 2020, https://wishforwheels.org.

11. The Polar Bike Project, accessed October 12, 2020, http://www.thepolarbike project.ca/; Ali Harper, email conversation with author, October 12, 2020.

12. World Bicycle Relief, accessed October 2020, https://worldbicyclerelief.org.

CHAPTER 2

1. Leanne Italie, "Dictionary.com Chooses 'Misinformation' as Word of the Year," Associated Press, November 25, 2018, https://apnews.com/article /entertainment-north-america-ap-top-news-religion-fake-news -e4b3b7b395644d019d1a0a0ed5868b10.

2. Channel 4 Entertainment, "Trailer: The Supervet," YouTube video, 0:40, September 15, 2017, https://www.youtube.com/watch?v=aQxFIjNW43o.

3. Netflix, "The Boy Who Harnessed the Wind: Official Trailer [HD]," YouTube video, 2:34, January 25, 2019, https://www.youtube.com/watch ?v=nPkr9HmglG0.

4. Gillie Collins, "Protagonist in 'Wadjda' Defies Saudi Gender Roles," *The Stanford Daily*, October 11, 2013, https://www.stanforddaily.com/2013/10/11 /protagonist-in-wadjda-defies-saudi-gender-roles/.

5. Hulu, "I Am Greta: Trailer (Official)," YouTube video, 2:38, September 10, 2020, https://www.youtube.com/watch?v=xDdEWkA15Rg.

6. Todd McLeish, "Winterized Frogs About to Thaw Out and Get to Work," ecoRI News, March 11, 2021, https://ecori.org/2021-3-9-winterized-frogs -about-to-thaw-out-and-get-to-work/.

7. "More Than 1,400 Frogs and Toads Saved on Denbighshire Road," BBC News, June 26, 2018, https://www.bbc.com/news/uk-wales-north-east-wales -44621387; Ximena Conde, "N.J. Crossing Guards Protect Amphibians Making Deadly Trek for Love," WHYY-PBS, March 4, 2020, https://whyy .org/articles/n-j-crossing-guards-protect-amphibians-making-deadly-trek -for-love/.

8. Nature, "Frogs: The Thin Green Line—A World without Amphibians," March 28, 2009, https://www.pbs.org/wnet/nature/frogs-the-thin-green -line-a-world-without-amphibians/4852/.

9. David Ellis, "Why Frogs Could Be Our Saviour Against Cancer," *Lumen: The University of Adelaide Magazine*, modified September 3, 2021, https://www .adelaide.edu.au/lumen/issues/16381/news16387.html.

10. SAVE THE FROGS!, accessed June 14, 2021, https://savethefrogs.com/.

11. Citizen Conservation, "Fighting Extinction," accessed June 14, 2021, https:// cms2.frogs-friends.org//fileadmin/user_upload/get _active/CC_Amph _Einfuehrungsartikel/Citizen_conservation _EN.pdf.

12. Patricia Valentine-Darby, "Reptiles and Amphibians—Threats and Concerns," *Southern Plains Network Inventory and Monitoring Program*, 2010, National Parks Service, accessed June 21, 2021, https://www.nps.gov/articles/reptiles-and -amphibians-threats.htm.

13. Department of Environmental Conservation, "DEC and Volunteers Prepare for Annual Salamander and Frog Migration: Spring Thaw and Warm Rains Will Soon Lure Amphibians to Woodland Pools for Breeding," March 15, 2021, https://www.dec.ny.gov/press/122522.html.

14. United States Environmental Protection Agency (EPA), "Wetlands Overview," December 2004, https://www.epa.gov/sites/default/files/2021-01 /documents/wetlands_overview.pdf.

15. The Nature Conservancy, "Wetlands at Risk," February 2, 2021, https:// www.nature.org/en-us/newsroom/indiana-sb389/.

16. Helping Ninjas, accessed October 31, 2022, https://helpingninjas.com /our-program/.

CHAPTER 3

1. World Health Organization, "1 in 3 People Globally Do Not Have Access to Safe Drinking Water–UNICEF, WHO," June 18, 2019, https://www.who.int /news/item/18-06-2019-1-in-3-people-globally-do-not-have-access-to-safe -drinking-water-unicef-who.

2. World Health Organization, "Drinking-Water," June 14, 2019, https://www .who.int/news-room/fact-sheets/detail/drinking-water.

3. WHO, "Drinking-Water."

4. United Nations Children's Fund (UNICEF), *Reimagining WASH—Water Security for All*, March 2021, https://www.unicef.org/media/95241/file /water-security-for-all.pdf.

5. UNICEF, *Reimagining WASH.*

6. UNICEF, "Water, Sanitation and Hygiene: Improving Children's Access to Water, Sanitation, Hygiene," accessed July 12, 2021, https://www.unicef.org /kenya/water-sanitation-and-hygiene.

7. UNICEF, World Health Organization, "Safely Managed Drinking Water," accessed July 12, 2021, http://www.prographic.com/wp-content/uploads /2016/11/UNICEF-SafelyMngDrinkWater-2016-11-18-web.pdf.

8. Dan Joling and Mark Thiessen, "Alaska Village Short of Water as Winter Approaches," NBC News/The Associated Press, October 11, 2012, https:// www.nbcnews.com/id/wbna49373022.

9. United Nations, "Global Issues: Water," accessed July 15, 2021, https://www .un.org/en/global-issues/water.

10. Copyright.gov, "What Is Copyright?" accessed October 1, 2021, https://www .copyright.gov/what-is-copyright/; "More Information on Fair Use," May 2021, https://www.copyright.gov/fair-use/more-info.html.

11. Water Science School, "The Water in You: Water and the Human Body," USGS (United States Geological Survey), May 22, 2019, https://www.usgs .gov/special-topics/water-science-school/science/water-you-water-and -human-body#overview.

12. Hippo Roller, accessed July 12, 2021, https://hipporoller.org/.

13. Water.org, accessed July 15, 2021, https://water.org/solutions/.

14. WATERisLIFE, accessed July 12, 2021, https://waterislife.com/impact /clean-water/#the-drinkable-book.

15. Thirst Project, "Our Story," accessed July 2, 2021, https://www.thirstproject .org/about/our-story/.

16. Gregory Johnson, email conversation with author, June 21, 2023; Ken Meyer, "Asked and Answered: President Obama Responds to an Eight-Year-Old Girl from Flint," The White House, President Barack Obama, April 27, 2016, https://obamawhitehouse.archives.gov/blog/2016/04/27/asked-and-answered -president-obama-responds-eight-year-old-girl-flint; Little Miss Flint Clean Water Fund, GoFundMe.com, https://www.gofundme.com/f/little-miss-flint -clean-water-fund.

17. Ryan's Well Foundation, accessed July 9, 2021, https://www.ryanswell.ca/.

CHAPTER 4

1. Smithsonian National Air and Space Museum, "Homing in on Pigeons' Contributions to World War II," March 16, 2021, https://airandspace.si.edu /stories/editorial/homing-pigeons-contributions-world-war-2.

2. London Gibson, "Tigers Are Endangered in Asia, but in Texas They're Backyard Pets," *Austin American Statesman*, updated November 27, 2018, https://www.statesman.com/news/20180501/tigers-are-endangered-in-asia -but-in-texas-theyre-backyard-pets.

3. RSPCA, "What Is the RSPCA's View on the Use of Tongue Ties in Horse Racing?" updated October 11, 2021, https://kb.rspca.org.au/knowledge -base/what-is-the-rspcas-view-on-the-use-of-tongue-ties-in-horse-racing/.

4. Victor Kiprop, "How Many Animals Are There in the World?" WorldAtlas, March 20, 2018, https://www.worldatlas.com/articles/how-many-animals -are-there-in-the-world.html.

5. Animal Welfare Institute, *Humane Education*, accessed August 17, 2021, https://awionline.org/sites/default/files/publication/digital_download/humane_education_brochure.pdf.

6. Animal Welfare Institute, "Dissection Alternatives," accessed September 5, 2022, https://awionline.org/content/dissection-alternatives; PETA, "Animals Used in Education," accessed September 5, 2022, https://www.peta.org/issues/animals-used-for-experimentation/classroom-dissection/.

7. Emily Smith, "Do You Really Know How Most Farm Animals Live?" The Humane Society of the United States, November 1, 2019, https://www.humanesociety.org/news/do-you-really-know-how-most-farm-animals-live.

8. Certified Humane, "Our Standards," accessed August 17, 2021, https://certifiedhumane.org/our-standards/.

9. Humane Society International Canada, "Asia's Dog Meat Trade: FAQs," accessed August 17, 2021, https://www.hsi.org/news-media/dog-meat-trade-faqs/.

10. Humane Society International Canada, "Saving Animals from China's Dog and Cat Meat Trade," accessed August 17, 2021, https://www.hsi.org/news-media/saving-dogs-from-chinas-dog-meat-trade/.

11. Congress.gov, "H.R.961—Safeguard American Food Exports Act of 2019," accessed August 17, 2021, https://www.congress.gov/bill/116th-congress/house-bill/961/text.

12. Lobby for Animals, accessed August 25, 2021, https://thomasponce.wixsite.com/lobby-for-animals; Thomas Ponce, email conversation with author, August 27, 2021.

13. Farm Sanctuary, accessed August 25, 2021, https://www.farmsanctuary.org.

14. *North State Parent*, "Lou Wegner: Kids Against Animal Cruelty," December 28, 2013, https://northstateparent.com/article/lou-wegner-kids-against-animal-cruelty/.

15. American Society for the Prevention of Cruelty to Animals (ASPCA), "Pet Statistics," accessed August 21, 2021, https://www.aspca.org/helping-people-pets/shelter-intake-and-surrender/pet-statistics.

16. The Humane Society of the United States, "Stopping Puppy Mills," accessed August 17, 2021, https://www.humanesociety.org/all-our-fights/stopping-puppy-mills.

17. Denise Kelly, "Captive Birds: No Way Home," *AV Magazine*, issue 1, June 7, 2016: 8–9, https://issuu.com/aavs/docs/aavs_av-magazine_2016-1_birds; Animal Groups' Historic Effort to Protect Birds Succeeds, February 28, 2023, https://www.avianwelfare.org/images/AAVS_AWC_Press_release_AWA.pdf; Rebecca E. Bazan, "Finally! Animal Welfare Act Bird Regulations Part 1:

Who Is Covered?" February 22, 2023, https://blogs.duanemorris.com /animallawdevelopments/2023/02/22/finally-animal-welfare-act-bird -regulations-part-1-who-is-covered/.

18. Vanda Felbab-Brown, "Wildlife and Drug Trafficking, Terrorism, and Human Security," PRISM, National Defense University, November 8, 2018, https://www.brookings.edu/articles/wildlife-and-drug-trafficking-terrorism -and-human-security/.

19. Antonia Ciriak, "10 Worst Countries for Wildlife Trafficking Today," WorldAtlas, February 16, 2020, https://www.worldatlas.com/articles /10-worst-countries-for-wildlife-trafficking-today.html.

20. Rene Ebersole, "How to Pick the Most 'Dolphin-Safe' Tuna," *National Geographic*, March 10, 2021, https://www.nationalgeographic.com/animals /article/how-to-pick-most-dolphin-safe-tuna.

21. Christina Sterbenz, "13 Surprising Things That Are Partly Made from Animal Products," *Insider*, March 24, 2014, https://www.businessinsider. com/15-surprising-things-that-contain-animal-products-2014-3?op=1.

22. PAWS: Performing Animal Welfare Society, accessed September 5, 2022, https://www.pawsweb.org/.

23. Bring Butterflies Back: Inspiring Youth to Protect Butterflies for Future Generations, accessed October 28, 2021, https://bringbutterfliesback.org/.

24. Save the Nautilus, accessed August 17, 2021, http://savethenautilus.com /about-us/.

25. The Blue Feet Foundation, accessed August 17, 2021, https:// bluefeetfoundation.com/about-me.

CHAPTER 5

1. NASA Global Climate Change, "Climate Change: How Do We Know?" updated August 9, 2021, https://climate.nasa.gov/evidence/.

2. NASA Global Climate Change, "The Causes of Climate Change," updated August 9, 2021, https://climate.nasa.gov/causes/.

3. UNICEF, "Fact Sheet: The Climate Crisis Is a Child Rights Crisis," December 6, 2019, https://www.unicef.org/press-releases/fact-sheet-climate -crisis-child-rights-crisis.

4. Rebecca Lindsey, "Climate Change: Global Sea Level," January 25, 2021, NOAA Climate.gov, https://www.climate.gov/news-features/understanding -climate/climate-change-global-sea-level.

5. Office for Coastal Management, "Fast Facts: Coral Reefs," NOAA, modified August 1, 2022, https://coast.noaa.gov/states/fast-facts/coral-reefs.html.

6. Habitat Conservation, "Shallow Coral Reef Habitat," NOAA Fisheries, updated January 21, 2020, https://www.fisheries.noaa.gov/national/habitat-conservation/shallow-coral-reef-habitat.

7. The World Bank, "Kiribati: Kiribati Adaptation Program—Phase III," September 15, 2011, https://www.worldbank.org/en/results/2011/09/15/kiribati-adaptation-program-phase-3.

8. Kate Samuelson, "This Olympic Weightlifter Danced Off Stage to Raise Awareness of Climate Change," *Time*, August 16, 2016, https://time.com/4453753/david-katoatau-kiribati-olympics-climate-change/.

9. Faena Aleph, "The Snow Guardian: The Hermit Who Inadvertently Recorded Climate Change," Faena.com, accessed September 5, 2022, https://www.faena.com/aleph/the-snow-guardian-the-hermit-who-inadvertently-recorded-climate-change#.

10. The Climate Reality Project, "Al Gore Leads Network of 20,000 Climate Reality Leaders in a Global, Grassroots Day of Climate Action & Education," July 31, 2019, https://www.climaterealityproject.org/press/al-gore-leads-network-20000-climate-reality-leaders-global-grassroots-day-climate-action.

11. The Climate Reality Project, "Our Mission," accessed August 19, 2021, https://www.climaterealityproject.org/our-mission.

12. Emily Malter, "The Oh-So-Bright Future of Wildlife Conservation: Meet Four Kids Working to Save Their Favorite Endangered Animals," *Sierra*, December 10, 2016, https://www.sierraclub.org/sierra/2016-6-november-december/green-life/oh-so-bright-future-wildlife-conservation.

13. Catherine Clifford, "Fierce Local Battles over Power Lines Are a Bottleneck for Clean Energy," CNBC, June 26, 2022, https://www.cnbc.com/2022/06/26/why-the-us-has-a-massive-power-line-problem.html.

14. IRENA, International Renewable Energy Agency, "Renewable Power Remains Cost-Competitive amid Fossil Fuel Crisis," July 13, 2022, https://www.irena.org/newsroom/pressreleases/2022/Jul/Renewable-Power-Remains-Cost-Competitive-amid-Fossil-Fuel-Crisis.

15. United States Environmental Protection Agency (EPA), "National Overview: Facts and Figures on Materials, Wastes and Recycling," accessed March 15, 2022, https://www.epa.gov/facts-and-figures-about-materials-waste-and-recycling/national-overview-facts-and-figures-materials.

16. UN Environment Programme, "Solid Waste Management," accessed August 30, 2021, https://www.unep.org/explore-topics/resource-efficiency/what-we-do/cities/solid-waste-management.

17. UN Water, "Water Quality and Wastewater," United Nations, accessed August 30, 2021, https://www.unwater.org/water-facts/quality-and-wastewater/.

18. Bebot Sison Jr., Cecille Suerte Felipe, "Payatas Tragedy: One Year After," Philstar Global, July 10, 2001, https://www.philstar.com/headlines/2001/07/10/91819/payatas-tragedy-one-year-after.

19. Ocean Portal Team, reviewed by Jennifer Bennett (of NOAA), "Ocean Acidification," Smithsonian, April 2018, https://ocean.si.edu/ocean-life/invertebrates/ocean-acidification.

20. Plant-for-the-Planet, accessed October 16, 2022, https://www.plant-for-the-planet.org/.

CHAPTER 6

1. Canadian Space Agency, "Why Do We Conduct Science Experiments in Space?" Government of Canada, June 12, 2018, https://www.asc-csa.gc.ca/eng/iss/science/why-do-we-conduct-science-experiments-in-space.asp.

2. NASA Technology Transfer Program, "NASA Spinoff," National Aeronautics and Space Administration (NASA), accessed September 21, 2021, https://spinoff.nasa.gov/.

3. Defense Intelligence Agency, United States of America, "Challenges to Security in Space: Space Reliance in an Era of Competition and Expansion," March 2022, https://www.dia.mil/Portals/110/Documents/News/Military_Power_Publications/Challenges_Security_Space_2022.pdf.

4. United Nations Office for Outer Space Affairs, "Treaty on Principles Governing the Activities of States in the Exploration and Use of Outer Space, Including the Moon and Other Celestial Bodies," accessed September 5, 2022, https://www.unoosa.org/oosa/en/ourwork/spacelaw/treaties/introouterspacetreaty.html.

5. United Nations Office for Outer Space Affairs, "Treaties," accessed October 18, 2022, https://www.unoosa.org/oosa/en/aboutus/history/treaties.html.

6. United Nations Office for Outer Space Affairs, Space Debris Mitigation Guidelines of the Committee on the Peaceful Uses of Outer Space, United Nations, 2010, https://www.unoosa.org/pdf/publications/st_space_49E.pdf.

7. United Nations Office for Outer Space Affairs, Guidelines for the Long-Term Sustainability of Outer Space Activities of the Committee on the Peaceful Uses of Outer Space, United Nations, Vienna, Austria, updated June 2021, https://www.unoosa.org/documents/pdf/PromotingSpaceSustainability/Publication_Final_English_June2021.pdf.

8. United Nations Office for Outer Space Affairs, *Committee on the Peaceful Uses of Outer Space: Membership Evolution*, February 24, 2023, https://www.unoosa.org/oosa/en/ourwork/copuos/members/evolution.html.

9. Asgardia: The Space Nation, "Frequently Asked Questions," accessed September 5, 2022, https://asgardia.space/en/pages/faq.

10. Seti Institute, "Unistellar and SETI Institute Expand Worldwide Citizen-Science Astronomy Network," May 25, 2022, https://www.seti.org/press-release/unistellar-and-seti-institute-expand-worldwide-citizen-science-astronomy-network.

11. R. Dick, "Applied Scotobiology in Luminaire Design," Society of Light and Lighting, August 27, 2013, https://rasc.ca/sites/default/files/Dick-Scotobiology_0.pdf.

12. DarkSky, accessed August 30, 2021, https://www.darksky.org/.

13. NASA, "Space Debris and Human Spacecraft," National Aeronautics and Space Administration (NASA), May 26, 2021, https://www.nasa.gov/mission_pages/station/news/orbital_debris.html.

14. Maya Wei-Haas, "Space Junk Is a Huge Problem—and It's Only Getting Bigger," *National Geographic*, April 25, 2019, https://www.nationalgeographic.com/science/article/space-junk.

15. Steven Freeland, "A Giant Piece of Space Junk from a Chinese Rocket Is Hurtling Towards Earth—Here's How Worried You Should Be," SciTechDaily, May 6, 2021, https://scitechdaily.com/a-giant-piece-of-space-junk-from-a-chinese-rocket-is-hurtling-towards-earth-heres-how-worried-you-should-be/.

16. The International Charter for Space and Major Disasters, accessed February 2, 2023, https://disasterscharter.org/web/guest/home.

17. Vito De Lucia, Viviana Iavicoli, "From Outer Space to Ocean Depths: The 'Spacecraft Cemetery' and the Protection of the Marine Environment in Areas Beyond National Jurisdiction," California Western School of Law (CWSL) Scholarly Commons, May 15, 2019, https://scholarlycommons.law.cwsl.edu/cgi/viewcontent.cgi?article=1551&context=cwilj.

18. Dave Mosher, "There's a Spacecraft Graveyard in the Middle of the Ocean. Here's What's Down There," *Business Insider Australia*, September 30, 2020, https://www.businessinsider.com.au/spacecraft-cemetery-point-nemo-google-maps-2017-10.

19. Maya Wei-Haas, "Space Junk Is a Huge Problem—and It's Only Getting Bigger," *National Geographic*, April 25, 2019, https://www.nationalgeographic.com/science/article/space-junk.

20. Luciano Anselmo, et al., *European Code of Conduct for Space Debris Mitigation*, issue 1.0, 3–10, June 28, 2004, https://www.unoosa.org/documents/pdf/spacelaw/sd/2004-B5-10.pdf.

21. United Nations Office for Outer Space Affairs, accessed August 30, 2022, https://www.unoosa.org/.

22. Centre National d'Etudes Spatiales, Deutsches Zentrum für Luft und Raumfahrt, European Space Agency, European Organization for the Exploitation of Meteorological Satellites, and Russian State Space Corporation, "International Charter: Space and Major Disasters 2020 Annual Report V4," accessed September 20, 2021, https://disasterscharter.org/documents/10180/14622/20th-Charter-Annual-Report.pdf.

23. Space Safety Coalition, "Best Practices for the Sustainability of Space Operations," September 16, 2019, https://spacesafety.org/best-practices/; Space Safety Coalition, "Space Safety Coalition Welcomes the Aerospace Corporation as Its Newest Member," January 14, 2021, https://agi.widen.net/s/gjf2bkm5pj/sscaerospace-release-final.

24. The Mars Society, "Frequently Asked Questions," accessed September 21, 2021, https://www.marssociety.org/faq/#Q20; Daniel Strain, "Science, Spacesuits, Dehydrated Food: Simulating Mars in the Utah Desert," University of Colorado Boulder, *CUBoulder Today*, April 8, 2021, https://www.colorado.edu/today/2021/04/08/science-spacesuits-dehydrated-food-simulating-mars-utah-desert.

25. National Space Society, "Rothblatt Space Settlement in Our Lifetime Prize Business Plan Competition," NSS, June 8, 2021, https://spacebizplan.nss.org/wp-content/uploads/2021/07/Rothblatt-Competition-info-7-8-21.pdf.

26. The Space Settlement Institute, "The Space Settlement Prize Act," accessed September 21, 2021, http://www.space-settlement-institute.org/space-settlement-prize-act.html.

27. Fabio Falchi, et al., "The New World Atlas of Artificial Night Sky Brightness," *Science Advances*, vol. 2, issue 6, June 10, 2016, https://www.science.org/doi/10.1126/sciadv.1600377.

28. DarkSky, accessed August 30, 2021, https://www.darksky.org/.

29. Aries Ramirez Licea, "Young Advocates Set Their Eyes on Tackling Light Pollution," International Dark-Sky Association (IDA), February 22, 2019, https://www.darksky.org/young-advocates-set-their-eyes-on-tackling-light-pollution/.

CHAPTER 7

1. "Peace and Violence," Compass Manual for Human Rights Education with Young People, Council of Europe, accessed August 2, 2022, https://www.coe .int/en/web/compass/peace-and-violence.

2. Jay S. Albanese, "Transnational Crime," Oxford Bibliographies, October 26, 2017, https://www.oxfordbibliographies.com/view/document/obo -9780195396607/obo-9780195396607-0024.xml.

3. "What Is Human Trafficking?" Kids Help Phone, updated December 7, 2021, https://kidshelpphone.ca/get-info/what-human-trafficking.

4. "Climate Action Holds Key to Tackling Global Conflict," UN Environment Programme, November 3, 2021, https://www.unep.org/news-and-stories /story/climate-action-holds-key-tackling-global-conflict.

5. "How Does Climate Change Impact Global Peace and Security?" *OUPblog*, Oxford University Press, June 11, 2017, https://blog.oup.com/2017/06 /climate-change-global-peace-security/.

6. "Threat to Global Security More Complex, Probably Higher than during Cold War, Secretary-General Warns Munich Security Conference," United Nations, February 18, 2022, https://www.un.org/press/en/2022/sgsm21146 .doc.htm.

7. "'Explosive' Growth of Digital Technologies Creating New Potential for Conflict, Disarmament Chief Tells Security Council in First-Ever Debate on Cyberthreats," United Nations, June 29, 2021, https://www.un.org/press /en/2021/sc14563.doc.htm.

8. "Rate of Fatal Police Shootings in the United States from 2015 to June 2022, by Ethnicity," Statista, June 2, 2022, https://www.statista.com/statistics /1123070/police-shootings-rate-ethnicity-us/.

9. Ellen Cranley, "These 10 Young Activists Are Trying to Move the Needle on Climate Change, Gun Control, and Other Global Issues," *Insider*, October 1, 2019, https://www.insider.com/young-activists-climate-change-guns-greta -thunberg-2019-9.

10. "Five Child Activists You Need to Know," UNICEF Australia, accessed June 30, 2022, https://www.unicef.org.au/blog/stories/five-child-activists.

11. Adam Schubak, "Read the Stories of 40 Incredible Kids Who Have Changed the World," *Good Housekeeping*, October 8, 2020, https://www.goodhouse keeping.com/life/inspirational-stories/g5188/kids-who-changed-the-world/.

12. Steve Peoples, Associated Press contributors Kevin Freking, Hannah Fingerhut, "Gun Safety Activists Decry Inaction As U.S. Mass Shootings Surge," PBS News Hour, April 19, 2022, https://www.pbs.org/newshour /politics/gun-safety-activists-decry-inaction-as-u-s-mass-shootings-surge.

13. "11-Year-Old Youth Activist Naomi Wadler Opens NCADV's 2018 Voices Rising National Domestic Violence Conference," *National Coalition Against Domestic Violence* (blog), August 27, 2018, https://ncadv.org /blog/posts/11-year-old-youth-activist-naomi-wadler-opens-ncadvs-2018 -voices-rising-national-domestic-violence-c.

14. "Maintain International Peace and Security," United Nations, accessed June 30, 2022, https://www.un.org/en/our-work/maintain-international-peace -and-security.

15. "Resolutions Adopted by the General Assembly, 53/243. Declaration and Programme of Action on a Culture of Peace," United Nations, October 6, 1999, https://documents-dds-ny.un.org/doc/UNDOC/GEN/N99/774/43 /PDF/N9977443.pdf.

16. Mo Rocca, "Samantha Smith, the Fifth-Grader from Maine Who Became 'America's Littlest Diplomat,'" *Sunday Morning*, CBS News, January 29, 2023, https://www.cbsnews.com/news/mobituaries-samantha-smith-americas -littlest-diplomat/; Lorraine Boissoneault, "The Surprising Story of the American Girl Who Broke Through the Iron Curtain," May 10, 2018, *Smithsonian Magazine*, https://www.smithsonianmag.com/history/surprising -story-american-girl-who-broke-through-iron-curtain-180969043/; Bunny McBride, "Samantha's Legacy: Kid-to-Kid Diplomacy. Foundation Formed by Her Mother Sponsors US-Soviet Youth Exchanges," *The Christian Science Monitor*, July 30, 1987, https://www.csmonitor.com/1987/0730/hsam.html.

17. "Resolution Adopted by the General Assembly 53/243 A. Declaration on a Culture of Peace," United Nations, September 13, 1999, http://www .un-documents.net/a53r243a.htm.

18. "UN International Day of Peace," United Nations, accessed June 30, 2022, https://internationaldayofpeace.org/.

19. Nobel Peace Center, "Behind the Peace Symbol," September 21, 2019, https://www.nobelpeacecenter.org/en/news/behind-the-peace-symbol.

20. "Meet the Black Lives Matter Global Network Foundation's Growing Board of Directors," Black Lives Matter, April 27, 2022, https://blacklivesmatter. com/meet-the-black-lives-matter-global-network-foundations-growing -board-of-directors/; Rebecca Shabad, Chelsea Bailey, Phil McCausland, "At March for Our Lives, Survivors Lead Hundreds of Thousands in Call for Change," *NBC News*, March 24, 2018, https://www.nbcnews.com/news /us-news/march-our-lives-draws-hundreds-thousands-washington-around -nation-n859716.

21. Jared Council, "Two Years After George Floyd, Black Leaders Reflect on Change," *Forbes*, May 23, 2022, https://www.forbes.com/sites/jaredcouncil

/2022/05/23/two-years--after-george-floyd-black-leaders-reflect-on-change
/?sh=43c0da7c6d1b.

22. Larry Buchanan, Quoctrung Bui, and Jugal K. Patel, "Black Lives Matter May Be the Largest Movement in U.S. History," *New York Times*, July 3, 2020, https://www.nytimes.com interactive/2020/07/03/us/george-floyd-protests-crowd-size.html.

23. World Population Review, "School Shootings by Country 2022," accessed June 30, 2022, https://worldpopulationreview.com/country-rankings/school-shootings-by-country; Jason R. Silva, "Global Mass Shootings: Comparing the United States Against Developed and Developing Countries," *International Journal of Comparative and Applied Criminal Justice*, March 21, 2022, https://www.tandfonline.com/doi/abs/10.1080/01924036.2022.2052126.

24. March for Our Lives: Mission and Story, accessed February 3, 2022, https://marchforourlives.com/mission-story/; "March for Our Lives," Iowa State University, accessed June 30, 2022, https://awpc.cattcenter.iastate.edu/directory/march-for-our-lives-marchforourlives-neveragain/.

25. Emanuella Grinberg, "How the Parkland Students Pulled Off a Massive National Protest in Only 5 Weeks," CNN, March 26, 2018, https://www.cnn.com/2018/03/26/us/march-for-our-lives/index.html; History.com Editors, "Teen Gunman Kills 17, Injures 17 at Parkland, Florida High School," A & E Television Networks, May 25, 2022, https://www.history.com/this-day-in-history/parkland-marjory-stoneman-douglas-school-shooting; March for Our Lives, accessed June 30, 2022, https://marchforourlives.com/.

26. Everytown for Gun Safety, accessed July 18, 2022, https://www.everytown.org/about-everytown/#what-we-do; "Gun Sense Action Network Team Signup," Gun Sense Voter, accessed June 30, 2022, https://gunsensevoter.org/gsan/.

27. "We Exist to End School Shootings—On Our K-12 Campuses," Protecting Our Students, accessed June 30, 2022, https://www.protectingourstudents.org/we-exist-to-end-school-shootings-on-our-k-12-campuses/.

28. Danuta Kean, "Bana Alabed, Seven-Year-Old Syrian Peace Campaigner, to Publish Memoir," *The Guardian*, April 13, 2017, https://www.theguardian.com/books/2017/apr/13/bana-al-abed-seven-year-old-syrian-peace-campaigner-to-publish-memoir.

29. "Bana Alabed," Simon & Schuster, accessed June 30, 2022, https://www.simonandschuster.com/authors/Bana-Alabed/2141414806; Liz Hoath (producer, *The Current*), "7-Year-Old Syrian Girl Who Tweeted from Aleppo Shares Her Story in New Book," CBC Radio: Radio-Canada, updated

November 6, 2017, https://www.cbc.ca/radio/thecurrent/the-current
-for-october-31-2017-1.4378789/7-year-old-syrian-girl-who-tweeted-from
-aleppo-shares-her-story-in-new-book-1.4378794.

CHAPTER 8

1. Canadian Centre on Statelessness, "Understanding Statelessness," accessed
   June 30, 2022, http://www.statelessness.ca/statelessness.html.
2. Bureau of Population, Refugees, and Migration, "Statelessness," US
   Department of State, accessed June 30, 2022, https://www.state.gov
   /other-policy-issues/statelessness/.
3. Cristela Jones, "'Being and Becoming a Fighter:' A Decade Since DACA
   Means No End in Sight for Dreamers," Border & Immigration, Texas
   Standard, August 19, 2022, https://www.texasstandard.org/stories/being-and
   -becoming-a-fighter-a-decade-since-daca-means-no-end-in-sight-for
   -dreamers/.
4. Betsy Lawrence, "The Biden-Harris Administration Celebrates the
   Contributions of Dreamers on Ten-Year Anniversary of DACA," The White
   House, June 15, 2022, https://www.whitehouse.gov/briefing-room
   /statements-releases/2022/06/15/the-biden-harris-administration-celebrates
   -the-contributions-of-dreamers-on-ten-year-anniversary-of-daca/.
5. "How Many Ukrainian Refugees Are There and Where Have They Gone?"
   BBC News, July 4, 2022, https://www.bbc.com/news/world-60555472.
6. Bree Steffen, "Website Connects Ukrainian Refugees with Hosts," Spectrum
   News1, May 16, 2022, https://spectrumnews1.com/ca/la-west/politics/2022
   /05/09/website-connects-ukrainian-refugees-with-hosts.
7. Shanifa Nasser, "Meet the 9-Year-Old Girl Whose Simple Act of Kindness
   During COVID-19 Spurred an Army of Volunteers," CBC, April 8, 2021,
   https://www.cbc.ca/news/canada/toronto/covid-kindness-good-neighbour
   -project-hana-fatima-1.5980113; Good Neighbour Project, accessed June 30,
   2022, https://www.goodneighbourproject.com/who-we-are.
8. Hristina Byrnes, "13 Countries Where Being Gay Is Legally Punishable by
   Death," USA Today, updated June 19, 2019, https://www.usatoday.com/story
   /money/2019/06/14/countries-where-being-gay-is-legally-punishable
   -by-death/39574685/.
9. "A Brief History of Our LGBTQIA2-S Pride Flag," Los Angeles County
   Department of Mental Health, June 16, 2022, https://dmh.lacounty.gov
   /blog/2022/06/a-brief-history-of-our-lgbtqia2-s-pride-flag/.
10. "United Nations Declaration on the Rights of Indigenous Peoples," United
    Nations, accessed September 5, 2022, https://www.un.org/development/desa

/indigenouspeoples/wp-content/uploads/sites/19/2018/11/UNDRIP_E
_web.pdf.

11. "Indigenous Peoples," Amnesty International, accessed June 30, 2022, https://
www.amnesty.org/en/what-we-do/indigenous-peoples/.

12. "Fulfilling Our Mission," Save the Children, accessed June 30, 2022, https://
www.savethechildren.org/us/what-we-do; "Canada Programs: National
Reconciliation Program," Save the Children, accessed June 30, 2022, https://
www.savethechildren.ca/what-we-do/canada-programs/.

13. Room to Read, accessed June 30, 2022, https://www.roomtoread.org.

14. Justice Rising, accessed June 30, 2022, https://give.justicerising.org/; Sarah
Whittaker, "The Storytelling Movement," 2014, accessed June 30, 2022,
https://inee.org/sites/default/files/resources/The%20Storytelling%20
Movement%20.pdf.

15. "244M Children Won't Start the New School Year," UNESCO, September 9,
2022, https://www.unesco.org/en/articles/244m-children-wont-start-new
-school-year-unesco.

16. "Global Youth Ambassadors," Theirworld, accessed June 30, 2022, https://
theirworld.org/projects/global-youth-ambassadors/.

17. Malala Yousafzai and Christine Lamb, *I Am Malala: The Girl Who Stood Up for
Education and Was Shot by the Taliban* (New York: Little, Brown, 2015); Malala
Fund, accessed June 30, 2022, https://malala.org/; Malala Fund, "Malala's
Story," accessed February 25, 2023, https://malala.org/malalas-story.

CHAPTER 9

1. Ronald Waldman, "Natural and Human-Made Disasters," Centers for Disease
Control and Prevention, accessed July 4, 2022, https://www.cdc.gov/eis/field
-epi-manual/chapters/Natural-Human-Disasters.html.

2. "Evaluation of the ALS Association Grant Programs Executive Summary
Report," May 2019, https://www.als.org/sites/default/files/2020-06/RTI
-Report-FINAL.pdf.

3. Mami Mizutori, "Our Work," United Nations Office for Disaster Risk
Reduction (UNDRR), accessed July 4, 2022, https://www.undrr.org
/about-undrr/our-work.

4. Annie Lowrey, "What the Camp Fire Revealed," *The Atlantic*, January 19,
2019, https://www.theatlantic.com/ideas/archive/2019/01/why-natural
-disasters-are-worse-poor/580846/.

5. "Fact Sheet: An Adjustment to Global Poverty Lines," The World Bank,
September 14, 2022, https://www.worldbank.org/en/news/factsheet/2022
/05/02/fact-sheet-an-adjustment-to-global-poverty-lines.

6. "Poverty Rate by Country 2023," World Population Review, accessed February 20, 2023, https://worldpopulationreview.com/country-rankings/poverty-rate-by-country.

7. "2020 Post-Enumeration Survey Results," United States Census Bureau, January 2022, https://www.census.gov/newsroom/stories/poverty-awareness-month.html.

8. "Canadian Income Survey, 2021," Statistics Canada, May 2, 2023, https://www150.statcan.gc.ca/n1/daily-quotidien/230502/dq230502a-eng.htm.

9. "Child Poverty," UNICEF, accessed July 17, 2022, https://www.unicef.org/social-policy/child-poverty.

10. Tanya Titova, Andrew Wilks, and Emrah Gurel, "Turkish Quake Victims Left Homeless Sheltering in Trains, Tents, Greenhouses," *PBS News Hour, Associated Press*, February 17, 2023, https://www.pbs.org/newshour/world/turkish-quake-victims-left-homeless-sheltering-in-trains-tents-greenhouses; International Committee of the Red Cross, accessed February 19, 2023, https://www.icrc.org/en; Doctors without Borders, accessed February 19, 2023, https://www.doctorswithoutborders.ca/content/about-us.

11. "Homeless Population by State," World Population Review, accessed September 5, 2022, https://worldpopulationreview.com/state-rankings/homeless-population-by-state.

12. "Habitat's History," Habitat for Humanity, accessed February 2, 2022, https://www.habitat.org/about/history.

13. Nick Gashed for Lexia Learning, "Illiteracy Is Costing America—Here's Why," *USA Today*, March 2, 2022, https://www.usatoday.com/story/sponsor-story/lexia-learning2022/2022/03/02/illiteracy-costing-america-heres-why/6848450001/.

14. "Literacy Statistics," ThinkImpact, accessed July 17, 2022, https://www.thinkimpact.com/literacy-statistics/.

15. Max Roser and Esteban Ortiz-Ospina, "Literacy," Our World in Data, revised September 20, 2018, https://ourworldindata.org/literacy.

16. "The Economic & Social Cost of Illiteracy," World Literacy Foundation, accessed March 9, 2023, https://worldliteracyfoundation.org/wp-content/uploads/2021/07/TheEconomicSocialCostofIlliteracy-2.pdf.

17. Little Free Library, accessed July 17, 2022, https://littlefreelibrary.org.

18. Madeline's Library, accessed February 8, 2023, https://www.madelineslibrary.com/; Joe Vithayathil, "'Read More, because It's Amazing': Young Girl Leading Charge to Bring a Library to Yamhill," Fox News, May 3, 2022, https://www.kptv.com/2022/05/03/read-more-because-its-amazing-young-girl-leading-charge-bring-library-yamhill/.

19. BeverlyCleary.com, "About Beverly Cleary: Bio," https://www.beverlycleary.com/about.

20. "Five Ways Reading Can Improve Health and Well-Being," Medical News Today, February 25, 2020, https://www.medicalnewstoday.com/articles/313429.

21. Avni Bavishi, Martin D. Slade, and Becca R. Levy, "A Chapter a Day: Association of Book Reading with Longevity," Social Science & Medicine, vol. 164 (September 2016): 44–48, https://www.sciencedirect.com/science/article/abs/pii/S0277953616303689.

22. "Life Expectancy by Country 2022," World Population Review, accessed July 18, 2022, https://worldpopulationreview.com/countries/life-expectancy; "Life Expectancy at Birth, Female (Years)—Central African Republic," The World Bank, accessed January 23, 2023, https://data.worldbank.org/indicator/SP.DYN.LE00.FE.IN?locations=CF; "Life Expectancy at Birth, Male (Years)—Central African Republic," The World Bank, accessed January 23, 2023, https://data.worldbank.org/indicator/SP.DYN.LE00.MA.IN?locations=CF.

23. "What Are the Other Health Consequences of Drug Addiction?" National Institute on Drug Abuse, July 2020, https://nida.nih.gov/publications/drugs-brains-behavior-science-addiction/addiction-health.

24. "World Bank and WHO: Half the World Lacks Access to Essential Health Services, 100 Million Still Pushed into Extreme Poverty Because of Health Expenses," World Health Organization, December 13, 2017, https://www.who.int/news/item/13-12-2017-world-bank-and-who-half-the-world-lacks-access-to-essential-health-services-100-million-still-pushed-into-extreme-poverty-because-of-health-expenses.

25. Computers for Kids, accessed July 18, 2022, https://www.cfkid.org/about-us.

26. "A Bold Aspiration 2022 Annual Report," Feeding America, accessed February 20, 2023, https://www.feedingamerica.org/sites/default/files/2023-01/FA_22ImpactReport_d9_FINAL_revised%20012723.pdf.

27. Shelby DuPont, "U.S. Department of Energy Uses ACS Data to Power the Low-Income Energy Affordability Data (LEAD) Tool," United States Census Bureau, February 23, 2021, https://www.census.gov/programs-surveys/acs/about/acs-data-stories/lead-tool.html.

28. Renewable Energy Transition Initiative (RETI), accessed July 28, 2022, http://www.energyhero.org/.

29. "Food Waste and Its Links to Greenhouse Gases and Climate Change," US Department of Agriculture, January 24, 2022, https://www.usda.gov

/media/blog/2022/01/24/food-waste-and-its-links-greenhouse-gases-and
-climate-change.

30. "IBBY and IBBY's Fund for Children in Crisis—An Introduction,"
International Board on Books for Young People (IBBY), accessed July 17,
2022, https://www.ibby.org/fileadmin/user_upload/CinC_Fundraising
_Flyer_2010.pdf.

31. International Board on Books for Young People (IBBY), accessed August 2,
2022, https://www.ibby.org.

32. Alex's Lemonade Stand, accessed July 27, 2022, https://www.alexslemonade
.org/alexandra-alex-scott-biography.

CHAPTER 10

1. "Cinema & Media Arts," York University, accessed August 16, 2022, https://
futurestudents.yorku.ca/program/media-arts; "What Is Media Arts?" Saint
Paul Public Schools, accessed August 16, 2022, https://www.spps.org
/Page/23303.

2. "The Demographics of Arts Participation in a Pre-Pandemic Year," National
Endowment for the Arts, December 2022, https://www.arts.gov/sites
/default/files/NationalReportforADPAccess.pdf.

3. *2020–2021 Get Lit Annual Report*, accessed February 8, 2022, https://drive
.google.com/file/d/1au-zyR16-YHauZzjuanYLZtmXfj_FVO4/view.

4. "Yankee Doodle: The Story Behind the Song," The Kennedy Center, accessed
August 16, 2022, https://www.kennedy-center.org/education/resources-for
-educators/classroom-resources/media-and-interactives/media/music/story
-behind-the-song/the-story-behind-the-song/yankee-doodle/.

5. David Segal, "That Diss Song Known as 'Yankee Doodle,'" *New York Times*,
July 1, 2017, https://www.nytimes.com/2017/07/01/sunday-review/that-diss
-song-known-as-yankee-doodle.html.

6. Christine Weerts, "A Short History of 'Battle Hymn of the Republic,'" *The
Federalist*, July 4, 2021, https://thefederalist.com/2021/07/04/a-short-history
-of-battle-hymn-of-the-republic/; "7 Facts about 'Battle Hymn of the
Republic,'" Parker Symphony Orchestra, October 18, 2018, https://
parkersymphony.org/facts-about-battle-hymn-of-the-republic.

7. BGS Staff, "Black Voices—Watch: Chris Pierce, 'American Silence,'" The
Bluegrass Situation, January 15, 2021, https://thebluegrasssituation.com/read
/watch-chris-pierce-american-silence/.

8. Heather (Jamie Frater, ed.), "10 Unique and Bizarre Ways Artists Make
Amazing Art," *Listverse*, April 30, 2015, https://listverse.com/2015/04/30/10
-unique-and-bizarre-ways-artists-make-amazing-art/.

9. Emmanuel Jal, "The Music of a War Child," TED Talk: TEDGlobal, posted August 2009, TED video, 18:03, https://www.ted.com/talks/emmanuel_jal _the_music_of_a_war_child?language=en; Emmanuel Jal, accessed August 16, 2022, https://www.emmanueljal.com/.

10. Lee Mokobe, "A Powerful Poem about What It Feels Like to Be Transgender," TED Talk: TEDWomen, posted June 2015, TED video, 4:12, https://www.ted.com/talks/lee_mokobe_a_powerful_poem_about_what_it _feels_like_to_be_transgender; Manoush Zomorodi, Diba Mohtasham, Sanaz Meshkinpour, "Lee Mokobe: How Can We Make Sense of Ourselves Through Poetry?" NPR and TED Radio Hour, May 14, 2021, 12:00, https:// www.npr.org/2021/05/14/996594214/lee-mokobe-how-can-we-make-sense -of-ourselves-through-poetry.

11. Sophie Prideaux, "Who Is Banksy? The Top Theories and How He Keeps His Identity a Secret," *The National*, February 10, 2021, https://www.thenational news.com/arts-culture/art/who-is-banksy-the-top-theories-and-how-he -keeps-his-identity-a-secret-1.1049700; Joe Syer, "Benevolent Banksy: 10 Times Banksy Has Done Something for Charity," MyArtBroker, accessed August 11, 2022, https://www.myartbroker.com/artist-banksy/articles /banksy-the-benevolent-10-times-banksy-has-done-something-for-charity-2.

12. Deborah Ellis, accessed August 11, 2022, http://deborahellis.com.

13. Nujood Ali, Delphine Minoui; Linda Coverdale, trans., *I Am Nujood, Age 10 and Divorced*, GoodReads, https://www.goodreads.com/book/show/6818019 -i-am-nujood-age-10-and-divorced.

14. Theatre of the Oppressed NYC, accessed August 16, 2022, https://www .tonyc.nyc; Theatre of the Oppressed, The Center for Applied Theatre, accessed August 16, 2022, https://centerforappliedtheatre.org/theatre-of-the -oppressed/.

15. Undercommoning, "Living Is Resisting: Street Dance Activism in Black Lives Matter," Undercommoning, June 29, 2015, https://undercommoning.org /living-is-resisting/.

16. James Estrin, "Striving for Justice and Equality with a Camera on New York's Streets," *New York Times*, August 24, 2018, https://www.nytimes.com/2018 /08/24/lens/builder-levy-justice-equality-new-york-streets.html.

17. Kristy Siegfried, "The Refugee Brief," The UN Refugee Agency (UNHCR), June 17, 2022, https://www.unhcr.org/refugeebrief/the-refugee-brief-17 -june-2022/.

18. Kathryn Syssoyeva, email conversation with author, August 15, 2022; Anomalous Co, accessed August 16, 2022, http://www.anomalousco.com /about.

19. Schellekens Peleman, "We Made a Giant Inflatable Refugee to Travel the World and Spread Awareness," Bored Panda, accessed August 12, 2022, https://www.boredpanda.com/inflatable-refugee-travels-the-world -schellekens-peleman/.

20. Bart Peleman and Dirk Schellekens, email conversation with author, February 8, 2023.

21. Taryn Grant, "Halifax Youth Express Refugee Experience through Art," *Toronto Star*, StarMetro Halifax, September 22, 2018, https://www.thestar .com/halifax/2018/09/22/halifax-youth-express-refugee-experience -through-art.html; Child and Youth Refugee Research Coalition (CYRRC), accessed August 12, 2022, https://cyrrc.org/who-we-are/.

22. Center for Artistic Activism (C4AA), accessed August 16, 2022, https://c4aa .org/about.

23. Alisha Rahaman Sarkar, "Afghans 'Selling Off Babies' as Child Carriage Booms Amid Starvation and Economic Collapse," Independent, November 24, 2021, https://www.independent.co.uk/asia/south-asia/afghanistan-child -marriages-food-crisis-b1963454.html; Emma Batha, Shadi Khan Saif, "Afghans 'Marry Off' Baby Girls for Dowries as Starvation Looms," Reuters, November 22, 2021, https://www.reuters.com/article/us-afghanistan -poverty-child-marriage-idUSKBN2I8075; Fazl Rahman Muzhary, "The Bride Price: The Afghan Tradition of Paying for Wives," Afghanistan Analysts Network, March 9, 2020, https://www.afghanistan-analysts.org/en/reports /context-culture/the-bride-price-the-afghan-tradition-of-paying-for-wives /#:~:text=Kandahar%20and%20Helmand%3A%201%2C000%2C000%20 to,)%20(see%3A%20here).&text=Bride%20price%20is%20known%20as,in%20 the%20draft%20marriage%20law.

24. "Asia Game Changer Awards: Sonita Alizadeh for Using Rap Music to Empower the Girls of Afghanistan," Asia Society, accessed August 16, 2022, https://asiasociety.org/asia-game-changers/sonita-alizadeh; Girls Not Brides, accessed August 16, 2022, https://www.girlsnotbrides.org/about-us/; "Bard College Student Sonita Alizada Addresses the UN on Child Marriage and Education for Girls," Bard News, February 19, 2020, https://www.bard.edu /news/bard-college-student-sonita-alizada-addresses-the-un-on-child -marriage-and-education-for-girls-2020-02-14; "Sonita Alizadeh," National Women's History Museum, accessed June 25, 2023, https://www.womens history.org/education-resources/biographies/sonita-alizadeh; Sonita, accessed May 16, 2023, https://www.sonita.net/about-sonita.

CHAPTER 11

1. "Why Downtime Is Essential for Brain Health," Cleveland Clinic, June 2, 2020, https://health.clevelandclinic.org/why-downtime-is-essential-for-brain-health/; Ferris Jabr, "Why Your Brain Needs More Downtime," *Scientific American*, October 15, 2013, https://www.scientificamerican.com/article/mental-downtime/.

2. Jackie Coleman and John Coleman, "The Upside of Downtime," *Harvard Business Review*, December 6, 2012, https://hbr.org/2012/12/the-upside-of-downtime.

3. Erica R. Hendry, "7 Epic Fails Brought to You by the Genius Mind of Thomas Edison," *Smithsonian Magazine*, November 20, 2013, https://www.smithsonianmag.com/innovation/7-epic-fails-brought-to-you-by-the-genius-mind-of-thomas-edison-180947786/.

4. Yitzi Weiner, "Young Change Makers: Why and How Anna DeVolld of Promote Our Pollinators Is Helping to Change Our World," Authority Magazine, October 9, 2022, https://medium.com/authority-magazine/young-change-makers-why-and-how-anna-devolld-of-promote-our-pollinators-is-helping-to-change-our-575023276e96.

5. Emmaline Soken-Huberty, "10 Exciting Career Paths for Activists," Open Education Online, accessed November 17, 2022, https://openeducationonline.com/careers/10-exciting-career-paths-for-activists/.

6. Fridays for Future, accessed November 17, 2022, https://fridaysforfuture.org/what-we-do/who-we-are/.

7. Fridays for Future, "Strike Statistics: List of Countries," June 21, 2023, https://fridaysforfuture.org/what-we-do/strike-statistics/list-of-countries/.

8. Alison Rourke, "Greta Thunberg Responds to Asperger's Critics: 'It's a Superpower,'" *The Guardian*, September 2, 2019, https://www.theguardian.com/environment/2019/sep/02/greta-thunberg-responds-to-aspergers-critics-its-a-superpower.

9. Masks4Canada: Canadian Doctors, Professionals, & Citizens for Masks, accessed November 18, 2022, https://masks4canada.org/about/.

10. Union of Concerned Scientists, accessed November 16, 2022, https://www.ucsusa.org/about.

11. Call Me Hannah, accessed November 16, 2022, https://callmehannah.ca/about/; "Youth and Social Media Activism: Hannah Alper: Social Media Week Toronto 2018," YouTube video, 14:30, posted by "Pinch Social," November 30, 2018, https://youtu.be/SDE9aVgDeMs.

12. DoSomething.org, accessed November 16, 2022, https://www.dosomething.org/us/about/volunteer-hours.

ACKNOWLEDGMENTS

S tudents attending my literacy presentations sometimes ask me, "Which of your books was the easiest to write? Which was the hardest?" Next time these questions arise, I'll be able to describe how I navigated this book's challenge to reveal often-sobering information while remaining encouraging and upbeat. This effort might have been on the top end of difficult if not for the inspiring individuals and organizations I discovered who are making a difference in our world as they tackle the causes they care about. I'm grateful to each person who took the time to speak or correspond with me as I pursued the most current details of their endeavors. Sharing their activities has allowed me to steer readers toward hope and empowerment.

My full appreciation extends to Lindsay Easterbrooks-Brown, Beyond Words managing editor, for her skillful and perceptive input. Her feedback was spot-on, and it has been a delight to work together to grow this work. Thanks also to Emmalisa Sparrow Wood, Beyond Words production editor; Sarah Heilman, copy-editor; Ali Shaw, proofreader; Brennah Hermo, marketing and public relations director; Bill Brunson, typographer; and Sara E. Blum for design, along with the entire Beyond Words team for their contributions to develop, design, and market *Make Your Mark, Make a Difference*. I'm thankful to Aladdin/Beyond Words for releasing titles that bring attention to important topics and to Stacey Kondla of the Rights Factory for her enthusiasm and drive to bring my writing to new readers. It is my pleasure to further acknowledge the Alberta Foundation for the Arts for its financial support. A special thank-you to Amy for the inspiration, along with the rest of my always supportive family, and to Grant Wiens for creating a home atmosphere that enables me to devote time to the themes I want to explore and share.